VISION AND RESONANCE

VISION AND RESONANCE
TWO SENSES OF POETIC FORM

JOHN HOLLANDER

New York
OXFORD UNIVERSITY PRESS
1975

Copyright © 1975 by Oxford University Press, Inc.
Library of Congress Catalogue Card Number: 74-22878
Printed in the United States of America

For Frank Kermode

PREFACE

Dr. Johnson could scarcely doubt "that on many occasions we may make the musick which we imagine ourselves to hear, that we modulate the poem by our own disposition, and ascribe to the numbers the effects of the sense." His caveat remains in effect for critics of poetic form, whether they treat it as affective instrument or as engine of intent. What interests us most today, however, is the blurriness of the distinction between "numbers" and "sense" which the observation takes so much for granted. It is also apparent that some of the most interesting and useful analysis of poetic effect constantly risks making its own music. In the following pages I shall both be concerned with the exact location of the sound in the sea-shell, as it were, and the mote in the eye; but I shall also be engaged in the kind of practical criticism which must proceed as though there were no dangers of the sort formerly and quaintly called "impressionistic."

These essays on the structure of verse reflect my concerns with formal aspects of poetic language over nearly two decades, but it was at a Christian Gauss Seminar at Princeton University in the Spring of 1962 that I first had a chance to cover systematically a number of related topics in metrical theory and history. At the time, structural linguistics seemed to provide a useful approach to many aspects of the problem of why English verse seemed to generate both such a rich array of metrical styles, and so desperate a horde of warring theories of how that richness was to be understood.

English prosody has tended to be a subject for cranks. A traditional descriptive terminology which could only fit the facts of practice by producing a number of conceptual ghosts; a radically independent written language invented to correct the eccentricities of English spelling; a loss of training in the classics, to which the ability to make deep sense out of the traditional terminology was tied; a profound linguistic and, in general, conceptual naïveté on the part of prosodists, enabling them to argue for years with each other without ever agreeing to anything but persuasive definitions of terms—all of these difficulties seemed then to yield to a therapeutic appeal to the facts of linguistic structure. At the time, Chomsky and Halle had not yet started to work on the fascinating problem of the stress accent in English; it seemed safe enough to say that English had phonemic word stress, that no easy rule like the penultimate syllable law for Italian, or the initial stress in Czech, could enable a stranger to the language to pronounce any word on sight. The consequences for English prosody at the time seemed quite straightforward. The major tradition of English accentual-syllabic verse—the line from Chaucer through Tennyson—constrained the wide variety of English syllables into one of two roles, and at least the way those roles were assigned was clear enough. In fact, in those days one could have described traditional English meter as implying an ad hoc phonology of English in which there was only one degree of syllabic stress. In it, monosyllabic words could be assigned stress-positions in an English line by treating them in phrases, like polysyllabic words. Thus *in the water* and *inattentive* could both be encoded in either of the following two situations. *A little feather, in the water yet* . . . or *And still in the water the feather is wet*. But in no case could we have *in the water* or *in the water* or *in the water*. Questions of quantity, feet, dipodies, isochronisms and so forth could be easily swept away. One could begin, with a minimum of terminology to talk about why poems seemed to sound like what they said, why a poet's submission to apparently absurd constraints could give his language wings, and so forth.

But this was only a beginning. The linguistic problems were even then beginning to grow more complex. Even then it was obvious to sensitive readers of verse, if not to structural linguistic theorists, that the relations between stress and syntax were most crucial, and most interesting, for a study of the dynamics of accentual-syllabic verse. And appeal to speech stress might not always do, at least as regards phrases: one of the most plangent modulations in Miltonic verse comes from his unspeakable syntax, to which we cannot appeal in the manner in which we do to Donne's, for a resolution of a metrical ambiguity.

I was also particularly concerned with the relation of verse to music, and, in particular, with the historical process whereby *song* became a figurative term, and wherein lyrical poetry lost its formal connection to melody in solo or choral songs. Poetry came to internalize music in the sounds and textures of its verse, leaving for setting only the empty husks of singable jingle. Along with this, many fictional and false notions had developed over the centuries locating the "musical" effects of verse in patterns of sound which could not be shown to be in operation, and some rather elementary conceptual analysis of the language used by critics about verse seemed in order.

In the intervening years, I became more and more interested in the idea of tradition and the way it operates in the poet's decisions about matters of form. Tradition is a matter of texts, not voices, and I began to question that automatic priority which we have generally assigned to the analysis of the spoken language in dealing with poetic structure. In addition, the interpenetration of theory and practice, the historical dimension with which synchronic structural linguistics seemed so impatient, and the analogous ways in which the phonological structures of one period of the history of verse would extend themselves, soundlessly but visibly, into others—all seemed particularly interesting for literary history.

Such problems, among others, are treated in the following pages both thematically and in connection with the formal styles of particular poets. The chapters move along an axis from the aural to the visual: speaking and writing are both language—indeed, it is that remarkable domain of language which connects the two in a unique way—and it is the region between them which poetry inhabits. It has become useful in the history of criticism to speak of poetry as being one or the other of these—song or inscription, utterance or text—and the discussions both of topics like rhyme, enjambment, ideologies about metrical form, and of individual figures like Donne and Campion, are arranged along the path which leads from music to picture. Several chapters have been written especially for this volume. These include the brief survey of certain problems of quantitative verse in English (I regret, as this book goes to press, incidentally, that Derek Attridge's *Well-Weighed Syllables* has not yet appeared), and the essays on titles, rhyme, and metrical experiment.

Of the others, "The Poem in the Ear" and "The Poem in the Eye," although considerably expanded and rewritten, started out as the Elliston Lectures at the University of Cincinnati in 1969. I am most grateful for having been given the chance to formulate two central problems in them. In general, these chapters are designed to be read as separate essays as well as in context, and I have allowed a few duplications of example and observation to remain to do their work in different contexts. I have added as an appendix an account of one aspect of the relation of words and music from a personal and practical point of view.

Other chapters were originally published as follows:

"The Poem in the Ear": part of this appeared in the *Journal of Aesthetics and Art Criticism* XV (1956), and part in *The Yale Review* LXIII (Fall, 1973).

"Donne and the Limits of Lyric": published in *John Donne: Essays in Celebration*, ed. A. J. Smith (London, Methuen and Co., 1972).

"The Case of Campion": part of this chapter formed an Introduction to the *Selected Songs of Thomas Campion*, ed. W. H. Auden (Boston, David R. Godine, 1973).

"Sense Variously Drawn Out": from *Literary Theory and Structure*, ed. Brady, Palmer and Price (New Haven, Yale University Press, 1973).

PREFACE   xi

"The Metrical Frame": part of this chapter appeared in *Kenyon Review* XXI (1959) under the title of "The Metrical Emblem."
"Ben Jonson and the Modality of Verse": adapted from the Introduction to *Selected Poems of Ben Jonson* (New York, Dell Laurel Editions, 1961).
"Romantic Verse Form and the Metrical Contract: reprinted from *Romanticism and Consciousness,* ed. Harold Bloom (New York, W. W. Norton, 1970), which in turn was expanded from an earlier essay on Blake in *From Sensibility to Romanticism,* ed. Frederick W. Hilles and Harold Bloom (New York, Oxford University Press, 1965).
"The Poem in the Eye": in a shorter form, this appeared in *Shenandoah* XXIII (Spring, 1972).
"A Poem for Music": published in *English Symposium Papers III* (Fredonia, N.Y., 1973); also drawn from "Notes on the Text of *Philomel*" in *Perspectives of New Music* (Fall-Winter, 1967).

Acknowledgment is made to the editors and publishers for permission to reprint here, as well as to the following:

The Estate of Robert Frost, Holt, Rinehart and Winston, Inc., and Jonathan Cape, Ltd., for permission to reprint "Never Again Would Birds' Song Be the Same," by Robert Frost.
William Carlos Williams, "The Red Wheelbarrow," from *Collected Earlier Poems.* Copyright 1938 by New Directions Publishing Corporation. Reprinted by permission of New Directions Publishing Corporation.
Ezra Pound, "Papyrus" and "In a Station of the Metro," from *Personae.* Copyright 1926 by Ezra Pound. Reprinted by permission of New Directions Publishing Corporation, and, from *Collected Shorter Poems,* by permission of Faber and Faber, Ltd.
The reproductions of the *technopaignia* from Renaissance editions in Chapter XII are from copies in the Cambridge University Library, whose permission to photograph them was most helpful.

I am indebted both deeply and widely to friends, colleagues, and institutions. It was during a term in the Society of Fellows at Harvard that the notion of doing systematic work on English prosody first occurred to me. I was directed from the music of poetry, though, to studies of both the music to which it was sung, and the ideas of music referred to in it. A chance to contribute to John Crowe Ransom's *Kenyon Review* series on meter, and to participate in the Conference on Style in Bloomington, Indiana, in 1958 and the Conference on Poetics in Warsaw in 1960, helped to focus my concerns again. A Morse Fellowship from Yale University and, most recently, a Senior Fellowship from the National Endowment for the Humanities enabled me to formulate, write, and rewrite much of the material in this book.

My colleagues Samuel Levin and Allen Mandelbaum have been generous and helpful with their advice and criticism. Conversations on a range of questions reflected in these pages with Geoffrey Hartman, Harold Bloom, W. K. Wimsatt, Richard Poirier, Stephen Orgel, Charles Rosen, David Bromwich, and Daryl Hine have been of the greatest value. The work of my students William A. Krohn and Elise Jorgens, on contrastive stress and on the settings of Stuart lyrics by Henry Lawes, respectively, has taught me much. At various times in the past, Donald Davie, Steele Commager, Edward T. Cone, Milton Babbitt, Howard Porter, Morris Halle, Edward Stankiewicz, Victor Erlich, David Ferry, Noam Chomsky, I. A. Richards, and Roman Jakobson have been of both minutely specific and broadly general help. Some of my students in a seminar in poetic form at the City University Graduate Center, and at the School of Letters some years ago, were effectively patient with my insufficiently qualified assertions. James Raimes and Vivian Hausch were of great help in editorial matters.

To the late W. H. Auden, whose ear for prosody was like a moral sense, my obligation is not easy to express in a sentence.

New York, N. Y.   J. H.
January 1975

CONTENTS

    I   The Poem in the Ear, 3
   II   Donne and the Limits of Lyric, 44
  III   Observations in the Art of English Quantity, 59
  IV   The Case of Campion, 71
   V   "Sense Variously Drawn Out": on English Enjambment, 91
  VI   Rhyme and the True Calling of Words, 117
 VII   The Metrical Frame, 135
VIII   Ben Jonson and the Modality of Verse, 165
  IX   Romantic Verse Form and the Metrical Contract, 187
   X   "Haddocks' Eyes": A Note on the Theory of Titles, 212
  XI   Observations on the Experimental, 227
 XII   The Poem in the Eye, 245

Appendix: A Poem for Music:
Remarks on the Composition of *Philomel*, 289

Index, 307

VISION AND RESONANCE

I
THE POEM IN THE EAR

In the world of the ear, poetry is a kind of music, as it is a mode of picturing in the context of the eye. Ordinarily, to discuss this musical dimension would be to talk about poetic language in its aspect of intonation—to concentrate upon meter, upon rhythm; to discuss the effects of sound that the urgencies of meaning produce when knotted into the fabric of tradition that conventionalized uses of poetic language always weave. It is always wise, when considering the so-called "music of poetry," to avoid, by evasion or scrupulous analysis, many of the metaphors and formal analogies by which literary poetry has been linked to, and has continually proclaimed its connection with, musical art. Discussions of English prosody, for example, have kept getting bogged down for hundreds of years in swamps of irrelevancy because of an archaic identity, in Greek times, of musical and poetic rhythm. And yet it is obviously the aspects of poetic language that are most like the resources of speech, rather than those of song, which come to the aid of poetic resonance.

Even as profound and usually unerring a critic as Northrop Frye, for example, can expose, tersely and devastatingly, the sloppy thinking behind the notion that Tennyson is a more essentially musical poet than Browning, and then go on rather disappointingly to suggest that, in truth, it is the other way around. What we might have expected from him was a discussion of the historical background of the concepts of "song," the "lyrical" and the musical in language that would identify Tennyson's primarily vocalic sound texturing with musicality, and not Browning's interplay of spoken intonation and rhythmic phrase structure with some of the most unbending of canonical meters. To put it crudely, it is felt that poetry which makes English seem more French or Italianate is musical; that which makes it seem more German is not. And yet what Professor Frye does, in an otherwise keen discussion of *opsis* and *melos*, is to reverse the arbitrariness and opt in effect for the Germans.[1] He has in fact provided an insight that reflects, rather than casts light upon, what is sometimes called the *Sprachgefühl* of English— the sense of its structure and that of other languages relative to it to which a native knowledge of English condemns its speakers. One should perhaps more properly ask: what has the history of English poetry and of European music generally had to do with this concept of the musical in speech? Why was it part of English poetic language's mythology about itself that vowels were more musical than consonants, for example?

In arguing for a hard look at the linguistic facts of sounded, spoken language in discussing the "life" of poetry in the ear, one is always attempting to demythologize. For example, a student, responding first to the fairly schematic movement of a standard set piece like Andrew Marvell's "Coy Mistress" poem, may exclaim appreciatively over the speeding up of the rhythmic pace of "But at my back I always hear / Time's winged chariot hurrying near" with its dactylic rush, and observe the continuation of the falling rhythm in "And yonder all before us lie / Deserts of vast eternity." Our demythologizing, here using a mode of exorcism no more arcane than historical grammar, would have to dampen his appreciative ardor with the observation that the last of these lines—the original form, "desárts," accented on the second syllable —was still for Marvell quite regularly iambic. Or, arguing at a kind of procedural extreme: one might wish to discourage analysts of poetic meter from using musical notation to simulate metrical patterns by appealing to facts about the structural function of either schematic

---

1. Northrop Frye, *Anatomy of Criticism* (Princeton, 1957), pp. 255-56.

"length" or actual clocked durations in English speech, prose, verse, and song. Or perhaps, one might take the example of a gifted, innovating, and envisioning poet like William Carlos Williams—triumphant in his ability to see humane magnificence in the ordinary, and to make us hear the most exciting rhythms of conscious life in the flattened cadences of the unrhetorical. Such a subtle practitioner can nevertheless, outside his poems, in his analytic and critical remarks about prosody in general, and his own metrical practice in particular, descend, in the rhetorical uneasiness and crankiness of the autodidact, to obfuscation at best and nonsense at worst.

Or even, there is the instance of the remarkable relation between Gerard Manley Hopkins's technical vocabulary for describing and naming some of his prosodic concepts, and the character of the imagery in his own poems. Surely the field of the latter yields up the former, and surely the expressive force of that vocabulary far exceeds its strictly conceptual utility. No real harm is done to prosodic theory by his use of terms like *hanger, outride, slack, sprung, running, rove over;* but, just as surely, Hopkins's brilliant and unique use of the words "pitch" and "stress," both in the language of his poetry and in his prosodic meta-language *about* it, takes us far away from the linguistic realities which either acoustic or articulatory phonetics might define. Indeed, his word "counterpoint" presents an extremely attractive scheme for dealing with actual instances of our English accentual-syllabic meter, that elusive dual citizen of the ear's kingdom and the eye's. But that attractiveness has led to adoption of the term as if it were a schematically fruitful analogy, instead of a startling metaphor, so that even today prosodists tend to follow its seductive song into dangerous waters.

For example, in using the term "counterpointing" to designate the relation between an iambic norm and a rhythmic actuality, prosodists follow Hopkins's more limited use of the word; he simply meant systematic reversal of iambic stress patterns and, as he says, "If however the reversal is repeated in two feet running, especially so as to include the sensitive second foot, it must be due either to great want of ear, or else is a calculated effect, the superinducing or *mounting* of a new rhythm upon the old; and since the new or mounted rhythm is actually heard and at the same time the mind naturally supplies the natural or standard foregoing rhythm, for we do not forget what the rhythm is that by rights we should be hearing, two rhythms are in some manner running at once and we have something answerable to counterpoint in music, which is two or more strains of tune going on together, and this is Counterpoint Rhythm."[2] And, we may add, this is the canonical use of "counterpoint" in prosody—notice how Hopkins's own metaphors of "superinducing or *mounting* a new rhythm on the old" lead him to an actually inaccurate musical analogy. The correct one would be rather one of syncopation. The problems of what Roman Jakobson has called *verse instance* as opposed to *verse design* respond to such a formulation. Just as, for example, any musician will understand how a string of syncopations in 3/4 time will yield an apparent sequence of 2/4 measures while yet not calling for actual rebarring, so the substitutions of Shakespeare's "Never, never, never, never, never" demand no description of the line as transcending the iambic convention of *King Lear*, momentarily trochaic as it may be.

Hopkins's image of counterpoint, as a matter of fact, results from musical sophistication rather than the lack of it—it is, conceptually speaking, most valid as a visual, rather than an auditory analogy. For Hopkins, counterpoint is generated by two musical lines, commensurate in category; but the two kinds of rhythm, the potential or schematic and the actual, are hardly so. What may have influenced him was some visual sense of the actual line of verse with two alternative strings of scansion marks above and below it, say, one of them marking the schematic iambic, the other the reversed or otherwise distorted actual rhythm. Together, these two strings of syllable markers might have seemed to Hopkins like a staff of musical notation, like two musical lines being simultaneously generated. The more independent they were, the more divergence there was between them, the more "contrapuntal" these analytic annotations might seem to be, and the more the text in question might be thought of as embodying them. (This seems certainly to be the case, for example, in T. S. Eliot's remark

2. Gerard Manley Hopkins, Preface to *Poems, 1876-1889*.

based on Hopkins's term: "I cannot help suspecting that to the cultivated audience of the age of Virgil, part of the pleasure in the poetry arose from the presence in it of two metrical schemes in a kind of counterpoint: even though the audience may not necessarily have been able to analyse the experience.")[3] But what Eliot points out in his last clause is often as true for poets and critics as it is for audiences. A good clarifier of the talk of prosodists—for English, arcane, contorted, and unduly quarrelsome as it so often is—would try to illuminate the ways in which linguistic and conceptual habit produced garbled descriptions of prosodic events nevertheless clearly and effortlessly being *perceived* and understood. But it must be confessed that, in another light, some of the mistakes and confusions that abound in so many studies of poetic form and its consequences for imaginative actuality are of a certain value. They are like the mistakes that poetry is always making about itself, and yet which we do not call mistakes but rather acknowledge as fictions.

The particular set of fictions identifying music and poetry are venerable and pervasive ones. The master figure, that of the music of poetry, has been in operation ever since Pseudo-Longinus (end of the first century A.D.?):

> We hold, then, that composition, which is a kind of melody in words—words which are part of man's nature and reach not his ears only but his very soul—stirring as it does myriad ideas of words, thoughts, things, beauty, musical charm, all of which are born and bred in us; while, moreover, by the blending of its own manifold tones it brings into the hearts of the bystanders the speaker's actual emotion so that all who hear him share in it, and by piling phrase on phrase builds up one majestic whole—we hold, I say, that by these very means it casts a spell on us and always turns our thoughts towards what is majestic and dignified and sublime and all else that it embraces, winning a complete mastery over our minds.[4]

3. T. S. Eliot, "The Music of Poetry," in *On Poetry and Poets* (New York, 1957), p. 20.
4. Pseudo-Longinus, *On the Sublime*, XXXIX, tr. W. Hamilton Fyfe, Loeb edition, p. 235.

The perfect identification of music and poetry in antiquity that has always been prized by Neoclassicisms of various sorts has already, by the time of the writing of this passage, been sundered. The bridge of an analogy has already been built.

Yet if that analogy covers a loss of actual music for poetry itself, signals the identification of poem with *text,* whether sacred to priest, teacher, or scholiast, we now find that we have gone a step further. We have lost total possession of the simile. Wallace Stevens, calls the notion of the music of poetry "old hat" and "anachronistic," and then goes on:

> . . . It is simply that there has been a change in the nature of what we mean by music. It is like the change from Haydn to a voice intoning. It is like the voice of an actor reciting or declaiming or of some other figure concealed, so that we cannot identify him, who speaks with a measured voice which is often disturbed by his feeling for what he says. There is no accompaniment. If occasionally the poet touches the triangle or one of the cymbals, he does it only because he feels like doing it. Instead of a musician we have an orator whose speech sometimes resembles music. We have an eloquence and it is that eloquence that we call music every day, without having much cause to think about it.[5]

The only way in which we might, indeed, save the analogy is by incorporating Stevens's evolution from song to speech; the music of poetry is one not of musical sounds, nor of the repertory of sounds that a particular language succeeds in segregating from the clamor of possibles. We are able today to think of music as structure, then, not feeling; and thus it is that what one reads, there on a page arranged in verse, hearing and vision joined in words, is music. *Ut pictura musicaque poesis:* the poem is song and picture at once, and the relation of scanning and hearing lies at the heart of all textual (rather than purely oral) poetry. But the musical analogy has been so compelling during its life, and has shaped so many poets' fictions about their own and

---

5. Wallace Stevens, *Effects of Analogy,* in *The Necessary Angel* (New York, 1965), pp. 125-26.

others' practice, that we might turn back to it for a while, reviewing some of its history and confronting its outworn presence.

2

By "the music of poetry" we generally mean all of the nonsemantic properties of the language of a poem including not only its rationalized prosody, but its actual sound on being read, and certain characteristics of its syntax and imagery as well. This poetic "music" has been assigned varied purposes in our literary history, from those of adornment, by the Neoclassicists, to those of intrinsic necessity, by the *symbolistes*. No matter what our commitment may be, we would probably agree that because of this "music," the effects of a poem operate on the reader in ways in which the words of a telegram do not.

Most of us would also agree that the elements of instrumental music do not carry meanings as do certain elements of language. We should also have to concede, however, that other units of language are akin to, and in some cases identical with, these musical building blocks. Aside from the phonemes, or ultimate significant sounds of a particular language, there are those properties of relative stress, pitch, and duration that can be perceived only as members of a series. These last have no existence individually: one cannot produce a single rhyming syllable, for example, just as he cannot clap one hand. All of these elements eventually become combined into meaning units of a language, but their organization, at a more primitive level, distinguishes that which is poetry from that which is not. As in the case of music, the more we realize the "meaninglessness" of these building blocks, the more we struggle to deal rationally with the ways in which they affect us.

Since antiquity, however, literary history has been continually confronted with various analogical couplings of music and poetry. A medieval Latin *conductus*, a troubadour *vers*, or a *virelai* of Machaut actually united forms and conventions, almost as in Greek music. The high Renaissance, after diversifying development of the two arts, sought to achieve its own version of the Greek unification of music and poetry. The baroque treated them as "Sphere-born, harmonious sisters," functioning as embellishment and instruction, almost like

Hobbes's "fancy" and "Judgment." Romanticism sought in the programmatic character of its music to identify it with poetry as transfigured experience. Scraps of all these doctrines remain in our vocabulary, and our own age has proliferated metaphorical descriptions of poetic entities in musical terms, and vice versa. Poetics today must thus face a tradition in which music and poetry are judged at various times identical, sister rituals with a mother in Classical antiquity, complementary intellectual processes, parallel channels for emotional floods, and, in our own day, dissimilar crafts that similarly ennoble and alienate their artisans.

Today, in our attempt to describe the "music of poetry," we find our language and habits of thought unnecessarily complicated by an intricate metaphor, yoking by violence together what have become dissimilar activities. Prosody is a particularly treacherous study. Unlike the metrists of antiquity and later ages, faced with the relatively simple task of describing canonical styles, "rules how to compose," in short, today we must understand conflicting rationales of the varied styles of an intricate tradition, and of a patchwork present descending from many areas of its simultaneously. Ever since Sidney Lanier hailed music and poetry as "the two species of the genus art of sound," prosodists, following his example, have felt free to turn to musical notation and terminology to help them unravel the problems they have inherited.

It was Leibnitz who first grasped the real nature of this difficulty when he declared music to be a kind of *"unconscious* exercise in arithmetic,"[6] thus implying in one phrase the ultimately determinative character of music's structure, as well as the compulsiveness of our tendency, on hearing it, to minimize all but its sensuous effects. For the Greeks, however, no such problem existed. Poetry was inseparable

6. *Monadology and Other Philosophical Writings*, tr. R. Latta (Oxford, 1898), p. 422n. Also, cf. *The Principles of Nature and of Grace*, same edition, p. 422, where Leibnitz insists that "Music charms us, although its beauty consists only in the harmonies (*convenances*) of numbers and in the counting (of which we are unconscious but which nevertheless the soul does make) of the beats or vibrations of sounding bodies. . . ."

from music, and the origins of Greek prosody lay in purely musical principles. Proper music was almost exclusively vocal, and hence the intended effect of any composition lay unambiguously exposed in its text. The notation of Greek vocal music is of great prosodic interest. It indicated pitches only, one or two for each syllable of text. A singer, then, could simply fit these pitches to the duration patterns indicated by the poetic meter and produce musical periods, corresponding to *lines* of verse, marked out in what we would call *bars* or *measures*, corresponding to *feet*.

But sequences of long and short durations cannot arrange themselves into musical patterns without the introduction of stresses, just as successively flashing red and green lights would require an accompanying click on every fourth red flash, for example, to produce perceptible groupings of an otherwise endless and unbroken continuum. Greek music employed the *thesis*, or stressed downbeat, and *arsis*, or unstressed upbeat, to mark off its feet or measures, even though Attic Greek, like modern French, possessed no phonemic stress itself. Stress patterns in Greek prosody may thus be seen to have served a musical purpose. The same sort of phenomenon can be seen, almost in reverse, in the development of bar-lines in baroque music. They became a necessity as instrumental music replaced vocal polyphony in predominance, since stress and syntactic patterns in the text could no longer give order to unbroken successions of notes.

Greek prosody, then, originated in systems of vocal music. It was when the speakers of an originally stressed Latin poetry took over Greek conventions that our traditional prosodic problems began to arise. The superimposition of schemata for the poetry of one language upon the hostile realities of another engender grave complexities; they may be seen in the effects of Romance prosodic conventions upon Old English, for example. But it was with the adaptation of Greek meters to Latin that poetry, originally inseparable from music, began to grow away from it. And it was then that poetry began to develop, in its meter, a seeming music of its own. The kinds of textual traditions that Curtius mapped so magnificently in his *European Literature and the*

Latin Middle Ages operated with a kind of internalized or figurative music. Inscriptions, in such a mode of tradition, were truly echoes of voices.

Aside from clarifying some of the historic confusions of stress and duration, however, too many musical prosodists have either swollen our lexicon or prosodical terms, or, without knowing it, needlessly proliferated marginal entities. Notating a poem for vocal reading is one thing; reifying prosodic elements whose existence is suggested by the notational symbols, and then employing these entities in a purported description of the poem, is quite another. Now it is description, adequate to various purposes of criticism, to which prosodical study has most frequently been committed. Historically, it has been continually stricken with inconclusive debate over ontology: "Does the foot exist?" "Is there quantity in English verse?" "Does 'hovering accent' exist, and if so, where does it hover?" Usually quite wisely, one's instinct leads him to avoid such questions. It must nevertheless be remembered that, as a famous logician has remarked, "What there is does not in general depend upon one's use of language, but what one says there is does."[7]

In attempting to keep this in mind in the following discussion of prosody and music, we should not attempt to offer a new method of scansion, decked out with new terms and symbols drawn from music, and selective redefinitions of older ones. Neither should we be concerned with stylistic similarities between the chromaticism of Gesualdo's madrigals, the texture of Crashaw's verse, and the *chiaroscuro* of Caravaggio. Rather, let us examine something of the history of music's identification with prosody in verse and attempt to describe the limits of usefulness of any further comparisons between the two that we might choose to make.

The first problem we shall have to face concerns the idea of the nature of music itself.[8] Classical antiquity bequeaths us no single line of doctrine on the subject. Actually, the Pythagorean view of music as a mathematical model of universal order, and what might be called the

---

7. W. V. Quine, *From a Logical Point of View* (Cambridge, Mass., 1953), p. 103.
8. The following matters are treated in considerable detail, especially with reference to English poetry, in my *The Untuning of the Sky* (Princeton, 1961).

Platonic view of music as a branch of rhetoric, have polarized and interacted throughout our history. The first of these, called by Boethius *musica mundana*, concentrates primarily on the organizations of musical structure, taking little interest in effects on a hearer, but making of them a *donnée*, like the apparent motions of the heavens. The second view, Boethius' *musica humana*, involves the effects of musical forms and conventions upon the hearer. In it, formal considerations are subordinated to ethical and psychological ones. At various times in the past, one or another of these views has predominated, with various admixtures of a third, or Plotinian, strand of tradition that makes of music an utter mystery.

The conflict between these two views is an important one for aesthetics generally, for it represents a traditional choice between concentrating on the structure of a work of art, and concentrating on its effect. It marks the gap between the word, sound or image, and the feeling that it may purport to invoke in the hearer. A grave confusion on this score is built, as it were, into the English language. For in the coalescence, shortly after Chaucer's time, of Latin *modus* (relating to structure) and Anglo-Saxon *mōd* (relating to feelings), a complicated redistribution of meanings between "mode" and "mood" arose to terrify lexicographers and betray all but professional aestheticians. Most important of all, however, is the fact that such confusions create a shaky bridge over the chasm between structure and effect. It is precisely this chasm which modern criticism has committed itself to filling in. It is the chasm which appears to lie between nature and convention, and the wealth of recent work in structuralist aesthetics has sought, by mapping the chasm, to bridge it.

Actually, this whole account is complicated by the fact that two schools of thought eventually arose within Greek music itself, and it was their differences, discussed in uncomprehending detail by Roman grammarians, that became responsible for so much terminological confusion. The *metrikoi*, primarily rhetoricians and grammarians, held to traditional principles of Greek verse, maintaining in particular that one long syllable should be made equal to two shorts. The *rhythmikoi*, musicians in our sense of the word, held for finer gradations in relative length. In essence, the latter group were arguing for melodies rhythmically independent of the text. Differences between "meter" and "rhythm" remained those of commitment to the independence of melody.[9] Acquired pairs of meanings, such as rational schema vs. actual sound, quantity vs. stress, and, more recently, the printed poem vs. the spoken one, have become pinned onto the terms "meter" and "rhythm" only since the Middle Ages.

Music in post-classical times, confined at first to the uses of the Church, eventually became an independent art with conventions, and eventually a history, of its own. Even the earliest theorists of the polyphonic period, during the tenth and eleventh centuries, were obliged to try to reconcile the respected authorities of Boethius, Cassiodorus, and Augustine, with the actual practice of their own day. The *Scholia Enchiriadis*, a tenth-century treatise, for example, discusses consonant intervals of the parallel *organon* that was unknown to classic times; then, to prove that such considerations only reaffirm the Pythagorean status of *musica mundana* as a branch of mathematics, the author invokes the following passage from Augustine's *De Ordine*: "*Thus reason has perceived that numbers govern and make perfect all that is in rhythm (called 'numbers' in Latin) and in song itself.*"[10]

It was just this use of the word "numbers" for prosody in general that the Elizabethan critics employed in trying to revive the prelapsarian marriage of music and poetry. Long after their divorce, and just at the time that their paths were departing from the parallel course to which Renaissance aesthetics had held them, a writer like Thomas Campion could argue from the ideology of *harmonia mundi* to the necessity of re-establishing classic scansion in English. The first chapter of his *Observations in the Art of English Poesie* (1602), "intreating of numbers in general," maintains that "the world is made by Simmetry and proportion, and is in that respect compared to Musick, and Musick to Poetry."[11] The conclusion follows that *numbers* (i.e., classic quanti-

---

9. I am indebted to Curt Sachs's discussion of this in Rhythm and Tempo (New York, 1953), pp. 115-46.
10. See *Source Readings in Music History*, ed. Oliver Strunk (New York, 1950), pp. 137-38.
11. Thomas Campion, *Works*, ed. Percival Vivian (Oxford, 1909), p. 35.

tative scansion) must replace rhyme and stress. The world had been redeemed from medieval ignorance, adds Campion: "In those lack-learning times and in barbarized Italy, began that vulgar and easie kind of Poesie . . . which we abusively call Rime and Meeter."[12] "Meeter" means stressed scansion here; it is even more confusing to note that other theorists like Puttenham use "numbers" to refer to a pure syllable-counting scansion, like that of Japanese verse. But Puttenham adds that "meeter and measure is all one . . . and is but the quantity of a verse, either long or short,"[13] and then cheerfully assures us that quantity in English consists in the fact that two or more syllables (shorts) make up a foot (long). Puttenham was the first really comprehensive English prosodist, and in his confusions he inaugurated the prosodical tradition of preserving inherited terminology at any cost.

The Elizabethan prosodists also produced some musical analogies which will be mentioned shortly. What must be remembered at this point is that throughout the Middle Ages music still usually depended on a poetic text for its *raison d'être*. By the fourteenth century, music had attained a stage of development that permitted stylistic controversy to concern itself not only with questions of sacred authority but with those of elegance, subtlety, and utility as well. Composers had been signing their names to compositions for over one hundred years, and instruments were being richly employed in the performance of vocal music. But music was still essentially singing; and although motets, up through the fifteenth century, were written to several texts simultaneously, one for each voice and often in different languages, only rarely could there be music without a text at all.

It was not until after 1500 that instrumental music received the continual attention of being notated, and it was not until the seventeenth century that, aside from lutes and keyboards, particular instruments were specified in score. It was during the sixteenth century, however, with its growth of both amateur and professional musical activity, that

---

12. Campion, p. 36.
13. George Puttenham, *The Arte of English Poesie* (1589), in *Elizabethan Critical Essays*, ed. G. G. Smith (Oxford, 1904), Vol. II, p. 70.

the utter separation of music and poetry was being prepared. Conditions apparently necessary to this final alienation began to emerge. A concentration of interest in instrumental music, and the birth of instrumental virtuosity, gave rise to a change from an emphasis on music as an activity in which one participated as a performer to an activity which one enjoyed as an audience. And finally, music became ideologically transformed from a microcosmic imitation of universal harmony, benefiting the hearer by bringing him into physiological and moral tune with the macrocosm, into a process operating instrumentally upon the emotions, affecting an audience through its senses alone. Renaissance apologists for music's virtues argued from its cosmological importance and venerable place in antiquity. But before 1620, Descartes could turn off the singing of the spheres as if with a switch when he began his *Compendium Musices* by saying: "The *object* of this art is sound. The end, to delight and move various affections in us."[14] Finally, hundreds of years after poetry had gathered the effects of music into its prosody, baroque music laid unequivocal claim to the powers of diction.

Even before the Renaissance, however, several situations urged further resemblances between music and prosody, in particular. One of these was the thirteenth-century musical system of *modal rhythm*, which used no time signatures or note values of different durations. Instead, six rhythmic modes, or schemata of duration and stress, called trochaic, iambic, dactylic, anapestic, spondaic, and tribrachic. The terminology of modal rhythm, as well as its exigencies, carried across to prosody, and influenced both the rationale and composition of *troubadour, trouvère,* and *Minnesinger* lyrics. Its effects may have reverberated in England in the beautiful lyrics of the Harleian Ms. 2253 that seem to show *troubadour* influence in their prosodic ambiguity.

There is not time to discuss the details of the influence of the folk tradition here. It lies at the roots of all vernacular poetry, and within it, music and poetry were so united as to preclude the existence of separate names for them. Throughout Western history, folk music and

14. René Descartes, *Oeuvres* (Paris, 1824), p. 445.

poetry alike have contributed richly to both sacred and secular forms of the two arts. The popular tradition is reflected somewhat in the peculiar status of the Elizabethan lyric poem, whose author could expect to find it set in a madrigal or ayre (himself remaining anonymous) at any time after its publication. The various ramifications of this convention included *contrafactum* or the writing of poems to pre-existent tunes. This reinforced the major premise of Barnfield's sonnet: "If music and sweet poetry agree,/As they must needs, the sister and the brother."

The early English theoretical writers, often making appeals to any myth or tradition and rarely to the bare phonetic facts of the language itself, started English prosodic thought from a mass of equivocations and quaint, but misleading analogies. From Gascoigne, who interpreted and used the Greek pitch accents as stress notation, through Puttenham, Harvey, Campion, and Daniel, who used terms like "numbers" and "measure" to apply to stressed or quantitative systems alike, such confusions abounded. It was a general tendency among them to etymologize "rhyme" from "*rhythmus*," and then to use this to force the argument that rhyming necessitates a stressed scansion. Much more confusing was Puttenham's division of "proporcion poeticall" into such divisions as "staffe," by which he meant stanza form, and "concord," "symphonie," or "harmony," by which he meant rhyme. Thirteen years after this, Campion was damning rhyme and stress in favor of the harmony of "numbers."

Such slipshod musical analogies persisted in English prosodical writings, but it was in the eighteenth century that such metrists as Gildon, Foster, and Lord Kames urged that "the prick'd notes of musick" be used to scan verse. They differed as to exactly how this was to be done. Most theorists held that English verse was measured by its own system of "accent," but whether "accent" named stress, pitch, quantity, or some indiscernible, continued to be debated. There did remain some holdouts to the old *harmonia mundi* systems: in 1744, Edward Manwaring published *Harmony and Numbers,* dedicated to Dr. Pepusch and the shade of Mersenne, and full of improbable correspondences between the intervals of musical pitch and the proportional divisions of lines of verse.[15] For the most part, however, music and poetry were treated as separate disciplines, alike primarily in that a set of symbols capable of describing one of them might possibly be forced into notating certain quantities of the other. Less and less appeal to the unity of the two continued to be contrived by metaphors, anecdotes, and myths, as in the manner of the Elizabethans.

Prosodical interest in music remained confined to attempts to utilize notation throughout the eighteenth century. Its one greatest exponent overshadowed all the others in scope and originality. The *Prosodia Rationalis* of Joshua Steele, published in 1779, was subtitled: *An Essay towards Establishing the Melody and Measure of Speech, to be Expressed and Perpetuated by Peculiar Symbols*, thus laying claim not only to the study of versification but to more general linguistic theory as well. By Steele's own admission, the work grew out of a controversy between its author and James Burnet, Lord Monboddo, the author of a remarkably perceptive work entitled *The Origin and Progress of Language*. Like John Horne Tooke in his *Epea Pteroenta*, Monboddo seems to have foreseen many principles of linguistic theory that were neglected until recent times. Much to Steele's dismay he declared, for example, that pitch, the prized "melody of speech" of so many musical prosodists, was insignificant within syllables and operated only upon word groups. (It would be called today "suprasegmental.")

Steele's book, on the other hand, took great pains to indicate the precise pitch patterns of individual syllables and used signs that resemble those used in teaching Chinese. Duration indicators were then attached to each syllable, below the staff stress symbols were added, and, still below these, dynamic indications that curiously prefigure drawings of the changing amplitudes of sound waves. Steele was compelled, throughout his book, to argue from the ontological commitments that his incredibly intricate notational system forced him to

---

15. I am not referring here to the kinds of pattern which Alastair Fowler investigates in *Triumphal Forms* (Cambridge, 1970). For a discussion of the eighteenth-century prosodic theories, see Paul Fussell, Jr., *Theory of Prosody in Eighteenth Century England* (New London, Conn., 1954).

make. But he often put his outlandish system to intricate linguistic uses, such as notating the intonation pattern of both a "ranting actor" and Garrick reading the "To be or not to be" soliloquy. He also carries on an enlightening debate with Monboddo on the nature of phonemic pitch, which he felt existed in English. Perhaps Steele's greatest difficulties as a prosodist, though, are exposed by his indulgence in a private whim. He wanted to re-establish declamation on musical principles; and, declaring the then-current fashions of Italianate *recitative* to be degraded, inserted a continuous tonic instrumental drone, with the occasional addition of the fifth for emphasis, into his "scores."[16] Something very much like this may have been a standard practice in the performance of many types of medieval secular song.

But Steele's use of the practice constitutes an avowed commitment to his use of a *performative* system of scansion, rather than a truly *descriptive* one. The second of these would aim at presenting schematically the whole "musical" structure of a poem, whether this consists, in any particular case, of the prosodic features of the language in which it is written, the arrangement of elements completely foreign to that language (syllable counting in English verse, for example), or even the arrangement of type on a page. A *performative* system of scansion, on the other hand, would present a series of rules governing a locutionary reading of a particular poem, before a real or implied audience. It would end up by *describing* not the poem itself, but the unstated canons of taste behind the rules. Performative systems of scansion, disguised as descriptive ones, have composed all but a few of the metrical studies of the past. Their subjectivity is far more treacherous than even that of reading poems into oscilloscopes and claiming that the image produced describes, or even *is*, the true poem.

Now it may be claimed that prosodical analysis is a form of literature in itself; that it is far more responsive to the pressures of its own history and conventions than to philosophic canons of truth imposed from without; and that it is just this kind of autotelic, subjective quality for which it is to be prized. I shall return to a consideration of this view

16. I am indebted to Donald Hall for insights into this in discussion many years ago, and for information about Steele.

shortly, but for the moment I wish to consider the final phases, and perhaps the most confusing ones, in the history of prosodical analysis, particularly in connection with its use of music.

To turn from Steele to the even more ambitious project of Sidney Lanier, published nearly one hundred years later, is to observe a fundamental change in the nature of the analogy we have been pursuing. Lanier, in some notes upon which he based *The Science of English Verse*, asserted that "Music is *not* a species of Language, but *Language is a species of Music*,"[17] and it is this tie which bound him throughout the work. Now Steele, despite his whimsicalities, was willing to let the almost trivial fact that both speech and music are composed of sound stand well enough alone, without risking the epistemological dangers of such a canonical assertion as Lanier's. Steele, consequently, remained a linguistic prosodist throughout his concerns with musical notation. But Lanier's Romantic notions of both poetry and music crippled him utterly, and he was further limited by a primitive phonetics which he attempted to construct from his not over-profound knowledge of musical acoustics. Like Steele, Lanier misplaced the significance of pitch in English but went beyond this to force a muddy identification of speech pitch with melody. His exhaustive rhythmical discussions produce at best a subtly notated individual reading of a particular passage. What appears to be his elaborate *mystique* about tone and color in speech sounds may originate in the synaesthesia of late Romanticism, or, more directly, in an extension of the rather unfortunate German word for timbre, "*Klangfarbe*." Perhaps some constructive analogy might be drawn between the quality of musical tones and the compositional characteristics of phonemes, but it is only through the use, by such scholars as Roman Jakobson, of distinctive feature analysis that such a comparison could efficiently be drawn. Lanier's "tone colors" often resort to the crudest impressionism. What may move us strongly in a poem of Rimbaud can only be perplexing in what purports to be "The Science of English Verse."

The interval between the publication of Steele's and Lanier's treatise

17. Sidney Lanier, *The Science of English Verse*, ed. P. F. Baum (Baltimore, 1945), p. 340.

saw music move from Haydn to Wagner and beyond, and included the poetry of both Chatterton and Swinburne. The aesthetics of musical romanticism that emerged at the beginning of the nineteenth century have persisted even into our own day. Schopenhauer, in the first quarter of the century, could deny for music the mimetic quality that he allowed, with considerable qualification, for the other arts, holding it to be "the copy of the Will itself," and, by reason of this, more penetrating emotionally. E. T. A. Hoffmann declared that music, "scorning every aid, every admixture of another art (the art of poetry), . . . is the most romantic of all the arts—one might say the only genuinely romantic one—for its sole object is the Infinite." Thus the cognitive or symbolic aspects of music were in some sense denied in order that it be understood as being sufficiently transcendental. But it was not long before it became personified to the degree that individual passages could be considered portentous, gay, longing, ambitious, or prostrate before the awesomeness of fate. Rather than evoking emotion, music somehow became transformed into it.

At the same time, however, such purists as Eduard Hanslick in Vienna could insist on a treatment of music, utterly divorced from all emotion, as pure Form manifesting itself in sound. Hanslick's purposes were those of his concern for structure, and a desire to clear the aesthetic air in their favor. The myth of "pure" music that took hold more generally, however, is better represented by Lanier's remark: "In a sense, any predicable is true of music; just as one may say anything of God, because, being infinite, there is nothing which He is not."[18] And finally, those poets who followed Verlaine in proclaiming the absolute priority of music, were invoking an extremely general concept of the Irrational.

By and large, modern prosody's musical heritage has followed the course we have been tracing. Recent accretions have included a few noteworthy confusions, however. Following Hopkins, the analogical use of the word "counterpoint" arose to describe the disparity between the actual sound of a passage of verse, and the rational schema simultaneously inferred behind it. Indeed, the perfectly proper use of the

18. Lanier, p. 341.

musical terms "syncopation" and even "hemiola" would avoid the trivialities and the inaccuracies incumbent upon the traditional misuse of "counterpoint." Impressionistic descriptions of verse continue to produce such vague metaphors as "cadence," "orchestration," "melody," "dissonance," etc. Often the rate at which new terms are proliferated seems only a function of the size of the commentator's musical vocabulary.[19] The prevalent influence of *symbolisme* and of Pater on all modern poetry has produced many equivocal aesthetic analogies between poetry and music on the grounds of the expository meaninglessness of both.

In general, the stock of musical expressions with which our tradition described the so-called "music" of poetry testified to an unstated commitment to two beliefs. The first of these is that the sound patternings in poetry, and even the suggestions of formal patterns which cannot be heard, affect us as music does. The second entails our assent to the proposition that these workings of verse must remain, as most of us feel that music must remain, rather like a kind of magic.

3

The magic wrought by language which has equal authority when spoken or written depends, then, on living fictions that survive the death of the more specific analogies which embodied them. If "the music of poetry" half embarrasses now, "the sound of poetry" still does not, nor does "the look of poetry" (printed text which does not fill rectangles of page, etc.). An important text for the consideration of the power of poetry as the efficacy not of music, but more generally of sound itself, is the first sixteen lines of Wordsworth's remarkable and quite neglected "Ode on the Power of Sound," begun in 1828 and published in 1835. They address themselves, at the start, to the primary sense of vision, but quickly shift to the auditory:

19. "Fugal" seems to be particularly overworked as a general formal term. Perhaps Joyce's misleading remarks to Stuart Gilbert about what is palpably the structure of an operatic overture, full of snatches of melody which are to be fully contextualized only in the opera itself ("Sirens" episode of *Ulysses*) helped this unfortunate term along.

> Thy functions are ethereal,
> As if within thee dwelt a glancing mind,
> Organ of vision! And a Spirit aërial
> Informs the cell of Hearing, dark and blind;
> Intricate labyrinth, more dread for thought
> To enter than oracular cave;
> Strict passage, through which sighs are brought,
> And whispers for the heart, their slave;
> And shrieks, that revel in abuse
> Of shivering flesh; and warbled air,
> Whose piercing sweetness can unloose
> The chains of frenzy, or entice a smile
> Into the ambush of despair;
> Hosannas, pealing down the long-drawn aisle,
> And requiems answered by the pulse that beats
> Devoutly, in life's last retreats!

The relation between the senses is fascinating here, eye and ear standing as thought and feeling; one is also tempted to dwell on the cave of Hearing as a Romantic fulfillment of Neoclassic traditions, in which sound, music herself, or echo inhabits a cave or a so-called "shell" (by tradition the "chorded shell," *testudo*, a synecdoche for "lyre" or even "lute"); but Wordsworth's musical shell is literally the seashell held to the ear, an exclusively Romantic invention. In this marvelous image—

> the cell of Hearing, dark and blind;
> Intricate labyrinth, more dread for thought
> To enter than oracular cave

—the shell merges with the *auricular cave* of the *cochlea*, the inner ear, whose logarithmic spiral mirrors that of the shell.

But our principal concern now must be with the totality of the sense of hearing as being made primary in this astonishing poem, a poem that will put sound, rather than light, in a privileged role in relation to the creating and prior *logos*. It is with Romantic poetry that we begin to get a poetic confrontation of the realms of the two reigning senses. In the Petrarchan centuries, the eye was closest to the mind and the heart—the eye spoke, shot its shafts, created, and benighted like the eye of heaven: "Wine comes in at the mouth / And love comes in at the eye," in Yeats's archaistic recapitulation. The Neoclassic enlightenment mistrusted the realm of the unmediated ear, almost echoing the uneasiness of Classical antiquity about textless (and, therefore, "irrational") music. Alexander Pope denounces bad critics who judge by the wretched ear alone, those "tuneful fools" whom he likens to those who "to church repair / Not for the doctrine, but the music there." Melody and meaning have parted company, poems have become primarily inscriptions, and there is no equivalent, in visual terms, for the ancillary quality of "music" in Pope's sense. But in Romanticism's concern with the visual and the visionary, a new attitude toward the realms of sense develops, and we observe, for example, the frequent event of the eye giving way to the ear at a particular kind of heightened moment. Not only in the continuous mistrust of optical vision by William Blake, but in Wordsworth, on the top of Snowdon, where the visionary prospect becomes penetrated by "the roar of waters, torrents, streams / Innumerable, roaring with one voice! / Heard over earth and sea, and, in that hour, / For so it seemed, felt by the starry heavens." We notice here that there is no equivalent term, in the ear's domain, for the word "visionary" in that of the eye; we must mix metaphors to characterize this acoustically improbable phenomenon as "visionary sound."

In Keats, too, the darkness falls at the end of the great Autumn ode leaving only the final night sounds of closure, the noises of gathering in; even more spectacular is the pursuit of the dark bird of myth, the nightingale, into the resounding and palpable forests of sound and touch where, "darkling," the poet can listen to more than birdsong. Or in Shelley's Skylark poem, where the imaginative attention soars after the heard but unseen point of eloquence that fills the great open room of English sky with sound as if, *we* would say today, a wall switch had been flipped on. Even Blake, for whom hearing is a bit more reliable than sight, can give us such fantastic synesthesias as in the London poem from *Songs of Experience,* where all of the apprehended phenomena are spoken of as "heard," and yet where sound turns into visual concretion:

> How the chimney-sweeper's cry
> Every blackening church appalls;
> And the hapless Soldier's sigh
> Runs in blood down Palace walls.

Here, the particular audibles condense, out of the waves they make in the air and the motions their impingings make on the consciousness, into a cinematic animation, becoming the blackening that is more than soot, and the reddening that bursts into blood on its contact with the surfaces of blame.

The imaginative regions of eye and ear in Romantic poetry are much more responsive to the phenomenology of the senses than were the musical and visual concerns of Renaissance and Augustan literatures. I refer to such matters as those of sweep and discontinuity—the ability of each sense to locate respectively point sources of light and sound in space; what it means that one can shut, or avert, the eyes but not the ears; how hearing outlasts vision as one falls through layers of sleep; and how sound can pierce the dark globe of sleeping consciousness, the planetarium in which are projected our dreams, without shattering it, while light cannot. Unlike the German Romantics, for whom music was the epitome of human imaginative activity, it was natural sound or, at most, music heard out-of-doors, blending with the wind and the sounds of trees and falling waters, which was of the greatest interest. The archetypal music of English Romanticism is not that of the concert hall, nor of the singer, nor of the ravishing modulation abstracted from a performance of it, nor of the demonic fiddling of Romantic fable. Rather is it the aeolian harp, activated by the wind, eventually coming to stand for the poet himself.

The wind harp was indeed so pervasive an image that it could even show up, in the work of a third-generation poet like George Darley, as a figure for poetic form, rather than the person of the poet himself. In the brilliant and sensitive Introduction to an 1840 edition of Beaumont and Fletcher (it anticipates Swinburne's critical sensitivity to Jacobean verse), Darley turns from his extremely detailed and pointed discussion of the accentual force of many particular lines to a more general meditation. It prefigures Whitman's figure of the rhythm and protean variety of the sea as a model for his own verse:

> I could easily imagine a fine system of versification, founded by some perfect modulator upon a very different principle from the *square;* upon a series of *triangles* for example, lengthening and contracting itself in turns like the rhythm of an Eolian lyre, now slowly, now rapidly—a swell now, now a swoon, till every mood of thought found its proper echo in the metre. But such a style of modulation is the last perfection of human language, which none has ever yet reached, perhaps ever will reach. Even to approach it demands much more consummate skill than our two dramatists possessed. Their peculiar rhythm has so little about it Eolian, that it has scarce any music at all except in some petted passages: ease is not music, gracefulness is not music, smoothness—nay suavity, is not music. To ensure music, lines must be full of sound, or *soundingness,* which results from principles in diametrical opposition to those of our authors—from single endings, even pauses, sonorous terminative words, sustained tone, and regular cadence or tread of the numbers. Reverse principles are useful now and then to give this system variety, and introduce apt discords, the resolution of which back again into concord, pleases beyond unbroken concord itself. There is more virtue in rhythm than it has credit for—a virtue productive of secret and remote effects, perhaps seldom thought of. Imagination and passion are beyond doubt the prime constituents of poetry, but to complete its distinct nature, rhythm would seem an attribute, however subordinate, little less useful than either. Thus to specialize man's nature, clay unites with the Spirit of God and the breath; these nobler adjuncts, reason and life, requiring as their presence-room the harmonical system of parts, called human form, ere they can render themselves apparent, like imagination and passion seeking the rhythmical form of language, called *Song,* wherein their divine properties might be rendered more manifest. . . .[20]

20. Beaumont and Fletcher, *Works*, with an introduction by George Darley, 2 vols. (London, 1840), reprinted in *Lives of British Dramatists* (Philadelphia, 1846), pp. 281-82.

I have quoted so much of this passage because it seems to me to reflect a considerable range of Romantic ideas about form. It includes the kind of interest in energizing the attention, in "excitement," of Wordsworth and Coleridge; a total recasting of the notion of speech sound into a new and stipulatively defined kind of music; an idea of form as being almost catalytic. The "soundingness" might be almost Emersonian. Finally, a bit further on, Darley expands upon the idea of *contrafactum*—the old practice in popular song of writing new words to an old and well-known tune:

> Every true poet has a *song in his mind*, the notes of which, little as they precede his thoughts—so little as to seem simultaneous with them—do precede, suggest, and inspire many of these, modify and beautify them. That poet who has none of this dumb music going on within him, will neither produce any by his versification, nor prove an imaginative or impassioned writer: he will want the harmonizer which attunes heart, and mind, and soul, the mainspring that sets them in movement together. Rhythm, thus, as an enrapturer of the poet, mediately exalts him as a creator, and augments all his powers. A good system of rhythm becomes, therefore, momentous both for its own sake to the reader, and because it is the poet's latent inspirer. If this be allowed, choice or change of rhythm may entail important consequences to our National Poetry.[21]

But the authenticating necessity of the wind, curling through the aeolian harpstrings with the rhythms of nature, had not always been requisite. From the middle of the sixteenth century onward, the celebration of music was an important subject for poetry, and evolved from being primarily an emblem of world order into the epitome of emotive rhetoric—the music of the spheres gave way to that of Orpheus, in a sense. But throughout the seventeenth and eighteenth centuries, the praise of music in poetry became more and more the praise of poetry itself. There are several reasons for this, not the least important being the Neoclassic awareness of the union of music and poetry in antiquity and the programmatic Renaissance attempts to reunite them in their

21. Ibid., p. 283.

original unfallen relation. Controversies about the relative role of text and music and how these are best to be served abound in the late sixteenth and early seventeenth centuries. Like the arguments over prosody in English literary criticism of that time, frequent agreements on principle produce the widest divergencies in mode of realization, so that while the greatest of the polyphonic madrigals were being composed in England by Byrd, Weelkes, Wilbye, and Gibbons, early experiments in monody were leading, in Italy, to thinly accompanied solo recitative and the birth of opera.

Despite these somewhat self-conscious attempts to reunite music with lyric and dramatic poetry, however, their paths diverged, and yet both were directed forward. Henceforth, the music of poetry and the poetry of music would have irreversibly contracted into metaphors, into concepts applying only to certain aspects of each art. There were specific problems shaping English poetry in its break with music; it is the early seventeenth century which hears the speaking voice, the Classical inscription, and the argumentative prose passage emerging, in metaphysical poetry, as the models for what are still called "songs." At the same time, mythologies of the kinship of music and poem proliferate in poetic imagery. By the later eighteenth century, "song" had become firmly established as a trivial poetic mode as opposed to meditation, epistle, and even totally unmusical formal ode. An interest in sound per se, rather than organized music, was developing. This interest finally flourished in what Harold Bloom has called the generally revisionary climate of Romantic poetry. This climate marks the renewed commitment with which Blake's Piper and his Bard, and the authors of *Lyrical Ballads,* adopt the literary modes of song text, popular and folk, and dramatic, as the forms which will release the deepest seriousness. They were the wings on which to fly out of the rhetorical and stylistic labyrinth of the *literary* and the *official* into the *poetic* which lay beyond.

When we consider the relation between text and music in song, we must be aware of three dimensions along which conventions may extend—poetic tradition, musical tradition, and convention of setting or underlaying or associating the two. Thus, for example, the very way in which a text would be treated musically in some fifteenth-century English secular song—no characteristic rhythmic impulse that either followed or substituted for that of the text; long (we would think) irrelevant melismata on unimportant words or syllables, and so forth—would seem to us to be "poor" setting. Or consider the alignment of textual and musical rhythms in a folksong or nursery rhyme and, on the other hand, the way in which another sort of "good" or "apt" setting might utterly distort the textual rhythm—Handel's setting, in *Semele,* say, of the couplets from Pope's *Summer* pastoral:

> Where-e'er you walk, cool Gales shall fan the Glade,
> Trees, where you sit, shall crowd into a shade,
> Where-e'er you tread, the blushing Flow'rs shall rise,
> And all things flourish where you turn your eyes.

These two couplets are the text for a ritornellic aria, and the whole rhythmic scheme of heroic iambic is lost in the movement of the setting, which nevertheless very cleverly maintains measure breaks at the syntactic caesuras. It is not that a simple setting is good and an ornate one bad: we implicitly admit a whole array of setting, let alone musical or poetic, conventions.

The polyphonic madrigal and the usually solo, strophic ayre or lute song were the two principal modes of setting texts in late sixteenth- and early seventeenth-century art songs in England. The second gradually came to supplant the first because of its purportedly greater fidelity to the poetic text; according to the best current French and Italian theories, a solo voice singing expressively modulated vocal lines, free of the entanglements and the obscuring fabric of polyphonic parts, could best express the emotional quality, and thereby the *meaning,* of a poetic text. It was certainly true that, as a passive listener, it was always possible to hear all the words in a solo ayre. In a madrigal, however, the listened-to texture is very peculiar indeed, with all sorts of episodic sections, fragments of phrase and word now clarified, now blurred, on frequent repetition in different voices; finally, one is reduced, as audience, to waiting hopefully for periods of homophonic, or foursquare harmonization of the kind we know from hymn tunes, where everyone sings the same syllable at the same instant. And yet those homophonic stretches were alien to the spirit of the true madrigal. In the accompanied ayre, a solo voice would sing a melody to a lute or viol accompaniment which might indeed make imitative counterpoint with the vocal part, but never contribute to the aural blanketing of the latter. The English madrigal was generally more of a household, and less of an esoteric, art than the Italian one, and we tend to find less idiosyncratic chromaticism, for example. But the distinguishing feature of the English art song during the Renaissance is the kind of rhythmic independence that the vocal lines must have in order to set the text well and expressively. For unlike French, in which the lack of syllabic stress accent can allow the same dissyllabic word to be set to two totally opposed rhythmic patterns in succession, or Italian, in which the penultimate accent and the generally vocalic, unstressed ultimate syllable tend to allow for certain smoothnesses of alignment of regularized, flowing melodies and the words they are sung to, English verse of the standard, accentual-syllabic sort poses grave problems for the musical setting. Precisely because the minute variations of stress accent in phrase structure account for so much of the rhetorical tone of English speech, precisely because of the ambiguities that accompany the process of getting the actualities of English sentences and phrases into the schemata of iambic verse, there is a kind of rhythmic richness about English poetry that is hard to find even in verse in Russian, which shares with English problems of word stress and concomitant vowel reduction, as well as a high proportion of consonantal clusters.

Now, the English madrigal was particularly good at working out all these ambiguities, at meeting the richnesses of impulse of the text with an appropriately complex array of rhythmic versions. It is just because of the independence of the various parts that it could do so. What sounds to an audience like a jumble can be appreciated by a singer of one of those parts as an extremely subtle variation on the rhythmic intricacies of a line other variations of which will appear in other parts. Necessarily, this makes the appreciation of madrigalian setting a *participatory* rather than an *audience* matter. Again, true madrigalian settings are never strophic; frequently, a particular poem will be set in a group of madrigals, so that the setting of a subsequent strophe or stanza, even though *metrically* equivalent to the first, will yet never depend on the intimate rhythmic interpretation given to that opening one. The ayres, on the other hand, were all strophic; and whatever the expressive attention given to the musical handling of one group of words, the unique exigencies of a subsequent group would make that attention irrelevant. Save in the cases of strophic songs whose rhythms are so mechanical, are so schematically close to the norms provided by the meter that they partake of syntactic woodenness and the rhythmic torpor of the mechanical, none but the first stanza can be set well. And even that setting will be a *frozen* version of the line's rhythm; far too often, even a magnificent composer of lute songs like John Dowland would choose the wrong version.

This effect of freezing a text in a setting, incidentally, poses some interesting problems for the prosodist. The legacy of the eighteenth-century "musical" metrists like Joshua Steele has been most unfortunate; prosodists, critics, and even casual (in the realms of linguistic theory, at least) classroom teachers continue to use musical notation to scan lines of verse. What is peculiar about such a practice is not that it cannot be used to specify properly which syllables, in accentual-syllabic verse, are stressed and which unstressed. It certainly can; the difficulty is that it over-specifies. Let me present some examples. The first is not in English, but I hope that it will be nevertheless familiar—the Schubert setting of Goethe's *"Heidenröslein,"* and the older, "folk-song" version of it. The text, it may be remembered, is like English, accentual-syllabic—in this case, trochaic tetrameter and trimeter catalectic: "Sáh' ein Knáb' ein Röslein stéh'n, / Röslein áuf der Héiden, / Wár so júng und mórgenschön,/Líef er schnéll es náh zu séhn . . ." etc. The two settings are in three and two, respectively, and they both handle the rhythm, even given strophic shifts in successive stanzas, extremely well:

32 VISION AND RESONANCE

The relative durations are irrelevant here: they are, in fact, over-specific as far as the prosody of the text is concerned. What the two settings have in common, is in fact the following

Sáh' ein Knáb' ein Rös-lein steh'n

or, to put it in the archaic and misleading terminology we still use, they both show that the text is trochaic, starting with what must be set as a downbeat. The extra length which the 3/4 setting gives to the stresses syllables we might think of as lying implicit in the text, just as the capacity for being equalized (as by Schubert) does. No use of musical notation to *scan* or analyze a poetic text will do any more than set it to a pitchless music. And as a setting, it cannot be correct or incorrect, save in giving a musical downbeat to a unstressed syllable, and thus distorting an English word. As a setting, it can only be better or worse, richer or thinner, sophisticated or plonking—indeed, like a critical reading of text in toto.[22]

Let me give an English example, from the period of English music and poetry we have been discussing. Thomas Campion's little poem in two stanzas of iambic pentameter *ababcc* beginning "Blame not my cheeks though pale with love they be" was set both by the poet-composer himself, and by Robert Jones in a collection published four years afterward. In both settings, the first and third lines are set to the same material which is repeated. Rhythmically, the two treatments go as follows:

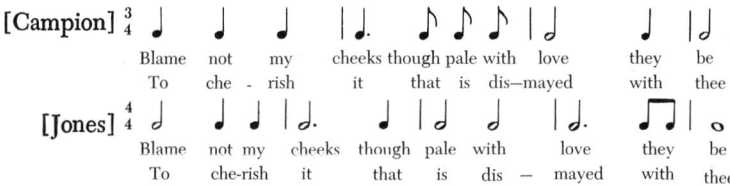

Whatever greater authority is to be given to Campion's own conception of the triple rhythm in the setting, it will be noticed that both composers are agreed on the contrastive stress pattern of the opening

---

22. What Schubert indeed does here is to point up the ordinarily lost, unstressed diminutive syllable "–*lein*" in a bit of brilliant vocal pointing.

phrase (a reversed opening foot, as the older prosody would call it, or a displaced stress-maximum): "Bláme nòt." Campion's setting is more declamatory; Jones's is slower and gives greater duration to the unstressed syllables "with" and "dis-," but with the intention of moving upward through a minor third (where Campion descends), on the three notes of "pale with love" and "is dis-mayed." Campion's setting is in D minor, Jones's in G major. Both promote the "it" of the third line willy-nilly, the accentual pattern having been "frozen" on the "cheeks."[23] Both, as with the Goethe settings, have something to say about the rhythmic complexities of the text, which as in all poems, result from various periodicities being overlaid upon each other. Syllable sequence, stress pattern, word boundary, modulations of stress pattern because of phrase grouping, additional prominence to syllables being given by internal rhyme, assonance, or alliteration—and all before we have considered anything semantic at all. It is inevitable that a number of different settings would all "mark up," scan, point out, diagram some of these overlaid rhythms, and pick them out. It was undoubtedly this phenomenon that Hopkins had in mind when he conceived of the concept of "counterpoint," as was observed earlier.

It should be understood, then, that while musical notation will *include* a perfectly verifiable marking of the accentuation as realized in the metrical scheme, it will provide other, ad hoc information that really constitutes a set of instructions for an oral performance. There are really three nesting sets of contingency patterns here.

METER

RHYTHM

SETTING OR PERFORMANCE

The meter (say, iambic pentameter) sets up certain contingencies, within which a vast array of different lines may be realized; given all

[23]. I am not suggesting that comparisons across setting genres be made; the differences might be too radical, although the common ground of word stress would remain. See, for example, the settings by Jones, in plain style, and by Alfonso Ferrabosco in declamatory style, of "Shall I seek to ease my grief?"

the possible compounding of rhythms mentioned before, the array is potentially infinite. To this extent, the conceptual matrix of the iambic pentameter is rather like a generative system, linguistically speaking. Any particular *instance* of a line, manifesting this design (to use Roman Jakobson's terminology) will have been derived from the constraints of the metrical system.

The next step is the relation of rhythm to performance or setting (which, for these purposes, are identical—the compounding of the rhythms in the musical setting, the melody, the harmonic rhythm if any, the modulating effects of other parts, rhythmically and harmonically, etc., are analogous to all the linguistic rhythms not specified by the verse design). That relation is usefully analogous: the rhythm of the line allows for, generates (in a grammatical sense) a host of possible settings, all within certain limits of contingency. To give a musical setting (pitchless as "musical scansions" are) to a line of verse, then, is as misleading as calling any particular line of *Paradise Lost* the poem's scheme, or meter. One says that the line exemplifies the meter, but then goes on to abstract. Such is the power of the musical mystique we examined earlier, the fiction of the music of verse, that it still flourishes in this pedagogical corner.

Hopkins, musician that he was, perceived an obvious fact about the way in which a musical setting can "freeze" a reading of a line's rhythm. We have been discussing monodic settings here, songs for voice and lute (or, in the case of the German song, piano).[24] In the polyphonic madrigals of the Elizabethan and early Jacobean periods, the fully independent contrapuntal vocal parts *could* (although they did not always) pluck out the ryhthmic ambiguities and possibilities in a text.

The virtues of the polyphonic setting of the madrigal can be exemplified by a brief and minor instance, a ballet, or "fa-la," as they were sometimes called, by Thomas Weelkes, from his 1598 collection. The text is a bit of fluff, perhaps Anacreontic in inspiration, and useful here only because of the rhythm of the last line of the first stanza:

24. See the more detailed discussion of these matters in Chapters II and IV.

> Hark, all ye lovely saints above,
> Diana hath agreed with love
> His fiery weapon to remove.
>   Do you not see
>   How they agree?
> Then cease, fair ladies, why weep ye?

Now a ballet differs from a true madrigal in that it is mostly homophonic, note against note, syllable against syllable in the various parts; only a mandatory section of fa-la-la-la-las is set polyphonically. Here, these fa-las come after "remove"; the voices then come back together homophonically on "Do you not see / How they agree," a neat little procedural pun typical of madrigals, which like to set verbs of rising or augmenting with an ascending melody and words like "sharp" with the appropriate accidental. All this might be barely worth observing, were it not for the ultimate line of the strophe. This is iambic tetrameter like the other longer lines, rhyming with the preceding two short ones but distinguished by the ambiguous stress pattern of its close. As far as iambic stressing is concerned, the line could read:

$$\text{Then céase, fair ládies, why wéep yé?}$$

The phrase "fair ladies," unless contrastively stressed "*fair* ladies" (as opposed, say, to the foul ones) enters the iambic pattern in just that way, and terminal "ye" picks up the extra prominence of being rhymed. But the last three syllables pose a rhetorical problem: contrastively accented, they can be "*why* weep ye?" or "why *weep* ye?" or "why weep *ye?*"—that is, "what are you crying for?" or "why are you crying about it?" or "why *you*, of all people?" It is the last of these that is certainly suggested by the metrical position of the phrase, reinforced by the rhyme. But in the context of the song, it should, if possible, be shown to mean all three. This is just what Weelkes does, by setting the line in a faintly polyphonic texture, with every voice repeating the phrase at least once, and, among the different parts, the various rhythmic patterns generating three different stressings of the text.

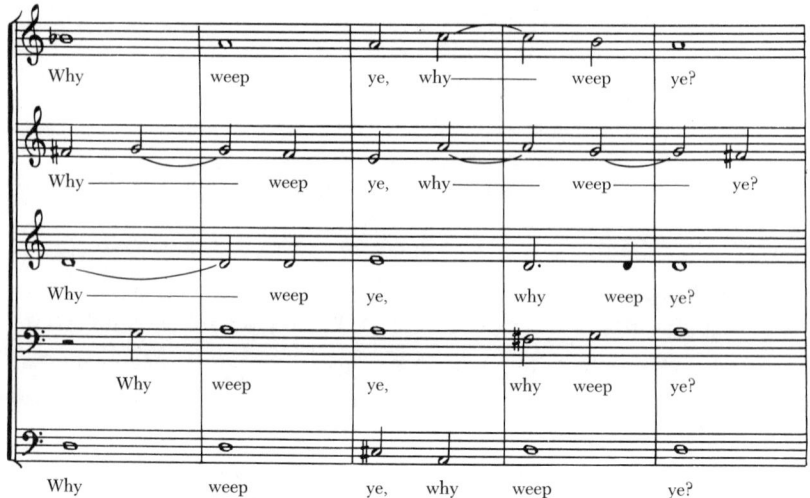

Another bout of fa-la-la-la-las closes the setting of the strophe. The point is clear: polyphonic settings can possibly get at the richness of rhythmic texture developed in accentual-syllabic English verse, while a single melodic line can probably not, at best perhaps managing to seize on part of a fruitful ambiguity and resolve it one way or another. But again, we must remember that the polyphonic setting's virtues can be apparent only to a participant. In a sense, the debased form of this almost coterie quality is the Restoration catch, where the frequent bawdy meaning that emerges when otherwise innocent single parts are sung in canon is apparent to the singers more than to the hearers.

Another example in the history of the separation between poetry and music is Henry Lawes. John Milton, who was his friend, praises him specifically as one who "first taught our English music how to span / Words with just note and accent, not to scan / With Midas' ears, committing short and long." In Lawes's setting of the great song to Echo in *Comus*, he manages throughout most of the song to prevent the interests of musical structure (the generation of sequences, for example, in the melodic line, the expressive prolongations and melismata that he would have felt requisite) from conflicting totally and crudely with the structures of the text. These structures involve the delicate modulation of line length and rhyme:

> Sweet Echo, sweetest nymph that liv'st unseen
>   Within thy airy shell
> By slow Meander's margent green,
> And in the violet-embroidered vale
>   Where the love-lorn nightingale
> Nightly to thee her sad song mourneth well.
> Canst thou not tell me of a gentle pair
>   That likest thy Narcissus are?
>   O if thou have
> Hid them in some flowery cave,
>   Tell me but where
> Sweet queen of parley, daughter of the sphere.
> So mayst thou be transplanted to the skies
> And hold a counterpoint to all heaven's harmonies.

Lawes's setting of these lines is in the Caroline declamatory style, programmatically monodic, devoted to setting an expressive but faithful recitative version of the text. Of necessity, this demands a subtler relation of musical to textual period than the older ayres provided, with their phrase-for-line patterns, strophic returns, and sub-strophic repeats. What is most interesting here is Lawes's attempt to handle the delicate, typically Miltonic enjambment at "have / Hid them" (measure 20), where the expected *contre-rejet* might have been "O if thou have / Seen them, tell me . . ." or the like. Lawes's prosodically awkward measure may indeed have been a go at rendering the effect of the "have," with its weak rhyme and its indeterminate active-auxiliary status as a verb. The echo of the attempt, at measure 23, generates too much rhetorical emphasis on "sweet" and displaces the rhyme, eventually, at "sphere."

What is interesting about Milton's praise of Lawes (for Milton was no musical illiterate himself) is its oblique thrust. He is praising him for being Italianate, for not being an old-fashioned polyphonist perhaps, and for his friendship and collaboration. Lawes does, in fact, "commit short and long," but he sounds, or perhaps *feels*, to Milton as if he doesn't. Nevertheless, the hopelessness of carrying over the deepest rhythmic impulses of the English poem into a musical setting was

as apparent to Milton as to anyone. This misplaced praise of Lawes, incidentally, is echoed in the twentieth century by Ezra Pound's rather uninformed remarks on seventeenth-century music, particularly his championship of Lawes and Jenkins on grounds rather inconsistent with his other literary-musical views. Pound's remarks on music and poetry are fascinating in this context because they embody certain literary attitudes toward the separation between the two that have been themselves the subject of poetry, but which, when stated as dogma, look rather shoddy. Thus, in *The ABC of Reading*, he announces portentously:

> The author's conviction on this day of New Year is that music begins to atrophy when it departs too far from the dance; that poetry begins to atrophy when it gets too far from music; but this must not be taken as implying that all good music is dance music or all poetry lyric. Bach and Mozart are never too far from physical movement.[25]

This is really either a banal musical truism, or quite false; that is, it either means that music must swing, that Bach's French suites must not be played as if they were classroom exercises in part-writing, or else, and here falsely, that Palestrina and Wagner on the one hand, and Milton and Wordsworth on the other, are the results of artistic atrophy. Doubtless Pound felt this to be true.

I should rather, at this point, invoke C. S. Lewis's remark about sixteenth-century lyric poems, although I think that it is far more true of the major seventeenth-century lyric, substituting as it does the authenticity of the spoken voice for the intonations of song. He observes that, "however happily married to their notes in the end, the poems had a rhythmical life of their own before the marriage, and it is their 'music'

---

25. Ezra Pound, *ABC of Reading* (Norfolk, Conn., n.d.), p. 14. Pound seems to have been unaware, for all of his celebration of Lawes and Jenkins, of the difference between the former's declamatory settings of texts, in 2, and his dance songs, in 3. This appears to be a Jacobean and Caroline convention, and one of great consequence for the future of English song.

in that sense that the literary critic is concerned with." Even more important, it is with that "music" that subsequent poets are concerned.

If the seventeenth century is that of the end of nostalgic Renaissance hopes for a re-creation of the original union of music and poetry, it is also the period in which poetry's own music develops most remarkably. The sounds of speech, instrumentalized within the framework of metrical conventions, become dominant in the organization of verse. The role of speech sound in the development of those unique and problematic English metrical conventions is quite limited, and in analyzing that development we remain, at the beginning particularly, in the realm of the eye rather than the ear. It is interesting, though possibly confusing, to note that, all this while, the linguistic music of poetry is being praised as though it were, in fact, actual vocal or instrumental music, as though, in fact, the separation between music and poetry had never occurred.

But this praise of music in poetry, this courting of its vanished partner, itself begins to be mechanical. In Neoclassic diction, all of the stiff personifications of music in such genres as the musical ode help to create the background of Romantic mistrust of the praise of the institutional music which has replaced the Renaissance notion of the harmony of the world, and for which the instrumental replaces the vocal as the epitome of human music. The Romantics turn to the celebration of natural sound, of human music authenticated by being heard out-of-doors and by blending with the music of nature. This outdoor music, the blending of the human with the natural, originates in pastoral. A *topos* is certainly to be found at the beginning of Virgil's first eclogue: "We have fled our homeland; you, Tityrus, at ease in the shade, teach the woods to echo 'fair Amaryllis.'"

> nos patriam fugimus: tu, Tityre, lentus in umbra
> formosam resonare doces Amaryllida silvas.

The woods learned their lesson well; the auditory mode of the pathetic fallacy came into being, as far as subsequent poetry is concerned. In the Renaissance, it is only pastoral tradition which maintains this notion of blending human meaning and natural assent; thus, for example, the April Eclogue of Spenser's *Shepheardes Calender:*

> "Contended I: then will I singe his laye
> Of fayre *Eliza,* Queene of Shepherdes all:
> Which once he made, as by a spring he laye
> And tuned it unto the waters fall."

The point here is not so much that the water might or might not have been that of Helicon, or the authentic source, in both original and applied senses of the word, of true poetry. Rather, it is starting to become legitimized within the pastoral mythology itself—it will be good poetry because it is tuned not to the music of the spheres (which in Renaissance mythology all well-tuned human music is, of necessity) but because it is tuned to the flow of water, the sound of eloquence in an uncorrupted garden. In the following two hundred years it will become cliché. But when Romantic poetry begins to take up the pastoral device, something else happens to it conceptually. A dialectic between the inner and the outer, being subject and object, takes it up, and it starts to involve the actualities of the ear and the way in which consciousness itself makes sense of these. Poetry becomes, for itself, something very like the "mingled measure," in Collins's and Coleridge's phrase, of the human music set against an undersong of wind or water or their resonances.

If a mythical starting point for the pastoral music of outdoor sound might be located in the Virgilian shepherd's liquid metronome, the more complex Romantic reading of nature demands a different sort of account. One poem by Robert Frost, harking back to Classical pastoral in one way, more directly invoking the biblical garden, may serve to illustrate this:

> He would declare and could himself believe
> That the birds there in all the garden round
> From having heard the daylong voice of Eve
> Had added to their own an oversound,
> Her tone of meaning, but without the words.

> Admittedly an eloquence so soft
> Could only have had an influence on birds
> When call or laughter carried it aloft.
> Be that as may be, she was in their song.
> Moreover her voice upon their voices crossed
> Had now persisted in the woods so long
> That probably it never would be lost.
> Never again would birds' song be the same.
> And to do that to birds was why she came.

This is an uncharacteristically mythopoetic moment for Frost. The myth is that of the imprinting of consciousness onto nature, not a visual one of, say, double exposure, or overlay of transparency that might fulfill technologically a wholly imagined Romantic device, but an aural one—"Be that as may be, she was in their song," and surely only because of the heightened power of eloquence in call or laughter, not weeping, the very sounds of which drop, like tears, into the ground. Hereafter, the poem says, nature would exist as a meaningful communicant—this is really a totally Emersonian poem—to be listened to because human meaning would always be in it. The final couplet of the sonnet is a blend of summation and inspired, crafty hedging: "Never again would birds' song be the same," says Frost, in the line that gives the poem its title. But then he withdraws, as if the point of the poem couldn't be the establishment of a major myth; the final line domesticates the story, turning into canny praise of Eve's beauty—"And to do that to birds was why she came." But of course the poem is not about Eve as woman at all, but, in an unavowedly Miltonic way, about a part of humanity.

"Her tone of meaning, but without the words"—undoubtedly what Frost had earlier formulated, in attempting to particularize the dimension of the music of speech to which his ear was most highly attuned, as "the sentence sound." He meant the delicate but crucial modulations of phrase-stress pattern, contrastive stress, the rhetorical suprasegmentals, that not only make oral communication what it is, but which a practitioner of classical accentual-syllabic verse must be aware of. It is the music of English verse in which syntax plays a necessarily important role. "Just so many sentence sounds belong to man as just so many vocal runs belong to one kind of bird," he writes to Sidney Cox in 1914. "We come into the world with them and create none of them. What we feel as creation is only selection and grouping. We summon them from Heaven knows where under excitement with the audile imagination."[26] The sound of sense: the music of speech, but of speech being watched, in its transcribed form, within a diagraming and punctuating and annotating grid of metrical pattern. To this degree, we all still dwell in the Romantic world of the ear, in which the song of birds is more like poetry than a Beethoven string quartet. Wordsworth's "Ode on the Power of Sound" is, of course, emphatically not about the power of music, but about the ear's larger, undomesticated vastnesses, those regions in which real poetry, rather than cultivated verse, is to be found, the realm of all the human and natural utterance, from cries of pain to shouts of discovery: the sounds of language and of the wind in trees.

26. *Selected Letters of Robert Frost,* ed. Lawrance Thompson (New York, 1964), p. 140. See also the letter of February 1914 to John T. Bartlett, pp. 110-13.

II
DONNE AND THE LIMITS OF LYRIC

So much has been written about Donne's metrical roughness that a comprehensive survey of commentary upon what the poet himself called "my words masculine perswasive force" would parallel the whole course of his reputation. Aside from the disagreements of his contemporaries about his metrical style—the strictures of a Jonson, the complex praise of a Carew—we can trace even in the revived but canonical twentieth-century phase of Donne's career a shift from an acceptance of Jonson's famous "not keeping of accent" to the commendation of it as a positive and unique virtue. Even though Jonson may have been complaining to Drummond of Hawthornden about the slightly more than fashionably irregular verse of the satires and even as, in twentieth-century criticism, a Browningesque rather than a Tennysonian sense of verbal music in verse began to be praised,[1] Grierson, writing before 1912, would find it necessary to apologize for "a poetry, not perfect in form, rugged of line and careless in rhyme" as being yet "a poetry of an extraordinary arresting and haunting quality, passionate, thoughtful, and with a deep melody of its own."[2] That "deep melody" of speech has since almost become a cliché of Donne

1. See for example, Sir Herbert Grierson's Introduction to his edition of the *Poems* (Oxford, 1912), Vol. ii, p. xv.
2. Grierson *op. cit.*, Vol. ii, p. lv.

criticism; it is used with force and clarity by the editor of a recent college text edition:

> To begin with, despite the absence of any facile smoothness of versification, the lines have a strange and original music, derived largely from an imitation of the accents of emotionally heightened conversation. . . . Donne's metrical control is of an astounding virtuosity, although that virtuosity is generally in the service of drama rather than of song.[3]

Coleridge, in some notes on Donne made in Lamb's copy of the poet in 1811, put the matter almost perfectly in observing that "*all* Donne's poems are equally *metrical* (misprints allowed for) though smoothness (i.e. the metre necessitating the proper reading) be deemed appropriate to *songs;* but in poems where the writer *thinks,* and expects the reader to do so, the sense must be understood in order to ascertain the metre."[4] This might just as well be about Browning. Whether they "imitate" or, in fact, embody, and whether they emulate "the accents of emotionally heightened conversation" or, as I shall try to show, are partly a necessary consequence of a speaker's trying to make himself understood—in any event, Donne's jagged rhythms, when considered against the smoothness usually demanded of strophic song texts, remain highly problematic, even when highly praised. "Donne," says Arnold Stein, "is a conscious master of harshness,"[5] and he is speaking for the literary temper of Modernism, for an age which approves of strong lines not for their wit, their "tension" alone, but for the rhythmic

---

3. John Donne, *Poetry and Prose*, ed. Frank J. Warnke (New York, 1967), p. xviii.
4. Reprinted in Roberta F. Brinkley, ed., *Coleridge on the XVIIth Century* (Durham, N.C., 1955), p. 521. This approaches one of the meanings of Robert Frost's notion of "sentence sound." Unfortunately, Coleridge can obscure the picture as well; elsewhere in the same notes (Brinkley, p. 519), he can start off "To read Dryden, Pope +c., you need only count syllables; but to read Donne you must measure *Time*, and discover the *Time* of each word by the sense of Passion." Unless he means by "time" something involving emphatic stress, this may not mean much.
5. Arnold Stein, *John Donne's Lyrics* (Minneapolis, 1962), pp. 24-25. Here again, it is "dramatic" expressiveness which is emphasized. Douglas L. Peterson in *The English Lyric from Wyatt to Donne* (Princeton, 1967), pp. 285-87, tries to connect Donne's roughness with the tradition of the plain, as opposed to the courtly, style.

insistence upon domination over the meter and its schemata which would place them in a line stemming from Catullus and Villon—the lyric of insistent talk, rather than the lyric of written flow (Horace and Ronsard). The Modernist sense of that tradition which makes of the speaking voice the most authentic singing has been one that has found the irregularity of Wyatt's experimental pentameters valuable per se.[6] It has found thinness and smoothness in what its Victorian forbears had thought of as lyrical language. And still largely unacquainted or unimpressed with Browning, it has made the rhythms of the *Songs and Sonnets* into touchstones for revision of prosodic theory.[7]

In these second thoughts on the nature of the unmusicality of Donne's lyrics, I should like to consider their roughness in a literally, rather than figuratively, "musical" context, and to inspect certain features of his rhythmic style, strophic patterning and rhetorical tonality which make the "songs" of their title so hard to take with an older, Elizabethan literalness. Some of these problems need no new discussion. Certainly the rhythmic variations within the versification of metrically identical strophes is not a problem peculiar to Donne. Composers of monodic airs like Dowland who set a great variety of texts would al-

---

6. Brought up on the invidious comparison of Tottel's reworking of "They Flee from Me" with the ms. text—almost a set school exercise in the early 1950s—I now find myself preferring the former. For an interesting discussion of this, see John Thompson, *The Founding of English Metre* (London, 1961), pp. 15-36.

7. Seymour Chatman, "Comparing Metrical Styles," in *Style and Language*, ed. Thomas A. Sebeok (Cambridge, Mass., 1960), pp. 149-72, uses the structural linguistic model of English stress, propounded by Trager and Smith in 1951, to compare the style of the *Satyres* with Pope's versions of them. Chatman's analysis was one of the first to try to systematize a description of some of the stress phenomena I shall discuss below. Roger Fowler, "'Prose Rhythm' and Meter," in Essays on *Style and Language*, ed. Roger Fowler (New York, 1966), pp. 82-89, is clear and useful. Disagreements with Chatman's methodology have been voiced eloquently and powerfully by W. K. Wimsatt and Monroe Beardsley in "The Concept of Meter: An Exercise in Abstraction," *PMLA*, LXXIV (1959), 585-98; also, in a revision of his own theory by Chatman in *A Theory of Meter* (The Hague, 1965). A more recent study of English accentual-syllabic meter from the viewpoint of transformational grammar is that of Morris Halle and Samuel Jay Keyser, "Chaucer and the Theory of Prosody," *College English*, XXVIII (December 1966), 187-219, where they establish linear syllabic position as a schematic unit. I adopt their useful concept of stress maximum to indicate the iambic handling of relative stress, particularly in groups of monosyllabic words.

ways work out a setting for the intial stanza and cheerfully ignore the lack of fit in subsequent ones, whether or not the performance of those following stanzas could be made possible with a little melismatic assistance. In the case of a rhythmically active line like the opening one of the great, anonymous peddler's song from Dowland's 1600 *Book of Airs*:

> Fine knacks for ladies, cheape, choice, brave and new

the equivalent line of the third strophe gets a weaker setting, requiring displaced word stress on the line's only two disyllables. Thus

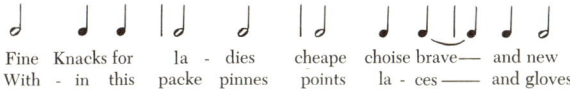

That is, in both cases the iambic norm is stretched by the rhythm of the text, but the *ad hoc* accentual underlining of one which a musical setting provides will not fit the cadences of another. With Donne, this situation is frequent and strongly marked. Let us consider one of the most interesting of the seven settings of Donne lyrics by seventeenth-century composers edited by André Souris and Jean Jacquot,[8] the version of "The Expiration" by Alfonso Ferrabosco from his 1609 book of airs. Here again, the setting cannot possibly hope to accommodate the second strophe in its rhythmic setting of the first one: "Any so cheape a death as saying goe."[9] The terminal line of the second strophe, for example, must be sung to this rhythm:

It is interesting to note that although the final imperative "Go!" is meant in both lines, it should be in inverted commas in the first in-

---

8. *Poèmes de Donne, Herbert et Crashaw, mise en musique par leurs contemporains* transcribed and realized by A. Souris, introduced by Jean Jacquot (Paris, 1961), to whose musical text I shall refer. Helen Gardner gives melodic lines from these in her edition of the *Songs and Sonnets* (Oxford, 1965), pp. 238-47.
9. The enjambment which leads to this line (". . . owe? Any . . .") is completely lost in setting. Here as elsewhere, when I am quoting from a text in its setting, I shall use the texts of the songbooks and mss., as transcribed in *Poèmes de Donne*, etc. These lines are from p. 9.

stance—"saying, 'Go!'" as a quick, easy death—whereas in the second, it is a direct but conditional command of the singer-lover. No matter how "expressive," by early-baroque or Modern standards, the setting is to be, it must surely comprehend the *sense* of the text. For example, the music in a good setting should punctuate the final two lines of the song, with its own rhythms, so as to do something like this:

> Except it be too late to kill me so,
> (Being double-dead—going and bidding), Go!

Now Ferrabosco's setting realizes neither the speech-rhythm of the phrase "saying, 'Go!'" in the first strophe, nor that of the complex syntax of the second. But at the crudest level of rhythmic fitting of musical downbeat to normal word stress (let alone to phrase stress among monosyllabic groups, or stress maxima in an iambic context) the second strophe will not work. It is rewarding to contrast Ferrabosco's setting of just these lines with another one, from an anonymous musical ms. of about the same time.[10]

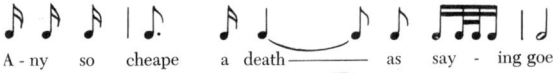

Here, at least the "saying, 'Go!'" phrase is plausibly treated; the syntax, and, hence, the rhetoric of speech is recognizable in the melodic interpretation of it. I mention syntax only because so much recent discussion of Donne's metrics has concentrated on declamatory and emotional effects of apparently abberrant stress-positioning in Donne's iambic lines,[11] without appeal to the basic complex relations between phrase-stress patterns and syntactic structure in English. But if the anonymous setting handles the terminal line of the first stanza well, its reciprocal is even more distorted than in Ferrabosco's version. It demands two sorts of accentual deformation.

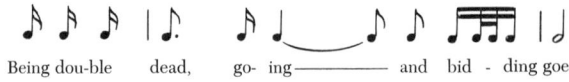

10. For lute and voice, from Bodleian ms. Mus. Sch. F. 575. f. 8ᵛ, *Poèmes de Donne*, pp. 10-11.
11. See, for example, Arnold Stein, *Donne's Lyrics*, p. 42.

—the first, on "going," exacerbated by the long tied, note value on the second syllable, the second, making the phrase "bidding go" syntactically equivalent—through rhythmic identity—to "saying go." But "bidding" is, as we have seen, part of another, complex parenthetical phrase, the very syntactical existence of which dissolves in song. Or, at any rate, this song.[12]

In other words, Donne's rhythmic modulation of language is such that even the most musicianly attention to word stress (and this, indeed, is not always Ferrabosco's strongest point) will frequently not suffice to accentuate correctly the textual syntax. In view of the increased attention, in early seventeenth-century monody, given to freeing the text from polyphonic labyrinths, in view of the growing influences outside of Italy of the *stile espressivo* of recitative, the unique problems of English prosody remained a stumbling block in the way of properly "committing short and long," not only in strophic settings but in through-composed ones as well.

One of these problems is that posed by contrastive stress. Even in the case of another poet, one who took pride—or at least believed himself undeserving of hanging—in keeping of accent, the accentual properties of English phrase structure posed a difficulty for musical setting. Ben Jonson's friend and collaborator Ferrabosco was, again, the victim; this time, the text in question is the final couplet of the famous seduction song from *Volpone*, out of Catullus, later included in *The Forrest* in 1616. " 'Tis no sinne loves fruits to steale,/But the sweet theft to reveale"[13]

---

12. Occasionally, strophic fitting can occur in these settings. Giovanni Coperario's version of "The Message" takes advantage of the alignment, in successive stanzas, of the word pairs "Which O"—"Which no"—"That I," for a repeated musical phrase. See *Poèmes de Donne*, pp. 7-8.

13. Another problem here is the relation of the two concluding couplets to each other. Jonson's folio text gives the punctuation "to reveale:/To be taken" and this suggests that Ferrabosco's setting is correct in its reading of the full stop. In that case, the penultimate couplet means "There's no sin in sex save for to do it openly," and "but" has the same sense of "except" that it does in the penultimate line of stanza 1 of "Drink to me only with thine eyes." I wonder about this: perhaps "but" means "nevertheless" here, and governs all three lines—"*But* (1) to reveal the theft, (2) to be taken, (3) to be seen—*these* are called crimes."

While the purely melodic effect is lovely and sophisticated—a stylistically forward-looking evaded cadence on the chord of the sixth at "beene," heralding the repetition of the words in a final phrase, etc.—it is almost as if the text laid under it were a fairly clever verse translation of that for which the music was composed. The sense of the couplet becomes clear only when we underline the emphatic stress:

> To be *taken,* to be *seene,*
> *These* have crimes *accounted* been.

"Crimes" needs no added stress, since it refers back to, rather than contrasts with, the "sinne" of the previous couplet. *"These"* (i.e. getting caught, not adultery itself), or, more subtly, "accounted" (morality is mere fashion) are the words which take an implicit contrastive stress in speech. According to the setting, the preceding lines of the text would have had to suggest that these were blessings, and "crimes" was then given emphatic development.

Ben Jonson's lyric culminates in the moral arguments of seduction which are frequently rhetorically contrastive. But we have only to turn to a far less schematic example, again from Ferrabosco's treatment of Donne's "The Expiration," to see how fundamental this problem is. Consider the third line of the first strophe:

> Turne thou (ghost!) *that* way, and let *me* turne *this*[14]

This has been italicized and repunctuated to gloss its meaning in the context of the stanza ("So, so, breake off this last lamenting kisse,/ Which sucks two soules and vapours both away,/Turne thou ghost that way, and let me turne this"). We may observe that, as in so many of Donne's lines, the "roughness" comes about as a result of ambiguities in reading the metrical disposition of stresses. "Let *me* turne *this*" falls

---

14. Text from Ferrabosco's song book of 1609 (*Poèmes de Donne,* p. 11). One could also read "Turne (thou ghost!) that way . . ." with a less archaic imperative form, but the larger problem would still remain.

perfectly into iambic position[15] because of the contrast with the preceding "Turne *thou* (ghost) *that* way." It also allows "kisse" and "this" to rhyme with greater reason, whereas if "this" were enjambed, for example (as in, say, ". . . and let me turne this/As yet unbloodied dagger from my heart"), any coherent musical setting would have to avoid a rhythmic ictus on "this." Similarly, another syntactic version of the line "Turne thou ghost that way which faces East" would call for a musical downbeat on "way" to make sense of it. But to emphasize "way" in the setting of Donne's line would be something like the way certain Romance foreign accents mis-stress English words. Here, then, is Ferrabosco's setting

which commits just that fault, totally missing, in its rhythmic generations, the point of the line. The other, anonymous setting cited before,[16] incidentally, manages this problem better:

The contrastive stress is pointed up in the setting, and at least gross syntactic grouping—aside from any nuances of expression which might grace that grossness—has been satisfied. But as we might expect, the consequences for the reciprocal line in the second strophe are more disastrous than merely a matter of musical rhythm wrecking word stress

♪ |♪. ♪♪ ♪♪ ৴ ♪♪♪ ♪ |♪
O——— if it have let my word worke on thee

Here, the gasping rest after the poorly treated "if it have, let . . ." is grotesque and irrelevant.

The setting of any poem to music recapitulates, in a strange way, the very process of metrical composition in a language; this is espe-

---

15. Or, with stress-maxima properly assigned, to use the Halle-Keyser terminology.
16. See note 10 above. With reference to the choice in note 16 above, note that the anonymous setting opts for the grouping "turn (thou ghost!)."

cially true in the case of English iambic verse. A particular line will make manifest certain possibilities implicit in the iambic schema (allowable reversals, promotions, or demotions in trisyllabic words, heightening of syllabic prominence by means other than stress, such as rhyme, assonance, alliteration, etc.). Just so will a musical setting of that line go one step further and resolve ambiguities that may remain yet exist in the fulfilled rhythmic line. For example, we know that line 21 from "A Valediction: Of Weeping,"

Weepe me not dead, in thine armes, but forbeare

is not dactylic only because of our knowledge of its context of versification, of the metrical convention of the poem itself.[17] For if the line had been preceded by a different one, the rhythmic possibilities would have gone the other way, as in, say,

Sweete though to drowne in the tides of thy haire,
Weepe me not dead in thine armes but forbeare . . . etc.

A good musical setting, like a proper scansion in the act of reading, or an actual oral performance of the line by a speaker, will resolve the ambiguity.[18] But let us take this back one step further: we know how frequently Donne's lines which look "rough" (or, in the precisely defined terms of a recent prosodic theory, "unmetrical"), turn out not to be so if the proper attention is paid to contrastive stress.[19]

A startling case of this occurs in "A Nocturnall upon S. Lucies Day," in such a way as to suggest an alternative reading of syntax and, thus,

17. Catherine Ing, *Elizabethan Lyrics* (London, 1951), pp. 234-35, considers this line, but her prosodic comments are hampered by her confusion of musical downbeat, word stress, emphatic stress, and metrical positions.
18. The composer Charles Wuorinen carries this analogy a step further into music itself, by considering the "freezing" of interpretation in taped, electronic music (whatever schematic randomizations may occur), as opposed to the interpretive choices of traditional instrumental performance. See his "Toward Good Vibrations," *Prose* #2, 1971, pp. 205-9.
19. A. J. Smith, *John Donne: The Songs and Sonets* (London, 1964), p. 44, observes this, albeit from an inverted viewpoint; I would disagree only in that I am arguing that "a reading with the natural speech rhythm" will often, indeed, scan, and that such elements as contrastive stress are part of natural speech rhythm.

of the nature of the image therein embodied. The mourning poet says
of the alchemist Love

> He ruin'd mee, and I am re-begot
> Of absence, darknesse, death; things which are not.

In order that the rhyme may function at all, let alone not set off what Milton called "wretched matter and lame Metre," the final syllable must be stressed; in order that Donne may not really deserve hanging, the semantic phrase stress must allow that to happen. Now assume for a moment that the phrase "things which are not" means "things which aren't, which don't exist." The rhythmic phrasal paradigm would be that of the phrases from Jeremiah 5:21, "which have eýes and seé not." "Thíngs which aŕe not" would in any case give either a truncated predicative, or else a totally existential meaning of the copula. We should then expect, in the first instance, a completion of predication in a contre-rejet in a following line (as, say, ". . . things which aŕe not/ Present, brighte, alive . . ."²⁰ But the stress on "not" suggests another reading, with a different paradigm of syntax and scansion; "things which are hót," for example, would take an iambic stress on the final adjective, "hot," (unless specifically stressed contrastively, of course, viz. "things which *are* hot"—as opposed to things which *aren't*). If Donne's phrase is modeled on this one, we must take "*not*" as adjectival, rather than as a negative particle, a nonce term meaning "not x, x being any predicate whatsoever." The ontological joke about reifying nothing is even stronger in this reading, and Love's alchemy far more impressive—the "quintessence . . . of nothingnesse" would certainly be, if nothing else, "not."

Recent theories of prosody have interested themselves in Donne's

---

20. Warnke in his edition (see note 3, above) omits a full stop after "not." I'm not sure whether this is a typographical error, or whether he means to read the enjambment as "things which are not/All others, from all things draw all that's good," where "not" is merely negatively predicative, an enjambment across strophes even more violent than "And there he lives with memorie and Ben/Jonson who wrote this of him . . ." from Jonson's Cary and Morison Ode.

emphatic stress for a variety of reasons.[21] The *Songs and Sonnets* and the *Elegies* seem encrusted with examples of lines which become fairly regular iambic pentameter when the purely contrastive stress is recognized:

> by that remorse,
> Which *my* words masculine perswasive force
> Begot in *thee*, and by the memory
> ("On his Mistresse," 3-5)

is a self-illustrating case. Pairs of pronouns frequently contrast in Donne; this is basic to the texture of his rhetoric. Phrases like "my words," normally stressed [·/], are shifted to [/·]. With the normal iambic option for trisyllables, "masculine" can be either [/··] or [/ ·/], and with the latter choice, the line becomes regularized, rather than "sprung" as in older ways of scanning Donne ("Which my words masculine persuasive force," for example). If the line is indeed as potent as the language it describes, then it is at least normally erect.

A few more examples, perhaps: line 20 of "The Anniversarie"—

> When bodies *to* their graves, soules *from their* graves remove.

—falls into its Alexandrine role more adroitly when the double contrasts of "to-from" and "their-their" are realized. Line 24 of the same poem—

> but wee
> Can be such Kings, nor, *of* such, subjects mee;
> (my punctuation)

—depends upon a contrastive elevation of "of." A particularly delicate effect is gained in "The Primrose," where, in line 8—

---

21. The most profound treatment of contrastive stress in Donne that I have seen is in an unpublished paper by William A. Krohn. But see, for example, the attempt to apply transformational principles in a somewhat crude way to the treatment of contrastive stress by Joseph C. Beaver in "Contrastive Stress and Metered Verse," *Language and Style*, Vol. ii, 1969, pp. 257-71. His examples from Donne are not very well handled.

$\overset{.}{\text{I}} \overset{/}{\text{walke}} \overset{.}{\text{to}} \overset{/}{\text{finde}} \overset{.}{\text{a}} \overset{/}{\text{true}} \overset{/}{\text{Love;}} \overset{.}{\text{and}} \overset{.}{\text{I}} \overset{/}{\text{see}}$

—the iambic irregularity obtained by reversal of stress in positions 7 and 8 rushes on toward an enjambment of "see"; this differs sharply from the situation in line 13

$\overset{.}{\text{For}} \overset{/}{\text{should}} \overset{.}{\text{my}} \overset{/}{\text{true-Love}} \overset{.}{\text{lesse}} \overset{/}{\text{then}} \overset{.}{\text{woman}} \overset{/}{\text{bee}} \ldots$

in the stressing of the compound. In the first instance, "true Love" with a plus-juncture, a spondaic accent, the stress pattern of Christian-name-plus-surname, or however an informal prosodic descriptive vocabulary would want to put it, is the usual adjective-noun pair. In the second instance, the name of the flower, the stress has regressed to the first syllable of the compound, and the four or six petals of the false floral emblem of love are matched by a skewed stress pattern on the words of its name as well.

It is just these contrasts which in English are far from being mere nuances, but engage fundamental grammatical relationships. To a French or Italian ear, particularly that of a musician, they might die away; and since the rhythmic generations of melodic lines were constantly being influenced by Continental music, the ability of English composers of the seventeenth century to embody and enhance in their settings the basic rhetorical stuff, the compelling speech-music of strong lines markedly decreased.[22] Smoother, post-Jonsonian lyric traditions, moving toward the thinness of Augustan song texts, provided easier materials for song settings than could poetic language rhythmically exciting in itself. Expressive formulae took precedence over rhetorical complexity, which, fortunately, texts began to abandon. Can we tell, for example, from John Hilton's (1599-1657) setting of "A Hymne to God the Father"[23] whether, in the rhythmic realization of

22. Even in the more recitative-like monody of the middle seventeenth century, this is evident. See Lawes's setting of "Sweet Echo" from *Comus*, for example, where the rhetorical music of "Tell me but where/Sweet Queen of parley, daughter of the Sphere" is turned, in the setting, into something rather strange.
23. From British Museum Egerton ms. 2013. f. 13^r, transcribed in *Poèmes de Donne*, pp. 18-19. This may be the setting which Walton says that Donne had sung by the St. Paul's choir, although it would have had to be in polyphonic form.

When thou hast done,   thou hast not done,   [for   I   have   more]

the composer has "set" the pun on the poet's name? At least he has not reduced the paradox to the more trivial one by implying with musical ictus a speech rhythm of "Whén thòu hást dóne, thou hást nòt dóne."[24]

No matter what the genres of the *Songs and Sonnets* lyrics are considered to be—and they embrace dramatic monologue, emblem verse, implicit dramatic scene (as when the insect is successfully threatened and killed in the white space between successive strophes in "The Flea"), argument, or whatever—the modulation of personal speech make the sounds of sense, and makes sense of the sound patternings of the meter. It is not the diversity of genres per se which makes so many of the songs un-song-like. Many a Jacobean composer, "his art and voice to show," would set and sing all manner of texts; William Byrd in his 1589 and 1611 books of madrigals set four passages from Geoffrey Whitney's emblem book, and, in an earlier volume, a quantitative translation of a group of lines from Ovid's *Heroides*. Musical and textual quotations from street cries and well-known tunes work their way into art songs by John Daniel and Thomas Campion. And the latter could insist on the similarity of lyrics and epigrams:

> Short Ayres, if they be skilfully frame, and naturally exprest, are like quicke and good Epigrammes in Poesie, many of them shewing as much artifice, and breeding as great difficultie as a large Poeme.[25]

It is ultimately a matter of modality that marks the metaphysical lyric from a musical point of view, a mixture of basic tonalities within a particular song. Whether polyphonic or monodic, the song is at a loss to handle the dialectic between lyric modes, the simultaneous presence of contrary impulses which even the formal musical dialogue (an increasingly popular seventeenth-century form) could only trivialize.

24. Beaver, p. 268, gives this reading, presumably because he never heard of the pun.
25. Thomas Campion, "To the Reader" from *A Booke of Ayres*, 1601, in *Works*, ed. Walter R. Davis (New York, 1967), p. 15.

This is particularly true in the case of the most complex kinds of post-Petrarchan love poetry. The Petrarchan poem will develop a mode and an emotional tonality of its own, and while it may turn against that tonality (particularly in the sestet of a sonnet) a sequential musical shift could represent it in a setting.

For example, in Thomas Campion's 1601 book of airs, there is a conventionally Petrarchan lyric whose first strophe goes as follows:[26]

> Mistris, since you so much desire
> To know the place of Cupid's fire,
> In your faire shrine that flame doth rest,
> Yet never harbourd in your brest.
> It bides not in your lips so sweete,
> Nor where the rose and lillies meete,
> But a little higher, but a little higher;
> There, there, O there lies Cupids fire.

The lady's eyes, a source of a higher, purer love than is her mouth, are here celebrated in the language of the sonneteers, and the air of sanctity, the forswearing of mere passion ("So meanely triumphs not my blisse," goes a line in the second strophe) are all familiar enough. But in his fourth book of airs, published *ca.* 1618, Campion parodied his own earlier song in some now-fashionable anti-Petrarchan second thoughts. The first strophe:[27]

> Beauty, since you so much desire
> To know the place of *Cupids* fire,
> About you somwhere it doth rest,
> Yet never harbour'd in your brest,
> Nor gout-like in your heele or toe;
> What foole would seeke Loves flame so low?
> But a little higher, but a little higher,
> There, there, o there lyes *Cupids* fire.

This is a satiric reduction, a literal lowering: here love starts, as Donne suggests that it should in "Loves Progresse," from below, that it may

26. Campion, *Works,* p. 41. See also below, p. 90.
27. Campion, *Works,* p. 190.

find its home in sex, at the body's center. Campion's setting for the second song is more chromatic in melodic line than is the first, and the lute part bawdily points up the repeatedly ascending "But a little higher" with contrapuntal nudging.[28]

These two songs represent two conflicting modalities. The major tradition of European song would have to differentiate between those modalities in setting them. Many of Donne's major lyrics embody a constant process of dialectic between modalities, conducted by an ingenuity masked as a reality principle, juggling hyperbole and abuse, insisting that the truest tenderness is the most feigning, that the most faithful caresses are those of wit and will combined. Art song could not begin to treat such complexity musically until Schumann began to set Heine *Lieder*. The poet of the *Songs and Sonnets*, double fool—perhaps even exponential fool—as he was, seldom ran the real risk of being a triple one.

28. Miles W. Kastendieck, *England's Musical Poet* (Oxford, 1938), pp. 114-15, discusses the sequence of rising repetitions of "but a little higher," each starting a whole tone above the end of the last one; but he appears to misunderstand the song and its relation, textually and musically, to the earlier one. Recent studies of Tudor and Stuart lyrics with regard to the music of their age are of much greater sophistication. A fine example is Frank J. Fabry's "Sidney's Poetry and Italian Song-Form," *ELR* III (1973), 232-48, which I have found most helpful.

III
OBSERVATIONS IN THE ART OF ENGLISH QUANTITY

The whole problem of quantitative verse has been so perplexing to the history of English poetry, and so inaccessible to modern critics with or without Classical background, that perhaps an excursus is in order. We might start out from any of a number of points—anecdotally, for example, by recalling how even as perceptive and probing a critic as the late R. P. Blackmur could quote the remark of Tennyson that he knew "the quantity of every English word except for 'scissors,' " without wondering exactly what it was that might be wrong with such a remark.[1] Clearly, even if he felt that some mysterious knowledge about the properties of words had died with nineteenth-century prosodic practice, that knowledge would either extend to all words (even, one would assume, the Tetragrammaton?) or it would be false knowledge indeed. But anyone discussing quantitative verse seems to most of us Moderns to be protected by a screen of mystique, if not a rebarbative air of the crank, and, after all, as wonderfully "Classical" a prosodist as Frost, himself capable of wielding the hendecasyllabic in a Catullan fashion, never talked about that sort of thing, so why need anyone? Frost's "hendecasyllabic" line of course, like those that Coleridge,

1. Tennyson's observation is preserved in the *Memoir* by his son, II, 231. R. P. Blackmur's essay entitled "Lord Tennyson's Scissors" appears in *Language as Gesture* (New York, 1952), where he calls the remark "irrelevant nonsense."

Tennyson himself, or any Romantic German might employ, is not in the least "quantitative"—it is simply an accentual-syllabic pattern, less flexible than iambic pentameter in allowing no substitution of syllables, "adapted from" the Latin meter for languages with phonemic word stress, as

This "hendecasyllabic" line is word-stressed.

And, to add to the confusion, the Italian *endecasillibo* is marked by other vastly different criteria. The whole area represents not only a host of historical confusions and analogies operating as identities, but modern ones as well; we are left largely either with the quantitative crank, someone with Classical training who for complex reasons fancies he hears true quantity in English verse, to the suspicious pragmatist who wisely ignores discussions of such matters as being mystique-ridden (but who then pays the price of being taken in by the misleading and misinformed accounts by poets themselves of what their practice is—W. C. Williams is a prime example of someone who did not really know what the term "quantity" *meant*).

We can dispose of the matter of Lord Tennyson's scissors easily enough. Tennyson was half-joking in any event, and his joke was in fact *about* the two different ways that "quantity" could be used, *both metaphorically*, in English verse. The first is simply the stress-analogue system, where the accentual-syllabic patterns of stressed and unstressed syllables correspond to patterns of long and short in Greek and Latin. This is the kind of so-called "metrical experiments" in which Tennyson himself indulged, although the analogy is deeply rooted in English verse practice from the Renaissance on. In its terms, "scissors," phonemically /'sizəz/, is "trochaic"—the syllables are stressed then unstressed, analogically "long-short" in that order. The other way in which quantity can be ascribed to modern English, however, is a more complicated problem, and I shall return to it specifically at the end of this brief discussion, hoping that by that time the reader will be able to solve it himself.

I should like to turn away from the "scissors" for a bit to what lies behind it, not only to make the other half of the explanation easier but because the history of the problem lies significantly close to the heart of what constitutes literary tradition itself. To say that the hankering after Classical quantity in verse (and after classical modality in the over-all relation of form, genre, style and audience response) was a manifestation of the sense of belatedness that haunts major poetry in the post-Classical world might sound merely modish, were it not for the testimony just to that effect by the so many Renaissance theorists of verse form, whether they crumble weakly, like Campion and other "quantitative" theorists, or resolve, like the heroic Sidney, out of the evil of the barbarous heritage of vernacular tradition, stress accent and all, to bring forth the good of a fulfilled poetic tradition. Indeed, in the Latin adaptation of the Greek meter itself, by Ennius in the third century B.C., we have the record of confirmation of a formal change as profound in its resonance in the dialectic of literary history as, for example, the use by Theocritus of the hexameter, reserved for epical narrative, in his very literary pastorals.

What was the function of the adaptation? I hope the even partially Greeked and Latined reader will bear with me for a brief run over well-trampled ground. Classical Greek, with no contrastive word stress, arranged its verse according to musico-prosodic measures, based on syllable length—certain vowels causing syllables to be long by nature, while a double consonant following any vowel (even crossing a word boundary) makes the syllable long by convention. Two shorts are by convention equal to long, as in our musical notation, two quarter notes or crotchets make up a half note, or minim. The arrangement of syllables in "feet" and feet in lines depended upon the length alone, for there was no stress accent to be heeded or ignored. The celebrated line from Homer (*Iliad*, XVIII, 576) describing the cattle on Achilles' shield, moving

par potamon keladonta, para hrodanon donakea

"along the murmuring river, along the slender reed" is a perfectly regular hexameter line, with six dactylic feet of a long followed by two shorts each, with a word boundary (here underlined more strongly by a syntactic parallel break) coming in the third foot. It would have been "scanned" (i.e. longs and shorts would have been marked) as follows:

par potamon keladonta, para hrodanon donakea

Notice that if we wished to use an isomorphic musical notation, with note values substituted for long and short indicators, we could only write the following, having no rule for placing up- and down-beats, whether with bar-lines or otherwise:

1. 𝅗𝅥 ♩ ♩ 𝅗𝅥   ♩ ♩ 𝅗𝅥   ♩ ♩ , etc.[2]

There existed, in fact, a rule of Greek prosody to clarify this. *Arsis* ("raising" of the foot), or upbeat, and *thesis*, or downbeat, were conventionally assigned to the first half of the foot (the long, or, when spondees of two longs were substituted for dactyls, the first one). Notice also that, had Classical Greek a stress accent, there would be no need for such a rule; if the first two words were accented pár potamón, for example, we could say that stress coincided with quantity—the *a* of *par* is short by nature, but *par* is long because *r* and *p* (of *potamon*) immediately follow—and we could group the notes in musical measures like this: 𝅗𝅥 ♩ ♩ |𝅗𝅥 . . . . The rule about *ictus*, or up- and downbeat, provided just such a way of grouping accents, regardless of the words involved. Therefore, we *can* write the scansion of the line in question in musical note values, properly grouped, thus:

2. Without a notated or conventionalized accentuation, and without a stress-accented text, such a string of notes might receive any sort of barring, such as 3/4, 5/4 or even an aperiodic irregular pattern of up- and down-beats. The whole point about the *ictus* rules was to normalize the rhythm. For a useful and sophisticated introduction to these problems, see William Beare, *Latin Verse and European Song* (London, 1957); for a much more detailed one, W. Sidney Allen, *Accent and Rhythm* (Cambridge, 1974).

or, if the musical "measures" cause the Classicist undue worry, then

Notice also that, during the Byzantine period and after, Greek did indeed develop a stress accent, like English or Russian, and that the words in line would have been pronounced

4. pár potamón keládonta, pará hrodanón donakéa

which would have aligned the accents with the long syllables, save for the case of *keladonta*, thus throwing the second and third feet out of the scheme. As a matter of fact, even as much alignment as does occur here is unusual.

The older, pre-quantitative Latin poetry was probably accentual, the basic line, called the Saturnian (it survives in perhaps 160 examples), consisted usually of five words, more rarely of six or four, with a word break most often after the seventh syllable. The number of syllables in the line varied from ten to sixteen or so; the number of stress-accented syllables, following the penultimate stress rule of Latin accentuation, was five or six. The canonical line: *málum dábunt Metélli Naévio poétae* represents the most common distribution of syllables and stresses. For Latin, with its word stress (albeit predictable, unlike that of modern Greek or of Russian), the adoption of the Greek quantitative measure posed the immediate problem that we observed in example 4 above, where there is the need for an alignment of stress and quantity because there is word stress to begin with. Thus, the *árma virúmque cáno* which opens the *Aeneid* is out of phase, while the end of the line is not. While the Latin language thus must ignore word stress in arranging the words in lines, the contingencies of Greek meter, meshing with the accentual condition of Latin, produce a new possible dimension of poetic variation. This is the first instance in our tradition, of a figurative poetic "music" that is not a matter of pure linguistic sound. For the Latin poet, a line can be relatively more or less aligned. It is significant that Virgil uses alignment systematically for line closure: just as the rules of Classical scansion call for an invariable [— ᴗ ᴗ — —], so an accentual cadence of [/ ·· / ·] invariably closes the hexameter line, almost like a rhyme. It is Virgil who seems to orchestrate his alignment (or, as W. F. Jackson Knight has called them, "homodyne" and "heterodyne" feet)[3] more remarkably than any other poet, and he can write a line like *sed nox atra caput tristi circumvolat umbra* ("but black night hovers above his head with mournful shades") where no short syllable receives a stress, and the last two stressed long syllables are connected by a deep assonance.

The attempt to adapt Classical meters to vernaculars, whether through Latin, with an awareness of alignment as a possible dimension, or later on, in the Romantic period, from Greek directly, poses various problems. Clearly French, with no word stress (save for the phrase-marking stress of the final syllable of a word in terminal position) and a purely syllabic verse system, could decide to adapt certain rules about short and long syllables, assigning them length either because of their phonemic quality or because of spelling conventions, and evolve a Classically derived verse system. This was done, in fact, by the members of the Baïf academy in the sixteenth century, in their *vers mesuré*. In English, with its strong accentual tradition, this becomes an awkward matter.

In the first place, English underwent a vowel shift between Middle English and Early Modern, so that the Indo-European *a, e, i,* become diphthongs based on each other, /ey/, /iy/, /ay/. Then there developed a spelling convention by which a doubled consonant following a vowel or diphthong would shorten it in internal position, *viz. pater/ patter*. Even if one were to try to adapt quantity systems to English, grave difficulties would ensue; length by position because of a doubled consonant within a word would produce, phonetically, shortening by position. Finally, the role of stress accent is so crucial that the alignment problem is vastly greater in English than in Latin. The alternative

---

3. W. F. Jackson Knight, *Accentual Symmetry in Virgil* (Oxford, 1939); he uses the word "heterodyne" to apply to a foot wherein stress and length clash, "homodyne" where they are aligned.

adopted by English verse tradition, and expanded by German Romantic poets, was to dignify accentual-syllabic verse patterns with Classical names, and to construct new line patterns using "feet" (i.e. pairs or triads of syllables) in which stress is substituted for length. For example, an "imitation" of the Homeric line cited above, composed in the stressed-analogue hexameter which we recognize from Goethe and Schiller (and, more unfortunately, Longfellow) would go:

$$/ \cdot \cdot \quad / \cdot \cdot \quad / \cdot \cdot \quad / \cdot \cdot \quad / \cdot \cdot \quad / \quad (/)$$
Heard by the murmuring river, the herds by the quivering rushes

Scanned, however, in the "quantitative" manner which treats written English as if it were written Latin, and with which the Elizabethans experimented, it would read:

$$- \; - \cup \; - \; \cup \; - - - \; \cup \; - \; - \cup \; - \cup \; - - \cup$$
Heard by the murmuring river, the herds by the quivering rushes

Reading one of these Elizabethan experiments is interesting, because the rules that the poets used for determining syllable quantity applied to the written text, but not necessarily to what one would hear. Sidney's Sapphic sung by Pyrocles to Philocleia[4] follows the formula: three lines of $[-\cup---\cup\cup-\cup-\cup]$ and a fourth of $[-\cup\cup-\cup]$ in each strophe. Consider the third strophe of the poem:

> Yet dying, and dead, doo we sing her honour;
> So become our tombes monuments of her praise;
> So becomes our losse the triumph of her gayne;
>   Hers be the glory.

The stresses suggest an interesting, loose, five-beat accentual rhythm, with a rhythmic parallel in the second and third lines, created by the grammatical one. Only the short line, "Hérs be the glóry," happens to suggest the stress-analogue pattern, the characteristic English Sapphic we hear, for example, in Swinburne's magnificent

---

4. From *The First Eclogues* of the *Arcadia;* text from W. A. Ringler, Jr. (ed.), *Poems* (Oxford, 1962), p. 30.

> Saw the white implacable Aphrodite,
> Saw the hair unbound, and the feet unsandalled
> Shine as fire of sunset on western waters;
>   Saw the reluctant
>
> Feet, the straining plumes of the doves that drew her,
> Looking always, looking with necks reverted,
> Back to Lesbos, back to the hills where under
>   Shone Mitylene;

In Sidney's "quantitative" version, even the characteristic "hanging" short syllable, audible as an accidentally unaccented one in the first line ("honour") vanishes in lines two and three. We must conclude that the quantitative experiment is somewhat like a written code—one needs to count and measure letters in order to determine the system, while the ear will infer that all sorts of accentual patterns it hears are indeed intended to be systematic. Indeed, one mistakes the rhythm of the lines for their schematic meter, which latter is hidden in an arbitrary and arcane system.[5]

Even though the quantitative experiments of the Elizabethans never really caught on (and Sir Philip Sidney's poems in these meters in the *Old Arcadia* are quite remarkable), the ghost of what was almost an obsession with them remains with us always. The Chaucerian accentual-syllabic line, rediscovered by Surrey although not understood to be Chaucerian at the time, was neither written, nor conceived of, nor to be comprehended, in "feet." It is an outgrowth of the Neoclassicizing turn of mind to talk about pairs of contrastingly stressed and unstressed syllables as "iambic feet"; it was both moving and silly that the convention developed, although to overthrow it completely would be like spelling "island" without the *s* because it was idiotic worship of Latin derivation that wrongly put it there. The ghost of the Classical scansion lives on, too, in our notation: the [⌣] of the classroom, standing for an unstressed syllable, is the quantitative short marker. The terms *iamb, trochee, spondee,* etc., are quite useful for talking about

---

5. See the discussion of Elizabethan quantitative experiments in the following chapter; also, the comprehensive treatment by G. L. Hendrickson, "Elizabethan Quantitative Hexameters," *Philological Quarterly,* XXVIII (1949), 237-60.

normal and displaced pairs of stress and unstressed syllables, and so forth. The accentual analogue of the Greek lyric, as opposed to the stichic meters—the patterns of lines arranged in strophes, and which did not allow of substitution of long for two shorts or vice versa—could be used so successfully by the German Romantics precisely because the stress patterns generated by the elegiac couplets, alcaic stanzas, and the like appealed so well to the demands of German stress and syntax. Milton's beautiful and profoundly experimental translation of Horace's ode to Pyrrha helped initiate this practice in English, as did— ironically enough—the unrhymed, accentual-syllabic poems in Campion's cranky pro-quantitative treatise, *Observations in the Art of English Poesie*.

Indeed, the stressed-analogue "Classical" meter has been displaced from the main stream of English verse only because the appropriate stylistic and generic analogue of the hexameter in Greek and Latin came to be the Chaucerian decasyllabic line, with stresses normalized to even positions—whether blank or in rhymed couplets—and standing indifferently for hexameters or elegiacs. It is not a question of any awkwardness that the Classically patterned accent groups might impose. Coleridge's two cases of the hexameter and the elegiac, "Described and Exemplified," are typical of the pretty models which learned poets from Sidney, Ben Jonson, and Milton on have ever enjoyed to build. The hexameter

> Strongly it bears us along in swelling and limitless billows,
> Nothing before and nothing behind but the sky and the ocean.

employs the same kind of assonance in the closure of the first line that Virgil used in the verse quoted earlier; the second has the assonance on the third and fourth downbeats, and a witty and learned array of the parallel phrases, "nothing before and nothing behind" across the caesura so that the second is broken, as if by a line enjambment, and the "behind" is tied assonantally to the "sky." The elegiac couplet is even more celebrated:

> In the hexameter rises the fountain's silvery column;
> In the pentameter aye falling in melody back.

But mostly it was the lyric meters, those scanned, as the Greeks said, *kata kolon*, in strophes with an unvarying line (rather than *kata metron*, by the measure or foot unit) that ever became attractive (the accentual Sapphic form, for example). Perhaps this is because their rhythmic effect was like that of a strophic song text already set to music, so that certain rhythmic configurations out of those implicit in the verse have been selected, underlined and established for all the successive strophes. Writing a stress-analogue Classical meter is like writing new words to an old tune. To be effective, such meters often need contextualizing: it is easy to "describe and exemplify" a line in the Coleridgean manner (this method, let us remember, going back to Pope's similar treatment of his own verse form in *An Essay on Criticism*), precisely because the exemplifying role provides its own rhetoric. The effect of the sudden trochee at the end of the iambic string in the scazon which made the Greeks think of it as lame can be shown in

$$\text{A lí}\text{ne of vér}\text{se that mó}\text{ves aló}\text{ng and é}\text{nds lí}\text{mping}$$

for example. One can not escape the effect of Robert Bridges's hendecasyllabics in "Would that you were alive today, Catullus," ending

> Not those two pretty Laureates of England,
> Not Alfred Tennyson nor Alfred Austin.

where it is hard to say whether it is the sublime-to-ridiculous echoing of the first name by the second which points up the movement of the meter, or the reverse. In any case the last line is a genius of finding.

Tennyson himself employed such stress-analogue meters with great facility and, one feels, sense of accomplishment. His remark about the scissors, to which we may now return, grows out of his immersion in Latin, and in the accentual syllabism he derived and expanded from Keats. One possible meaning of the observation—namely, the role of *scissors* in this kind of stress-analogue meter—we have already settled. The other should now be apparent: applying some kind of Elizabethan written code system, based on purely graphic questions, how would the word read? The problem is, obviously, with the double *s*, standing for the single phoneme /z/; the matter of the silent *c* is simply part of the joke—it makes the word look even sillier, brings out the paradoxical impossibility of being Classical in English verse even more. Tennyson's antiquity had to be Chaucer and Spenser and Milton, as far as his verse went; the Virgil and Ovid he pillaged had to enter his poetry transformed.

Tennyson, incidentally, seems to have composed only three poems in experimental, Elizabethan-style "quantitative" verse. In two cases, the alcaics to Milton and some joking Catullan hendecasyllabics, he carefully aligned stress accent, à la Campion, with syllables "long" in his written system. His superb ear for accentual syllabism (save in a few incunabula like "When Claribel low lieth," or a rare late lapse like "Clara, Clara Vere de Vere!" where the comma after the first Clara, alas, struggles to no avail) helped him here, as always. Thus, the first stanza of his "Milton" reads purely as a stressed-analogue alcaic, and counting letters to try to decode the quantities only confirms the effect of the analogue:

> O mighty-mouth'd inventor of harmonies,
> O skill'd to sing of Time or Eternity,
>   God-gifted organ-voice of England,
>   Milton, a name to resound for ages. . .

Tennyson's use of alliteration and internal assonance here is identifiably his own, and the quantitative coding is rather like a door prize. So, too, in the hendecasyllabics ("All composed in a metre of Catullus,/All in quantity, careful of my motion"), where the quantitative positional rule for short syllables allows the word "of" in the quoted lines to take on more quantitative prominence than they have accentually—Tennyson would hardly ever use "of" in a stressed position, if at all. There is only one case of Tennyson's writing pure or Elizabethan-type quantitative lines without consistent regard for accent, and here he clearly intends the effect to be exasperating. These lines are a burlesque of the whole practice:

> These lame hexameters the strong-wing'd music of Homer!
> No—but a most burlesque barbarous experiment.
> When was a harsher sound ever heard, ye Muses, in England?
> When did a frog coarser croak upon our Helicon?

> Hexameters no worse than daring Germany gave us,
> Barbarous experiment, barbarous hexameters.

Here he even avoids at times aligning stress and quantity in the last five syllables of the line, which even the Latin poets tend so often to do. He obviously had contempt for the whole quantitative undertaking, and we must conclude that he knew better than to ascribe his magnificent ear for rhythm to a dubious cryptographic skill.

And so at the last, we must see Lord Tennyson's scissors error in a more generous light than we did at the beginning. For while he erred in believing that even an arbitrary decision procedure for ascertaining English quantities could exist, he is to be held free of the charge that his knowledge of it could be much more than a kind of game. And, of course, the whole remark, quoted out of context in the fragmentary and humorless memoir of his son, might just be a little joke after all, as was observed earlier. It is simply that jokes are always about something.

One would hope that dissolving the problem of Lord Tennyson's scissors would lay the last ghost of quantitative hankering in English and American poetry. Unfortunately, specters continue to appear: the mere fact, for example, that *length*—of syllable, word, phrase, utterance, etc.—is a phonetic reality, that the syllable "it" takes less time to emit than the syllable "crunched," leads many theorists of meter and rhythm to call such a phenomenon "quantity," and thereby to conjure up a few more flapping sheets. Even what should be harmless—using musical notation to scan a line—makes for trouble, as we have seen in Chapter I, by tending to reify entities in the notational system that are secondary to the function of the notation itself. Poetry occurs in time, it is true; but unlike music, the eyes can play back material in the region of any poetic moment, scan, riffle through line or pages without altering the character of the reading experience as radically as the revision of musical listening would. Quantity is a linguistic entity, and its phonetic basis was argued even in Classical times. And for the making of verse in new and old ways in English there are far more productive fictions to employ as catalysts.

IV
THE CASE OF CAMPION

In most discussions of the relation between music and poetry in the realm of post-Classical song, Thomas Campion is eventually invoked. Poet-composers are always rare, and one who was also a theoretician of verse (his treatise on part-writing is undistinguished as musical theory, at any level), even rarer. There are also some intriguing paradoxes about his career: his theory was based on the notion that what he did in his practice of verse was quite wrong, and yet the examples he constructed in that theoretical treatise of how to write correctly were carefully hedged so as to square more with his practice than with the theory they were supposed to illustrate. But along with Sidney, Donne, and Jonson, Campion is one of the founders of English lyric verse, writing handsomely constructed short poems and setting them to music himself. There are larger modes of the lyric—one would have to acknowledge the revolutionary character of Spenser's *Epithalamion*, for example, in expanding the notion of "song" beyond anything that might be literally meant. But slight and tactful though he is, Campion remains of great interest for any attempt to puzzle out the strange separation of speech and song in the history of English lyric poetry. Our idea of lyric originally comes from a Classical Greek distinction between solo songs, sung to the lyre, composed in short stanzas and usually of an erotic character, and choral ode, composed in triads of long strophes and of public, celebratory character (when not occurring as part of tragedy or comedy). There were many other Classical poetic styles: elegiac verse was composed in couplets (always unrhymed as in all Classical verse) and was used for satire and epigram inscription and witty or pointed observation. Iambic verse had other ranges of use, from speeches in plays to drinking songs and love lyrics. Then there was, of course, the continuous hexameter line of epic poetry, and the originally almost startling adaptation of it by Theocritus for his pastoral eclogues.

Latin poets followed and adopted these Greek models, but the actual association of meters with musical forms and styles began to disappear. The Renaissance, extremely self-conscious as it came to be about Classical antiquity, sought to emulate it with a deliberate reunification of music and poetry. England lagged behind the Continent in the development of its music after the death of John Dunstable (1390-1453), one of the most renowned musicians of his day. By the 1580's, however, Italian influences and the invigoration of a native tradition led to a remarkable burst of secular musical activity, and the emergence of a group of composers of the first rank, among them William Byrd, Orlando Gibbons, John Dowland, Thomas Weelkes, Thomas Morley, and others. Aside from solo keyboard and lute composition, their main activities were in the field of song. Madrigals were polyphonic settings of poetic texts for several voices, either unaccompanied or, more often, with instruments either doubling the voices or taking their parts. They were often florid, chromatic, and complex, and went to such lengths to avoid stanzaic repetition of different words to the same tune, that they confined themselves to monostrophic poems, like sonnets, or else frequently set two stanzas of the same poem as two different madrigals. Airs, or solo songs, were written for voice and lute (although usually printed with four-part settings included). They were more oriented to a performer-audience situation than the madrigals, whose musico-poetic delights would appear primarily to one of the singers, hearing the complexities of the setting of the often-repeated words weaving around him. Airs, in addition, were primarily stanzaic: the composer would find a text and set the first stanza, allowing the subsequent ones to be "sung to the same tune," as it were. In the case of frequently banal, metrically smooth poems, this "fit" worked very well. In the case of Donne's *Songs and Sonnets*, the tense, wrenched, individualized rhythmic patternings of almost every line made stanzaic settings almost impossible. With Donne's poems we begin to see texts whose musical settings can best be thought of as the verbal "music" of their own, intense speech cadences, as was observed in a previous chapter.

By the 1580's, a variety of poetic conventions had become assimilated to the notion of "lyric poem," including "sonnets" in both the strict and loose senses (that is, the familiar fourteen-line iambic pentameter poems as well as any short, Petrarchan love poem), epigrams, pastoral lyrics, and so forth. A musician (as Donne puts it in "The Triple Fool"), "his art and voice to show,/Doth set and sing my pain"—and composers frequently raided miscellanies and anthologies as well as published books and poems in manuscript. Almost any poem might, after publication, show up in a musical setting, sometimes altered for the convenience of the composer.

Although the composers of these songbooks used to be credited, in older and unscholarly anthologies, with the words to their songs, this was rarely the case. Except for an occasional amusing anomaly, like Captain Tobias Hume in his *Poetical Music,* there is only Thomas Campion to maintain, in the English Renaissance, the ancient traditions of the poet-composer. The reputation of another such figure, Chaucer's great contemporary Guillaume de Machaut, has undergone a strange revision in the last fifty years. Before then, philological scholars thought of him as a lyric poet, and it is only modern musicology that has shown how much more interesting his ballades, virelais, and rondeaux were as musical structures than as verse patterns. In short, Machaut is ranked as one of the great composers, and his musical glory has eclipsed his fame as a poet.

Not so with Campion. As a composer he is idiomatic and graceful, seldom tactless but seldom inspired. He worked within the framework of the strophic air always, and never responded to the influence of the new Italian *stilo recitativo* like Alfonso Ferrabosco, or developed an insistent and personal chromaticism, like John Daniel (brother of the poet Samuel, who refuted Campion's prosodic theories). Neither did he, like John Dowland—who was a virtuoso lutenist of great fame—do anything remarkable with his lute accompaniments: for the most part, they lie easily under the hand, with a minimum of fugal writing and a rather four-square texture.

His minor talents as a composer are most exposed, perhaps, when we can compare his setting of one of his own texts with that of another composer. In the case of a little song from Campion's fourth book,[1] we have just such an opportunity. The text itself works through a rather hackneyed Elizabethan theme, but presents one feature of interest for the setting:

> I must complain, yet doe enjoy my Love.
>   She is too faire, too rich in bewty's parts.
> Thence is my grief; for Nature, while she strove
>   With all her graces and divinest arts
> To form her too too beautifull of hue,
> She had no leasure left to make her true.

The degree of enjambment of the third line would hardly be noticeable were it not for the exigencies of setting, where in the style Campion usually employs, a musical period coincides with a line. Not only is Dowland's setting superior in every way—the lute accompaniment, for example, is polyphonic and inventive—but the better composer approaches the transition from line 3 to line 4 with great musical and metrical sophistication. His lute accompaniment covers the enjambed break "strove/With" by a rapidly moving figure, but picks out the *contre-rejet* "With" with a single bass note. It is a bit of musical setting that would correspond almost exactly to a sophisticated oral performance of the poem. And yet this all occurs within the convention of the Jacobean strophic lute song: this is not yet a matter of the breaking up of lines of verse into syntactic and rhetorical units by the kind of declamatory setting that comes to be a Caroline vogue (settings of Carew by Lawes would be a case in point).

1. It will be observed that Campion's poems, largely because they were published in songbooks, do not have titles, as do Donne's *Songs and Sonnets*. See Chapter II.

But as a master of the structure of the stanzaic lyric song text, Campion is unsurpassed in English. He is Sidneyan to the degree that he is absorbed with elements of what the earlier poet called *architectonike*—the patterning and symmetry of parts of language: lines, grammatical structures, stanzas, and so forth. He is Jonsonian in his response to Latin lyric and elegiac poets, rather than to Sidney's shaping Italian. But he is in a different lyric world from John Donne's, dominated as it is by a rhetorical necessity which overrides repetitive stanzaic principles in the generation of its rhythms and its images. "Strong lines" was the seventeenth-century critical term for metaphysical verse of the Donne tradition. Campion's remain always smooth.

But by no means weak. If his modes was not the skewed, the emphatic and the paradoxical, it remained all the more the delicate, the precise, and the epigrammatic. We tend to think of epigram or aphorism primarily in terms of written inscriptions, rather than chant or song—and indeed, Classical tradition assigned epigram to the meter of the elegiac couplet. Yet there were lyrical poems—like the Anacreontea—which Renaissance writers assimilated to such poems as those of the Greek Anthology, and it is not strange to find Campion remarking as follows about the poetic form he made his own:

> Short Ayres, if they be skilfully framed, and naturally exprest, are like quicke and good Epigrammes in Poesie, many of them shewing as much artifice, and breeding as great difficultie as a large Poeme.

Let us look at an instance of this. Catullus' famous lyric "*Vivamus, mea Lesbia, atque amemus*" was a background text for many seventeenth-century poems of erotic invitation. Shakespeare reworked some of it in *Venus and Adonis*. Ben Jonson's adaptation of it occurs first as a song in *Volpone* and later in his selection of his own favorite poems called *The Forest*. It was set by Ferrabosco, as we saw in an earlier chapter, but it remains most powerful as a spoken text:

> Come, my Celia, let us prove,
> While we may, the sports of love;

> Time will not be ours for ever:
> He, at length, our good will sever.
> Spend not then his gifts in vaine.
> Sunnes that set may rise againe:
> But if once we loose this light,
> 'Tis, with us, perpetuall night.
> Why should we deferre our joyes?
> Fame and rumour are but toyes.
> Cannot we delude the eyes
> Of a few poore household spyes?
> Or his easier eares beguile
> So removed by our wile?
> 'Tis no sinne, loves fruits to steale,
> But the sweete theft to reveale,
> To be taken, to be seene,
> These have crimes accounted beene.

Campion's reworking of the same Latin original is another matter. Here, he abandons Catullus after the first strophe, and turns the *nox est perpetua una dormienda* from the middle of the poem into a slightly varying refrain, seeing in it unfulfilled lyrical and expository possibilities:

> My sweetest Lesbia let us live and love,
> And though the sager sort our deedes reprove,
> Let us not way them: heavn's great lamps doe dive
> Into their west, and strait againe revive,
> But soone as once set is our little light,
> Then must we sleepe one ever-during night.
>
> If all would lead their lives in love like mee,
> Then bloudie swords and armour should not be,
> No drum nor trumpet peaceful sleepes should move,
> Unles alarme came from the campe of love:
> But fooles do live, and wast their little light,
> And seeke with paine their ever-during night.
>
> When timely death my life and fortune ends,
> Let not my hearse be vext with mourning friends,

> But let all lovers rich in triumph come,
> And with sweet pastimes grace my happie tombe;
> And Lesbia close up thou my little light,
> And crowne with love my ever-during night.

This is the *carpe diem* theme further humanized and matured by an awareness of the *memento mori* aspect of it: the vision of dying in love, and for it, and having love made on one's tomb, is a sweeter one than we find in Jonson's "let us do it while we can," or, later on in the century, the sardonic energy of Marvell's "To His Coy Mistress."

In this poem, too, it is as if the stanzaic limitations were a source of creative energy for Campion, rather than a restraint. Throughout the corpus of songs we can see this energy at work—whether in a hymn, like the lovely "Never Weather-Beaten Saile," a magic spell like "Thrice Toss These Oaken Ashes in the Aire," or a half-parodic comment on the burning brands of Eros in "Fire, Fire, Fire Fire." The development of a theme and its disposition throughout the successive strophes is always his forte. Take, for example, the justly famous "Cherry-Ripe," which takes off from the most common of street cries, the *"Cherry ripe ripe ripe!"* of the cherry vendor, sung, as we know from other early seventeenth-century evidence, through an ascending third:

Whether the sung phrase as Campion recalled it suggested the garden conceit (Herrick wrote a little poem starting with the same repeated words of the street cry), or whether it crept in as the basic image was unfolding, the result was a wonderful transformation of a whole series of commonplaces:

> There is a Garden in her face,
> Where Roses and white Lillies grow;
> A heav'nly paradice is that place,
> Wherein all pleasant fruits doe flow.
> There Cherries grow, which none may buy
> Till Cherry ripe themselves doe cry.

> Those Cherries fairly does enclose
> Of Orient Pearle a double row;
> Which when her lovely laughter showes,
> They look like Rose-buds fill'd with snow.
> Yet them nor Peere nor Prince can buy,
> Till Cherry ripe themselves doe cry.
>
> Her Eyes like Angels watch them still;
> Her Browes like bended bowes doe stand,
> Threatning with piercing frownes to kill
> All that attempt with eye or hand
> Those sacred Cherries to come nigh,
> Till Cherry ripe themselves doe cry.

In the first strophe, we may let the significance of "heav'nly paradice" go by, thinking it a mere hyperbole as conventional as the roses and lilies of the blazon, or Petrarchan catalogue of delights—the red of feeling and the white of purity which combine in the "carnation" or flesh tone in emblematic color language (the Elizabethans seem not to have had our term "pink"). We may even miss an echo in the use of "flow" for "abound," of the Biblical "flowing with milk and honey," seeing only the image extending through the refrain: the lady's lips, which alone are able to say "yes" for her, are like wares that advertise themselves. But then, in the second stanza, both rosebuds filled with snow and pearl jewels growing in a vegetative garden underline the neglected "paradice." Here are all seasons at once, and the natural and artificial are confounded: We are in the neighborhood of the earthly paradises of Spenser and his followers. The final stanza, in which the cherries become "sacred" and assimilated mythologically to the golden apples of the Hesperides, shows us the garden as being angelically protected (the old Petrarchan cliché about frowning eyebrows being like drawn bows is redeemed in this new association). The courtly compliment now turns out to be central moral vision: the only *paradiso terrestre* or Earthly Paradise is to be found in beautiful sexual attainment, in the plucking of cherries that are no forbidden apples, and just for that reason, such attainment isn't always easy. Campion's stanzaic development has served the imaginative purpose of taking seriously what might be, in a weaker song by a less serious and joyful singer, a bit of lyrical rhetoric.

In his musical setting of the poem in his *Fourth Booke of Ayres*, Campion cannot help but work in the melodic phrase of the street cry itself into his refrain. Imitative and referential bits of musical setting like this abound in later Elizabethan and Jacobean musical practice, and Campion employs them occasionally with a certain amount of delight. Thus

> When to her lute Corinna sings,
> Her voice revives the leaden stringes,
> And doth in highest noates appeare,
> As any challeng'd echo cleere;
> But when she doth of sorrow speake,
> Ev'n from my hart the strings do breake.

and there is an expressive downward turn of the vocal line underlined by a chordal sweep on the lute to suggest the breaking strings.[2] The second strophe, incidentally, moralizes the anecdote in conventional fashion, applying it to the poet's own feelings, and concluding with a familiar Elizabethan invocation of "heartstrings" (the term's literary popularity resulted from a Latin pun on *cor, cordis*, "heart," and *chorda*, "string"). But the musical setting of the first stanza must remain effective for the second, and the heartstrings must "break" as well, the figurative heartbreak echoing the anecdotal damage to the instrument:

> And as her lute doth live or die,
> Led by her passion, so must I,
> For when of pleasure she doth sing,
> My thoughts enjoy a sodaine spring,
> But if she doth of sorrow speake,
> E'vn from my hart the strings doe breake.

Many of Campion's songs concern, or involve imagery about, music and its effects as celebrated in mythology: "Follow Your Saint"; "To Musicke Bent Is My Retyred Minde"; "Tune Thy Musicke to Thy

2. See the discussion of these lines in Rosemund Tuve, *Elizabethan and Metaphysical Imagery* (Chicago, 1947), p. 15.

Hart"; "To His Sweet Lute Apollo Sung the Motions of the Spheres," for example, and much in the masques and court entertainments celebrate music and thereby, given Campion's personal and learned Neoclassical association of the two, of poetry as well. Even in his metrical version of the 137th Psalm ("By the waters of Babylon"), Campion pays special attention to the musical possibilities of "We hanged our harps upon the willows in the midst thereof," and gives us

> Aloft the trees, that sprung up there,
> Our silent Harps wee pensive hung

playing deliciously on the etymological connection of "pensive" and the Latin *"Pendere":* "to hang."

Even, too, the metrical example, "Rose-cheekt Lawra"—surely the most successful "exercise" qua poem, in our tradition—affirm a Platonistic correspondence between actual and ideal, based on an avowed relation between heavenly harmony and human music:

> Rose-cheekt *Lawra,* come
> Sing thou smoothly with thy beawties
> Silent musick, either other
>   Sweetely gracing.
>
> Lovely formes do flowe
> From concent divinely framed;
> Heav'n is musick, and thy beawties
>   Birth is heavenly.
>
> These dull notes we sing
> Discordes neede for helps to grace them;
> Only beawty purely loving
>   Knowes no discord:
>
> But still mooves delight,
> Like cleare springs renu'd by flowing,
> Ever perfect, ever in them-
>   selves eternall.

This beautiful little poem occurs in Campion's cranky *Observations in the Art of English Poesie,* a treatise on poetic meter whose attack on rhyme and championing of Classical prosody over native English verse structure seems pointless to us today. The Elizabethans are, after all, our poetic Greek and Latin poets—the English past is our linguistic and imaginative antiquity, the iambic pentameter is our Classical verse. But at the end of the sixteenth century, the desire to legitimize a national English literature by giving it good Classical credentials still led some poets and critics to espouse a literal adoption of the quantitative meters of Greek and Latin poetry. We have seen in the previous chapter how this cannot be done in English, with its prominent word stress, save by assigning Latin vowel lengths to the written English, and simply patterning what amounts to a typographical code which cannot be heard as verse. Thus, a translator of a passage from Ovid in a songbook of William Byrd starts out with one of those pseudo-quantitative lines which reads

    Constant Penelope sends to thee, careless Ulysses

and which *sounds* like a five-beat dactylic line in English rhythms: *bumpity, bumpity, bumpity, bumpity, bum-bum*. The poet, however, by a dark process of giving values to letters in syllables rather than to sounds, intended

    — — —ᴜᴜ— —   — —   — ᴜ ᴜ — —
    Constant Penelope sends to thee, careless Ulysses

at least, this is what Byrd assumed he meant, from the note values he gave it in setting. This may make sense to the sufficiently learned eye, perhaps, but to no ear.[3]

There were many treatises which opposed Campion's theory of Classical verse in English. Samuel Daniel wrote one specifically to refute Campion's views (rather than his practice). The *Observations* must be understood as a contribution to an ideological battle of the end of the sixteenth century; it would be a great mistake, for example, to construe its definition of what he calls "*Ditties* or *Odes*" as "*Lyricall*,

---

3. These are quantitative scansions, not accentual marks. For more background on the theory of quantitative scansion in vernacular languages, see Chapter III.

because they are apt to be soong to an instrument, if they were adorn'd with convenient notes" as applying to Campion's own lute songs. He is simply talking theoretical language, invoking definitions of Classical scholiasts and Renaissance scholars. The strategies employed by those who defended writing the way Campion in fact wrote poetry vary widely; they range in quality from the grotesque and misinformed treatment of English accent as if it were Greek or Latin, to the extremely sophisticated arguments of a major poet and theorist like Sir Philip Sidney. Some treatises simply refer to stressed and unstressed syllables as "long" and "short," and mention iambs, trochees, dactyls, spondees, and anapests in English as if the substitution of stress accent for quantity were a perfectly simple matter, and as if the magic of the old names completely justified accentual practice. Others, less confused but no less zealous, used the old terms in a more or less consciously figurative way. An extremely complicated example of this would be Milton's words in praise of Henry Lawes. When he esteems his composer friend for "committing short and long," he is really saying "he knows how to set stressed and unstressed syllables in an expressive way to the new declamatory style which itself has managed to regain some of the famed expressive power of the music of antiquity." In any case, Milton knew perfectly well that he was using "long" and "short" metaphorically. Some of the Elizabethan writers on prosody seem to have been considerably less sure of themselves. Their legacy to us, of course, is this metaphoric use of words like "foot," "iambic," and the rest to stand for groups and arrangements of groups of stressed and unstressed syllables in English verse.

But some of the defenses of the traditional practice were much more interesting. In Sidney's "Apology for Poetry" we see a constant, reasoned attempt to justify contemporary practices of genre, form, and style by showing their proper analogy, rather than their identity, to Classical concepts. When it comes to meter, Sidney simply argues that the glories of Classical scansion utilized certain structural elements of the Greek language, and that English poetry must make full use of the analogous resources of the English language for the same purposes (I quote a modernized text):

Now, of versifying there are two sorts, the one ancient, the other modern: the ancient marked the quantity of each syllable, and according to that framed his verse; the modern observing only number (with some regard of the accent), the chief life of it standeth in that like sounding of the words, which we call "rhyme." Whether of these be the more excellent, would bear many speeches. The ancient, no doubt, more fit for music, both words and time observing quantity, and more fit lively to express divers passions, by the low or lofty sound of the well-weighted syllable. The latter likewise, with his rhyme, striketh a certain music to the ear: and in fine, since it doth delight, though by another way, it obtaineth the same purpose. . . .

Ben Jonson, too, in his *English Grammar*, puts the major position clearly in stating that "our Verses and Rythmes (as it is almost with all other people, whose language is spoken at this day) are naturall. . . ." We might observe in passing that Sidney is echoing standard Renaissance opinion about the Orphean power of ancient music and poetry to move the passions, and that he praises rhyme as the modern analogue of this "musical" quality. By and large, Sidney's argument becomes the traditional one in following centuries.

The other strategy for confronting the monolith of Classical poetry was to try to adapt Classical quantitative scansion in English, by means of a written code, as it were (English orthography having ceased to spell the spoken language since the great sound shift). If it is hard to have sympathy today for such an endeavor, it must be remembered that the poets and critics in question had been writing Latin, and often Greek, verses by means of just such a system—after all, the English pronunciation of the Classical languages had little to do with the sounds running through the heads of the poets they imitated. More important, there was no critical tradition for dealing with accentual-syllabic verse. Chaucer was thought to have written a loose, four-beat accentual (called "riding rhyme"). Surrey had helped, in his Petrarch translations and imitations, to formalize the iambic pentameter as the English line. But this was a tradition established by practice alone, with no conceptual defense for it. In an effort to overcome this obstacle, many scholars and critics, from the humanist Ascham on through Gabriel Harvey, Spenser, and others to Campion, writing in 1602, decided to classicize English verse by adopting Greek prosody. After all, the Romans starting with Ennius had done the same. Not only was rhyme to be held in contempt, but the lack of metrical variation possible in accentual-syllabic verse made it inflexible. This was accompanied by the abandonment of accent and syllabic counting as well. According to the transformation rules of Archdeacon Drant invoked in the series of letters that passed between Spenser and Gabriel Harvey on the subject of quantitative scansion, English written syllables could be classified long and short, and Classical meters produced by the arrangement of them.

We are not sure exactly how these rules worked, particularly for such matters as elision and the treatment of certain vowels and diphthongs. Certainly, there was little appeal to the spoken language as it actually sounded. Since the great vowel shift that occurred in English during the early fifteenth century, the vowel letters of the Latin alphabet had come to stand in English for diphthongs based on sounds utterly different from those which they had represented in Greek and Latin, and continued to represent in modern Romance and Germanic languages. Such an attempt to use Classical scansion could have little more than phonetic effect of a written code. For the average literate reader, even one well versed in Classical poetry, English quantitative verse cannot be "heard," or resolved into patterns by mere inspection, but must be worked out rather elaborately. It is almost a process of deciphering but since this kind of visual decoding represents the English reader's approach to the Classical poetic texts as well, few of the Elizabethan theorists saw anything wrong with this. Nevertheless, they continued to employ stock references to the musical power of verse in antiquity to justify their use of this code. Whenever one of these Classicizing theorists seems to feel any desire to reconcile his prescriptions with the phonetic facts of the English language, it only confuses the issue more, for, as we shall see, the concepts and terms at his disposal, such as "heavy" and "light," "grave and acute," "high and low," "accent," and "number," all had a long history of use in connection with

Classical meter. They had no simple terminological tools for distinguishing stress accent from pitch accent, for example. They continued to write as if the differences between a spoken and a written language were often irrelevant, and sometimes nonexistent. But we must remember that neither the Elizabethans nor any Classical scholars since actually spoke the language encoded in their written texts. And if Spenser may have been made to play the sixteenth-century equivalent of baseball in Latin at the Merchant Taylors School, the sounds he emitted would have been largely misconstrued in Augustan Rome, in all probability.

The Elizabethans were very much aware, however, that Classical spoken Latin was stressed according to the antepenultimate rule, and that, except in certain interesting cases, the reader of Latin verse must shut his ears to the disposition of stressed and unstressed syllables in the poetic line. Thus there was an ancient precedent, too, for a rationale for verse that excluded the most audible rhythmic elements in English speech. Any doubts that theorists like Gabriel Harvey must have had about the differences between patterns of sound and patterns of written characters could probably have been eased by the reflection that Classical poetry involved such uncertainties also!

Aside from all their polemic and theorizing, the Elizabethans actually produced some poetry written in the spirit of what Gabriel Harvey had called the "reformed versifying." These range in pretention from short, casual examples that are little more than casual metrical models or dummies, written to illustrate a point in an argument, to long ambitious poems like Abraham Fraunce's *The Countess of Pembroke's Emmanuel*, a life of Christ in Classical hexameters, rhymed, surprisingly enough, in couplets. Let us look for a moment at a poem falling somewhere midway between these extremes.

$$\smile — \smile — | \smile — \smile — | \smile — \smile —$$
Vnhappie Verse, the witnesse of my vnhappie state,
$$\smile — \smile — | \smile — \smile — | \smile — \smile$$
Make thy selfe fluttring wings of thy fast flying⁴

---

4. The text is given without normalization of "u" and "v." The word "Thought" clearly belongs at the end of this line, as demanded by the meter. Most Spenserians accept this emendation.

$$\text{[Thought,] and fly forth vnto my Loue, whersoeuer she be:}$$

$$\text{Whether lying reastlesse in heauy bedde, or else}$$

$$\text{Sitting so cheerelesse at the cheerfull boorde, or else}$$

$$\text{Playing alone carelesse on hir heauenlie Virginals.}$$

If in bed, tell hir that my eyes can take no rest;
    If at Boorde, tell hir that my mouth can eate no meate;
    If at hir Virginals, tel hir I can heare no mirth.
Asked why? say, Waking Loue suffereth no sleepe;
    Say that raging Loue dothe appall the weake stomacke;
    Say that lamenting Loue marreth the musicall.
Tell hir that hir pleasures were wonte to lull me asleepe;
    Tell hir that hir beautie was wonte to feede mine eyes;
    Tell hir that hir sweete Tongue was wonte to make me mirth.
Nowe do I nightly waste, wanting my kindely reste;
    Nowe do I dayly starue, wanting my liuely foode;
    Nowe do I always dye, wanting my timely mirth.
And if I waste, who will bewaile my heauy chaunce?
    And if I starue, who will record my cursed end?
    And if I dye, who will saye, *this was Immerito?*

This little poem, entitled simply "Iambicum Trimetrum," was written by Spenser and sent by him to Gabriel Harvey in a letter published in 1580, "Immerito" being his *nom de plume*. It is a kind of self-referential presentation poem on the model of many Latin ones (Catullus' iambics, etc.), but full of local Elizabethan influence. The rhetoric is Petrarchan, the relation between poet, poem, and lady being almost standard for sonneteering. The alliterative packagings are typically early Elizabethan. The arrangement is in triplets, with the imagery of bed, food, and music disposing itself consistently in the first, second, and third lines of the triplets throughout the poem, in heavy-footed conceits. There is also an element here of a kind of figurative patterning that we associate most strongly with some of Sidney's lyrics in the *Arcadia*. Each triplet contains two groups of three names or predicates, appearing in the first and last halves of the lines; the conceit is one of figure, we might say, rather than one of trope. The images develop from elaboration rather than from the frenzied metaphysical chase through the metaphor for other points of comparison.

Metrically, this is some kind of passable iambic trimeter, which, as will be remembered, is the standard dialogue meter for Classical drama, and which uses three pairs of iambs for the line. (The iambic, trochaic, and anapestic feet were always used in pairs or "dipodies" in Classical verse.) Substitution of a long for a short was allowable in the first iamb of any pair, and anapests were also substituted, sometimes only at the beginning of the line, sometimes throughout. If we follow these criteria, making allowance for the fact that the ubiquitous Master Drant must have given some method for deciding some of the quantities which remain ambiguous for us, we can make these lines scan.[5] But, if, as in the case of the hexameters set by Byrd, they are read aloud, what one hears is something else. Here, it is a kind of free English Alexandrine, with six stressed syllables per line, fairly strong syntactical breaks at the caesuras, a consistent " · / · /" at the end of each line, and enough parallels of syntax and conceit to allow any hearer to know where the line breaks come. The audible poem is in a free meter that any twentieth-century poet might employ, and that no Neoclassical poet would dare use, either (1) because it has no Classical basis, or (2) because it is a debased, limping form of one of the acceptable analogues of a Classical meter, the accentual-syllabic six-beat line showing French influence. And clearly, to produce such a meter was

---

5. For a discussion of these rules and how Sidney applied them, see W. A. Ringler's elaborate notes to *The Old Arcadia* in his edition of Sidney (Oxford, 1962), pp. 389-93. John Thompson's admirable *The Founding of English Metre* (New York, 1961) discusses the Classical meters on pp. 128-38; on p. 137, he commends the movement of the Spenser lines discussed above, but construes them, accentually, rather differently than I do. Undoubtedly this is because he uses the unemended text, and allows the accentual and syntactic pattern of "Make thy selfe fluttring wings of thy fast flying Thought" to serve as a matrix, or reference line for the rest of his reading. All these discussions on the sixteenth century were complicated by the fact that most prosodists confused the concepts of stress and quantity, used "long" for "accented," etc. Thus Richard Stanyhurst, in the Preface to his quantitative translation of Virgil (1582) confuses these utterly. See the Spenser-Harvey correspondence, also, for confusions about the relation of quantity in verse to accent in speech.

not Spenser's intention; here is a clear case where the schematic rationale for the construction of the poem is completely at odds with the rationale that the inference of an enlightened reading would discover. And this leads us to an important point.

Let us distinguish between the "two meters" of these lines by calling the Classical scansion the *"meter,"* and the patterns of sound that emerge upon reading (rather than decoding) the actual linguistic *"rhythm"* of the lines.[6] The first of these is a programmatic scheme for the construction of lines; the second is the characteristic movement of the lines themselves. The meter is some kind of signification of the poet's intention here; the rhythm represents some of the range of his poem's effect upon a reader. It is obvious here that the elements of the rhythm—phonological, lexical, and syntactic—are in no way specified by the metrical scheme, or even included in its frame of reference. One could construct English verse, for example, written in this same Classical meter, which would give the rhythmic effect of early alliterative verse:

> Harshest of harp-musics, horrible mockery
> Of ancient cadence, the oldest of the arts

If these lines are decoded, they will yield the hidden message of iambic trimeter. Without the key, only the rhythm remains to be talked about.

In the Spenser poem, it is only the rhythm which is of interest to the reader of the poem as a poem. It is only the actual rhythm of the lines themselves which could possibly represent any of the *expressive* function of meter, which is to be distinguished from the *formal* or *conventional* function. As a matter of fact, the latter is provided for here by the arcane *meter*, not by the rhythm. I shall have occasion to use this distinction between meter and rhythm throughout these pages, and shall comment in greater detail on the distinction later on. It should be obvious at this point, however, that even when the meter is quite prominent or obvious, certain elements of language will be patterned in the lines written in that meter which will not come under its rules.

6. See Chapter VII.

For example, the so-called English iambic line carries with it no prescriptions about assonance or alliteration or rhyme or whether the lines are to be end-stopped or enjambed or whether there is to a clear syntactical break or caesura anywhere or how long words are to be or what syntax is to be like, etc., etc., etc. And yet two actual specimens of English iambic pentameter verse will differ so remarkably because of their different arrangement or ignorance of such elements that it seems trivial to point out that they are both cases of five-stressed, decasyllabic verse. We can say that any line has a rhythm of its own, and that it may share this rhythm with associated, neighboring lines of poetry. But only lines considered in the context of others have or can be said to represent a meter.

Campion was a loyal Neoclassical ideologue in the controversies about metrics. In his preface, To the Reader, in his 1601 book of airs, he speaks slightingly of the normal English accentual-syllabic verse in which all his airs but one are composed; they are, he says, "after the fascion of the time, eare-pleasing rimes without Arte." Fortunately, he never rode his hobbyhorse over the living bodies of his songs. Even in his treatise, he adapts the prevailing sort of quantitative written coding of English so that his "long" syllables are always the ones bearing the stress accent of the word. "Rose-cheekt Lawra" is therefore merely an unrhymed English trochaic poem, perfectly plain to the ear. Campion's one song in Classical meters which concludes his first book of airs, "Come let us sound with melody the praises" is set for voice and lute, with note values corresponding to syllable length, in a fashion followed in Byrd's setting mentioned above, perhaps derived from a French tradition. But his unerring sense of iambic rhythm and its controlled rhetorical possibilities prevailed over his schematic beliefs.

That rhythmic sense is everywhere paralleled by other modes of stylistic tactfulness—of degree and depth of allusion to Classical models and themes; of length to which a conceit is drawn out; of the subjugation of wit and literary ambition to the limits of the song form he could make his own. His conventional Petrarchan vocabulary and imagery of love are never used mechanically, and his wit never allows empty gesture to depose verbal act. I can think of no better example of Campion's lyrical good humor than his ability to undercut even his own conventional delicacy with an equally graceful anti-Petrarchan move in the self-parodying "Beawty, since you so much desire" from the fourth book.[7] With its chaste original, "Mistris, since you so much desire" from the 1601 book, the one idealizing, the other faintly bawdy, we are shown two sides of the same Elizabethan coin. To have been unable to toss it and cope with head or tail at equal ease would have evidenced a want of invention and a false decorum from which Campion, in all the limitations of his poetic chamber music,[8] can never be said to suffer.

7. See above, p. 57.
8. I do not mean hereby to slight the beautiful rhythmic textures of Campion's verse, nor its internal "music" of assonance and alliteration. These patterns have been analyzed in an excellent article by John T. Irwin in *Studies in English Literature*, X (1970), 121-41.

V
"SENSE VARIOUSLY DRAWN OUT": ON ENGLISH ENJAMBMENT

"The music of the English heroic line," said Dr. Johnson, "strikes the ear so faintly, that it is easily lost, unless all the syllables of every line cooperate together; this cooperation can only be obtained by the preservation of every verse unmingled with another as a distant system of sounds; and this distinctness is obtained and preserved by the artifice of rhyme. The variety of pauses, so much boasted by the lovers of blank verse, changes the measures of an English poet to the periods of a declaimer; and there are only a few happy readers of Milton who enable their audience to perceive where the lines end or begin. *Blank verse,* said an ingenious critic, *seems to be verse only to the eye.*"[1] To an age like our own which is so accustomed to purely graphic meters and visual formats for poetry, such a comment seems hard-of-hearing; we would more properly want to say this of pure syllabics, for example. Of more central concern, however, is the short shrift given to "the variety of pauses," a variety not only basic to the metrical system of *Paradise Lost,* but one which has become more and more important in the recent history of prosody.

Johnson's concern here was with the integrity of the poetic line. There is a long tradition for his anxiety about line terminus as a guardian of that integrity. The Virgilian hexameter, overflowing with syntax,

1. Samuel Johnson, "Milton," *Lives of the English Poets.*

nevertheless marked its rim with an almost inevitable accentual close, a stress pattern of [′ ·· ′ ·]² accompanying the unvarying quantitative schema [—◡◡——] no matter how little alignment of stressed syllable with long one had occurred in the first four feet.³ Dryden, in an amusing anticipation of Dr. Johnson's disparagement of blank verse as opposed to more powerful rhymed couplets, hankered after just this kind of marked terminus which he knew the Classical, heroic hexameter to possess: "For imagination in a poet is a faculty so wild and lawless that, like an high-ranging spaniel, it must have clogs tied to it, lest it outrun the judgment. The great easiness of blank verse renders the poet too luxuriant."⁴ The unbridled forward surge of language, Dryden argues, is specifically to be curbed by linear closure. This same marking function, whether considered in its melodious, chiming role or as a more prosaic ticking, is invoked by other arguments for rhyme, down to a very different sort of neoclassicism from Dryden's, in Paul Valéry's remark about how "Rhyme establishes a law independent of the poem's theme and might be compared to a clock outside it."⁵

If rhymes are clogs, dampers, or restraints, it is an exuberantly generative linguistic faculty upon which they operate. Milton himself, in

2. I shall use [·, ′] to mean unstressed and stressed syllables in accentual-syllabic verse; our commonly used, casual [◡ ′] notation borrows its two markers from quantitative and accentual notational systems, and is rather like a mixed metaphor or a Graeco-Latin compound.
3. Whether or not this effect is merely statistical, given the consequences of the penultimate stress rule in Latin, is problematic. See Charles Gordon Cooper, *An Introduction to the Latin Hexameter* (Melbourne and New York, 1952), for an excellent treatment of these matters, as well as the discussion of applications to English in G. L. Hendrickson, "Elizabethan Quantitative Hexameters," *Philological Quarterly*, 28 (1949), 237-60. The reader of modern English, too, can perceive the effects of a terminus marked by features *outside* the metrical system: consider three lines of pure syllabic verse, à la Marianne Moore or W. H. Auden, with ten syllables and no assigned stress patterns. In the following example they will all terminate in an accentual iambic close; or, if one prefers the terminology of Halle and Keyser, stress maxima in even positions:

    Open windows in the morning are bright;
    Closed transoms give on the hallway and spill
    No intriguing pale yellow squares of sun. . . .

4. John Dryden, *Epistle Dedicatory to "The Rival Ladies"* (1694), in *Essays* (Everyman edition), pp. 187-88.
5. Paul Valéry, *Analects*, tr. Stuart Gilbert (Princeton, 1970), p. 102.

defending his own "variety of pauses," denounced rhyme, "the Invention of a barbarous Age," as a "troublesome and modern bondage."⁶ It is, however, poetry itself, lines handcuffed together, rather than the poet's creative faculty, which he specifically wished to liberate (" 'ancient liberty recover' to Heroic poem"). In this he was preceded by Ben Jonson, whose image of the fetters of rhyme applies wittily and profoundly to its internal constraints—

> Joynting Syllabes, drowning Letters,
> Fastning Vowells, as with fetters
> They were bound!⁷

—as he was followed, strangely, by Blake: "Poetry Fetter'd, Fetters the Human Race."⁸ Even though Blake was talking here of the chains of Miltonic blank verse (now having outgrown the antithetical role it played, as against rhymed couplets, in *Paradise Lost*, and become the primary mode itself), he could quote Milton in claiming it to be "derived from the modern bondage of Rhyming." It might be observed in passing that the tying down of line endings comes to stand for such a restraint—on the generative wit that races across them—primarily in a Neoclassical reaction against Miltonic verse.

Milton's own reference to his "variety of pauses" appears in the prose preface on "The Verse," added after the first 1667 printing of *Paradise Lost*, rejecting rhyme as being of "no true musical delight; which consists only in apt Numbers, fit quantity of Syllables, and the sense variously drawn out from one verse into another." Allowing for a terminological confusion between stress and quantity common in Renaissance English poetic theory (where, actually, stress is thought of as English quantity), Milton is asserting that the music of his verse will lie in its being in fact accentual-syllabic blank verse, and in its instrumentalized enjambments. "*Sense variously drawn out*"—this is clearly the heart of the matter. He is arguing specifically against the

---

6. John Milton, *Paradise Lost*, prefatory note on "The Verse." The text, as in all quotations from Milton throughout, is that of M. Y. Hughes (New York, 1957).
7. Ben Jonson, "A Fit of Rime Against Rime," ll. 10-12.
8. William Blake, "To the Public," Preface to *Jerusalem;* the text is that of David V. Erdman and Harold Bloom (New York, 1970), p. 144.

notion that only rhyme is musical, the notion that "stumbled" many readers, and for this reason it is the figuratively "musical" variation in the character of his line termini which he underlines. Recent sophisticated discussions of Milton's style during the last decade have begun to analyze the amazing repertory of effects, at once both subtle and profound, of which Milton's language in *Paradise Lost* was capable. Within the context of such discussions, it should now be clear that, as with all "musical" devices in *Paradise Lost*, the intricately related demands of local meaning and larger vision are being served by the many ways in which Milton's line endings variously fetter and spur the exuberance of syntactic production.

One need only look at a celebrated example, the opening line of *Paradise Lost:*

> Of Man's first Disobedience, and the Fruit
> Of that Forbidden Tree, whose mortal taste . . .
>
> (1.1-2)

Here we have a paradigm of the poem's unique mode of linearity: a line characterized by an architectonic structure in its unfolding array of syllabic distribution (three monosyllabic words, then, central in every sense, a word of five syllables, then three monosyllables again) exhibits a closed unit of what Alastair Fowler has discussed as "triumphal form."[9] But its stasis is immediately disturbed by the brilliant line-ending. "Fruit" might well have led to something like "Thereof" in the following line, thus being taken in the figurative sense of "results"; actually, the line which follows thrusts us into the primary, literal sense of *that* fruit of *that* tree. "Disobedience" has the importance of staged centrality, "Fruit" the urgency of a terminal place which reveals both its own positional ambiguity and that of the word occupying it. These two impulses—the one toward systematic, static pattern, the other toward periodic flux and articulated paragraphing—are the warp and weft of the verse fabric of *Paradise Lost*. Whenever brilliantly framed and patterned lines occur, they are opened out at their closing to allow their apparent syntactic closure to flow forward. Thus, for example, when the inner state of Satan on Mount Niphates is being described:

9. Alastair Fowler, *Triumphal Forms* (Cambridge, 1970).

> horror and doubt distract
> His troubl'd thoughts, and from the bottom stir
> The Hell within him, for within him Hell
> He brings, and round about him . . .
>
> (IV.18-21)

The perfect schematic chiasmus of line 20 swirls up as a momentary picture in an agitated phantasmagoria, until our attention moves on, dragged by the force of continuing syntax and its tugging toward completion (we must have the verb, however inverted, for which "Hell" is an object, as well as a symmetrical tessera in a mosaic pattern). But consider the "stir" in line 19: it produces nothing that we would ordinarily call a prominent enjambment. The pattern [verb / Object] (where the slant-dash stands, as usual, for line break) represents no more than a moderate flow of sense. But what hangs on at the end of the line is the likelihood of the verb's intransitivity, i.e., it might have gone on: "stir / From their dark slumbers Thoughts more troubl'd yet." The *contre-rejet*, or continuation of the enjambed unit, shows it to be surprisingly transitive, and it is this surprise which lights up the following line. Even more shocking is the dissolution of the linear façade a few lines further on, where conscience

> wakes the bitter memory
> Of what he was, what is, and what must be
> Worse; of worse deeds worse sufferings must ensue.
>
> (IV.24-26)

Here the static pattern of line 25, framing the formula from the prayer-book ("As it was in the beginning, is now and ever shall be"), is jolted by the revelation that "be" was merely predicative (and of "worse," at that), rather than existential. As if to confirm the intention of that jolt, "worse" is repeated twice in the line.[10]

---

10. Further study may show this to be a widespread convention for assuring the attentive reading that the shock it felt was deliberately intended. Thus, in "The Tunnel" section of Hart Crane's *The Bridge*, in an almost exclusively closed iambic pentameter environment, we get: "That last night on the ballot rounds did you / Shaking, did you deny the ticket, Poe?" The repetition can also echo ironically, as in *Paradise Lost*, I, 508-9: "Th'Ionian gods, of Javan's issue held / Gods, yet confessed later . . ."

In short, Milton's "variety of pauses" is a powerful and delicate device, "musical" if one must, for choreographing the reader's attention, for directing, focusing, and moving the highest and finest perceptions both of the text he reads and of his own act of reading. Closure and flow, the opposed features of Milton's verse form, oppose themselves in ways parallel to the opposition of visual and acoustic modes, respectively, of poetic language. More interestingly, the "pauses" are employed to point up other conceptual dimensions in the meanings of the text—not merely the local sense of the lines which they connect, but of the mind of the whole poem. The opening line of Book I moves us from the general to the concrete and local, and from the figurative sense of a word to the literal one. These are both crucial categorical pairs in the poem, confusions in which will entangle both Satan's thought and its echoes in human dialectic. Throughout the poem, the dynamics of line terminus will point up such dimensions as can be revealed by grammatical shift—a verbal-nominal ambiguity points up another kind of lexical one, such as that of original (Latinate or Greek or Hebrew) meaning versus a derived one (itself a metaphorical dimension of the poem, emphasizing the distinction between the Original and the Fallen). Thus

> this *Assyrian* Garden, where the Fiend
> Saw undelighting all delight, all kind
> Of living creatures . . .
>
> (IV.283-87)

where a shade of the *O.E.D.* adj. 5 sense of "kind" ("benevolent"), reinforced by an off-rhyme and by internal assonance, hangs over the line end, as if to continue "all kind / And loving creatures," for example. Or, again, the line break can affect the lexical quality of a word lying beyond that break, playing an unfallen against what Christopher Ricks has designated an "uninfected" meaning.[11] So as in Satan's cry of delight

> O fair foundation laid whereon to build
> Thir ruin!
>
> (IV.521-22)

11. Christopher Ricks, *Milton's Grand Style* (Oxford, 1963).

Donald Davie has called attention to the "oxymoron revealed" in the line transition,[12] but he neglects the dimensions of "ruin." Owen Barfield has commented on the shift in meaning of the word from that of a process ("ruining") to the residues of that process ("rubble");[13] here there is indeed an oxymoron only when "build" is literal and "ruin" equals "ruins." But we are led also to consider the other case, where "build" is figurative, and "ruin" means undoing, and where there is no oxymoron at all.

Often, the Miltonic line juncture will startle in a complex mimetic way, operating on words and their designata at once. Thus, of the two contiguous trees in Paradise—"And next to Life / Our Death, the Tree of Knowledge" (IV.220-21)—it is "Our Death," not just "Death," which is imminent even in the garden, Free Will being what it is. Or again, Satan (at IV.197-98) "sat devising Death / To them who lived" and the ambiguity of "devising" first suggests the creation and institution of death itself, until, with the *contre-rejet* of the new line, the mere sense of "plotting" is revealed. And here, too, the axis of general versus particular is underlined.

These examples show us that it is always a grammatical operation which the "sense variously drawn out" effects, and only thereby a semantic and, ultimately, an imaginative one. In the lines given below, it is actually a matter of a shift in antecedent—from the "expected" to the "discovered"—which forces an ironic point:

> Satan, now first inflam'd with rage, came down,
> The Tempter ere th'Accuser of man-kind,
> To wreck on innocent frail man his loss
> Of that first Battle, and his flight to Hell:
>
> (IV.9-12)

Linearity itself shapes our expectations in blank verse, and our first impulse is to take a line like 11, far from being an architectonic one as it

---

12. Donald Davie, "Syntax and Music in *Paradise Lost*" (in *The Living Milton*, ed. Frank Kermode, London, 1960, pp. 70-84), opened up many of the problems of line ending in *Paradise Lost* and was able to argue, before many other critics of Milton's verse, from the phenomenology of the act of reading.
13. In *Poetic Diction* (2nd ed., New York, 1957), pp. 120-22.

is, as completing a period. "His" would then, given lexical richness of "wreck," refers to "man"; the enjambment revealed itself reveals the true antecedent, but the ambiguity of the pronoun reflects the fact that, in the poem, Satan's loss is not only a type of Adam's, but a cause of it.

Paradise Lost bristles with such instances, and one is tempted to quote dozens of them. From Book IV again, Eve's account of her displacement of narcissistic admiration onto a recognition of Adam's as an objectified beauty, concludes "and from that time I see / How beauty is excell'd by manly grace" (ll. 489-90), where the literal sense of "see" dissolves into a figurative one ("see how" as "understand that"), with a lingering hedging of her commitment. Or

> hideous ruin and combustion down
> To bottomless perdition there to dwell
> In Adamantine Chains and penal Fire
>
> (I.46-48)

where, again without a conserving pattern, "down" has a fleeting, illusory (because, ultimately, grammatically impossible) adjectival quality, "dwell" seems first to be followed by a stop, and the following *contre-rejet* maintains the effect of bottoms dissolving into mirages as dropping continues. Again, in Book VI (ll. 876-77), in a similar context, the postpostive adjective is uncovered in all its force: "Hell their fit habitation frought with fire / Unquenchable."

The taxonomy of the "variety of pauses" would yield some interesting results for students of Milton's imagination,[14] perhaps with respect to a way he seems to have of making metaphoric use of a phenomenol-

---

14. Seymour Chatman set up the category "alternative" lines (midway between "run-on" and "end-stopped") in which, loosely defined as it is, these Miltonic examples might fall. See "Comparing Metrical Styles," in *Essays on the Language of Literature,* ed. Seymour Chatman and Samuel R. Levin (Boston, 1967), pp. 148-49; but the insensitively performatory approach to the nature of the poetic line (as in "Caesura, end-stoppage, and enjambment exist only in actual performance, since they are phonological, not orthographic phenomena," p. 148) tended to confirm the suspicions of W. K. Wimsatt and others that Chatman's methods could contribute little to the understanding of English meter and its role in the poetic process.

ogy of language: grammar, syntax, and diachronic morphology, as the reader is aware of them, become elements of experience which are, in subtle ways, moralized in the poem. But at this point I should like to abandon the gathering of instances, and turn from the "variety" to the "pauses," to some of the procedural problems for prosodic analysis which the notion of "pause" sets up.

What we have in fact been considering is a variety of enjambments, even though we usually reserve that term only for what appear to be the more abrupt or sharp of these. In discussions of caesura in various languages, the word "pause" is misleadingly used to describe a situation whose necessary and sufficient condition is a word boundary;[15] such a boundary will coincide with a wide array of junctures, some of which would indeed be projected into speech as "pauses," or be represented by punctuation in writing. In enjambment, however, linear terminus exercises an even more marked cutting effect; ironically enough, our convention of separating lines of verse with a slant-dash in prose format suggests a more useful model for treating enjambment than the usual pair of opposed terms "enjambed" versus "end-stopped" evokes.

Let us choose instead a kind of spectrum, along which we would arrange all the possible ways of terminating lines, considered not as boundaries or termini, but as the kinds of cutting into syntax which the slant-dash notation illustrates. At either end of this spectrum, we would put a trivial case, one of extreme "softness" of cut, where the slant-dash really divides nothing, and the other of "hardness," where an unusually strong linkage is severed. In order to accommodate a diachronic view of the English poetic line since Chaucer, the spectrum must be sufficiently wide to include such normally trivial cases. Thus, on the right, the terminus of

> Through *Eden* took their solitary way. /

15. See, for example, "Caesura," in the *Encyclopedia of Poetry and Poetics*, ed. Alex Preminger, Frank Warnke, and O. B. Hardison (Princeton, 1965). In Classical verse, the rule that a caesura must fall within a foot serves to give it a *linking* role, and diaeresis, the coincidence of foot and word boundary, falling at the end of the third foot of the heroic line, would have a cutting function.

makes a total closure—of phrase, clause, period, book, and *Paradise Lost*. At the other end of the spectrum, let us place a cut so sharp as to be analogously senseless, so sharp that it has no phonetic, let alone grammatical, consequences whatsoever, a cut not even between graphemes (as in b/ Etween) but between two subcomponents, as in the disyllabic couplet

> And al-
> Though Paul[16]

In between these, we might arrange the possible cuts in a kind of ordered array.[17] Certainly [xxxxx; / Xxxxx] would be far over toward the right, while [a / (any noun)] would be toward the left or "hard" side. The best way to show such an array might be to consider the effects of alternative cuts, of pathological versification, in a familiar passage. Consider the famous "self-descriptive" couplet from Pope's *An Essay on Criticism*:

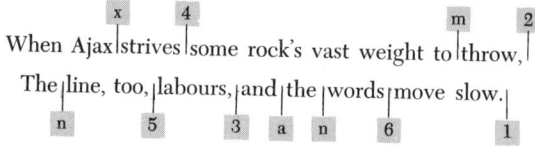

I have numbered from 1 to 6 in this diagram some possible points at which a contemporary poem in free verse might, in quoting Pope's

---

16. A line should be drawn at this point between a linguistic, and a purely graphic, effect. This extreme left-hand end of the spectrum is engaged only by twentieth-century verse in any case, but certainly an accentually syllabic strict couplet like "O, now / A Cow," done as

> O, NOV / V A COW

is "concrete poetry," and hence a branch of graphic art; cutting a grapheme as it does, it is not annotating language, but abstracting forms.

17. My colleague Samuel R. Levin recognized, in "The Conventions of Poetry" (in *Literary Style: A Symposium*, ed. Seymour Chatman, New York, 1971, pp. 172-74), the need for some kind of hierarchy of junctural features. In another context, Roger Fowler observed that the shorter the lexical unit, the less likely it is to be enjambed. See also Viktor Žirmunskij, *Introduction to Metrics* (s'Gravenhage, 1966), pp. 158-68.

lines, break them. I have also shown the possible ordered array [n <
m < a] (where [<] means a harder cut), and I have raised a question
whether the consonantal clusters at [x] enforce a different order of cut
from the one its merely grammatical status of [subject / Verb] would
make.

The effect of such a spectrum is to allow a treatment of line breaks
as marking or indicating syntactic groups, and sometimes as perform-
ing a trick not unlike covering up one end of a line of English inscription, inviting the reader to guess at the nature of the hidden text, and
then revealing it. Milton, and Blake when he follows him, is in effect
employing the half-covered line, the guess, the correct "answer" and
even the moment of *anagnorisis*, of discovery of the truth with its slight
rebuke, as part of the marking process. Certainly the marking or annotating is done within the metrical resources of the verse. But just as
certainly is it being effected by a kind of metalanguage—not one as
sharply differentiated from its object language as are prosodic signs,
brackets, the symbols of sentence-diagram, and so forth, but clearly as
separated. This operation is an concrete an instance of the abstractness
of meter, in the sense argued for it by W. K. Wimsatt and Monroe
Beardsley,[18] as one could hope to find.

The Miltonic tradition of enjambed blank verse deploys its variety
of line endings to annotate syntax, primarily; when a lexical ambiguity
is being developed, it is a control exercised over the act of sequential
reading which points it up. But even within the line, accentual-syllabic
meter can do its work of notating and annotating the syntax of a text.
Contrastive, or other sorts of emphatic stress, provide the most obvious
surface upon which the effects of iambic positioning can operate, even
when the results are not specifically those of contrast. Let us consider
an ambiguous sentence cited by Chomsky as requiring two syntactic

18. In "The Concept of Meter: An Exercise in Abstraction" (1959, reprinted in
Essays in the Language of Literature, pp. 91-114), some problems raised by
Chatman's approach led to a formulation tacitly assumed throughout the present
essay, and affirmed in different form in the author's own "The Metrical Emblem"
(1960), reprinted in the same volume, pp. 115-26. "The Rule and the Norm," in
which Wimsatt and Beardsley refined their argument with respect, this time, to
the schematic treatment of English iambic meter by Halle and Keyser, appeared
in *Literary Style: A Symposium*, pp. 197-215.

descriptions,[19] but whose ambiguity is easily resolved by the informal notation of italics:

1. They don't know how good meat tastes

can be immediately associated with one of its two possible syntactic descriptions (the one involving the relation, as Chomsky gives it, "meat tastes good") by means of italicization in ordinary prose:

2. They don't know how good *meat* tastes

Here there is an implicit contrastive treatment of "meat" ("They don't know how good meat can taste, having fed only on rice and fish"). Note, however, that an alternative treatment

3. They don't know how *good* meat tastes

while assigning a different syntactic description still retains some ambiguity because of the emphatically contrastive "good." That is, 3a, "how *good* meat tastes (not just pleasantly *salty*)" versus 3b, "how '*good*' meat tastes (*Prime* meat, not that stringy 'U.S. Good' you've been eating").

Now, because of its conventionality, accentual-syllabic verse can do its own sort of italicizing. We could just as easily use versification to resolve the syntactic ambiguities in our example. When recast into iambic pentameter, the ambiguity of 1 can still be preserved, although shaded toward the readings of 3:

4. "But they don't know how good meat tastes," he said

This line retains another possibility as well, one to which Chomsky might have assigned a third syntactic description, and which emerges in the italicized version:

5. They don't know how good meat *tastes*

and where the emphatic stress could yield 5a, "how good meat *tastes*, rather than *looks*" versus 5b, a noncontrastive terminal emphatic stress

---

19. "Topics in the Theory of Generative Grammar," in Noam Chomsky, *Selected Readings*, ed. Allen and Van Buren (London, 1971), p. 11.

that we might style the girlish petulant, a version, in meaning of either 2 or 3b, but not, I think, of 3a.

As a line of verse, 4 could certainly yield readings 2, 5a, or 5b, and, less likely, 3a. This uncommitted quality is characteristic of self-consciously iambic modern metrical styles (in this case, for example, Robert Frost's in his blank-verse eclogues). But consider another iambic treatment of our example, from another hypothetical Frost poem:

> 6. "They don't know how good meat tastes."
> "Silas does."

Here 3a and 3b are ruled out, by the implicit italicization of "meat." It is obvious, too, that other accentual-syllabic rhythmic settings could reinforce the effects of 4 or 5 even more obviously. Thus, we could render the sense of 3 more clearly as

> 7. They don't know how good meat tastes!
> The missing joys! the needless wastes!

Alternatively, an elided anapestic movement could do the work of 6, as in

> 8. They don't know how good meat tastes
> In the misty mid region of Weir!

But all of these effects are much more powerful when deployed around the line terminus than among iambic positions alone. In the case of this example, let us consider

> 9.   they don't know how
> Good meat tastes

and

> 10.   they don't know how good
> Meat tastes

and

> 11.   they don't know how good meat
> Tastes

and

  12.   they don't know
    How good meat tastes

Here we must decide not only which of the meanings charted in 2, 3, and 5 are assigned by the positioning of the line break, but how the discovery of the *contre-reject* may revise that decision. As we actually read 1, Chomsky's unannotated string in its unavowedly literary context (that is, as an *example* in a linguistic treatise), the various possibilities of 2, 3, 5, etc., flicker on and off, within the transparency of the line of text, like the alternating readings of the duck-rabbit cited by Wittgenstein.[20] With the discovered *contre-rejets* in these lines, we are prodded into one decision or another; thus, in 9, the primary revelation is that "how" will *not* be followed by "to" and its infinitive, while the secondary one is that we are left with a case of 2 because of the stressed position of "meat."

In 10, the possibilities of 2, 3, and 5 do not waver so much as jam up against each other, and we are required to consider the possibility of simultaneous readings. 11 tends to rule out 3, combining 2 and 5—except for the hint of 3b in 5b. Finally, 12, of all the possibilities, retains the slow ambiguity of 4, and, through it, of 1.

Now to return to the enjambment spectrum discussed earlier: while it is clear that 12 represents the softest of these cuts in syntax, dividing verb and complement, 9 and 10 both present interesting problems. In order to assign them places along the scale, we should not only need an extremely sophisticated system of gradation, but we should have to resolve ambiguities about where the cut, in fact, occurs. In 10, for example, the reader arrives at the line ending believing that the cut is being made as in

  10a.   they don't know how good
    He is

20. Ludwig Wittgenstein, *Philosophical Investigations*, II.11; I think this is more appropriate an analogy than the alternating readings of, say, the Necker cube, as the graphic conventions being punned upon in the first instance are more like linguistic ones of the kind at work in our example.

where, because of the inversion, the cut is being made between predicate adjective and its verb. But the discovered *contre-rejet* reveals the possibility of an adjective-noun (and thus, initial foot-reversal as well). If previously introduced material has prepared a reading of 3a or 3b—for example,

> 10b. Their beef is rotten; they don't know how good
> Meat tastes

—then the enjambment will have been harder than in

> 10c. They love its hue, but they don't know how good
> Meat tastes

Some of these distinctions may seem overly delicate, but they are very powerful in determining the pace and texture of metrical style, and not for the music, but the doctrine there—not merely for their abstract rhythm of percussiveness, however clothed in the melody of rhyme or assonance, however modulated by alliteration the attack. Operating within the line, through the action of stress-maximum positioning on monosyllables, they hum out a melody which can be hauntingly characteristic. Thus the lines about the hen

> Who cackles every morning from her perch
> To tell the servant girl new eggs are laid

and, later on in the same poem, about the boy who

> takes his hat and hopes to find it full,
> She's laid so long so many might have been
> (John Clare, "Hen's Nest")

sound particularly like Robert Frost in his mode of wielding the controlling tool of positioning. Similarly with Dante Gabriel Rossetti's

> Our speed is such the sparks our engine leaves
> Are burning after the whole train has passed
> ("Antwerp to Ghent")

which sounds equally like Frost, and where the colloquial syntax allows a clause, with an ellipsis of the relative pronoun, to glide into terminal position before the main verb of the *contre-rejet*.

Neither of these metrical gestures brandishes its implements as do those of Browning. I am thinking of an instance like

Sétebos, Sétebós, and Sétebós!
("Caliban upon Setebos")

where the two possible ways of handling an initially stressed trisyllabic word in an iambic context are flourished with a kind of measured panache: [′ · ·] or [′ · ′] will both do (but never [· ′·, · ″, or ″ ·]), and so *do* they both. There are so few problems in the accentual-syllabic accommodation of polysyllabic words that many areas of metrical controversy of the past two decades might have been bypassed if there were no monosyllables in English. In these remarks I am only indirectly concerned with the theoretical background of the iambic pentameter line, and shall merely suggest that in the present discussion, I have been thinking of phrases as polysyllabic words,[21] and clauses as phrases built from these. "Naturally dactylic" words like "Setebos" or "Trumpington" and compounds like "scatter-brained" and "whistle-stop" are stressed in the same ways as phrases like "scatter it," and their stress-positioning in a line would be isomorphic to Browning's (i.e. "Scatter it, scatter it, and scatter it").[22]

Much of what happens in strong or hard enjambments, then, forces a reinterpretation of the position of the syntactic cut at the line break, based upon the discovered *contre-rejet*. As we have seen from Milton, other revisions can depend upon the syntactic rereading: the discov-

---

21. As Hopkins seems to do in the hard cut at the end of the first line of "The Windhover": "morning's minion, king- / Dom of daylight's dauphin."
22. But note that in "A halfpenny will help you scrape a knee," the allowable stressings for "hálfpenny" and "scrápe a knee," permit one to give way, and the iambic context to dissolve (when sung, for example, to the tune of Richard Rodgers's "To Keep My Love Alive"). The [′ · ′] metrical treatment mediates between two other extremes:

[′ · ·] halfpenny→ ′ · ′ ←scrape a knee [· · ′]

One of the reasons that trisyllabic rhyming played such an important part in the history of the light verse from Browning through Old Possum is that it allows for the momentary comic fiction that syllables or morphemes are punning words in another syntactic context—as in Lorenz Hart's sequence "Like a wreck to me—appendectomy" from the song mentioned above. See also p. 126.

ered transitivity or intransitivity of a verb, the verbal status if a participle, can also force an accompanying acceptance of an etymologized or earlier historical usage. Particularly in contemporary English, a level of diction might be implied by a *contre-rejet*. Consider the following possibilities:

> . . . and I go.
>
> . . . and I go
> Homeward
>
> . . . and I go
> Home on Wednesdays
>
> . . . and I go
> Without my lunch

where the difference of aspect between the second and third cases reinforces the difference between the archaic and the colloquial levels upon which the cases are arranged.

There are other metrical considerations which can affect the hardness or softness of enjambments. English adaptations of Classical meters, whether stressed analogues of quantitative meter, or visual codings of the meters themselves (by which I would include all the Elizabethan experiments from "Master Drant's rules" to Campion's experiments), can modulate enjambed effects:

> Glory too God, the father, and his onlye
> Son, the protectoure of us earthlee sinners,
> Thee sacred spirit, labourers refreshing,
>   Stil be renownèd
> (Richard Stanyhurst, "A Prayer to the Blessed Trinity")

These lines compose a stressed Sapphic strophe (perhaps Stanyhurst had given it a quantitative coding as well—he did this elsewhere). "Onlye / Son" is rather hard; "refreshing / Still" is rather soft, and yet the boundary between lines 3 and 4 is frequently violated by hyphenation (and hence, one of the hardest of cuts) in Classical authors (Sappho, Catullus), as if the stanza really were a three-lined one, with two

Lesser Sapphics and a longer terminal. Thus Campion: "Author of number that hath all the world in / harmony framèd" forms the conclusion of a Sapphic strophe. In both these cases, normal accentual-syllabic line end expectations are suspended as a result of the reader's recognizing the Sapphic pattern, which will allow none of the variation, in the accentual version of it, generated by the English iambic line (if a purely quantitative version, the line will have no audible integrity in any case).

Rhyme is, of course, another factor in modulating the effects of terminal cuts. Robert Herrick ("Upon Himself"), echoing in his small way Ben Jonson's powerful and famous enjambment across not only a line, but a labeled strophe break "And there he lives with memorie: and *Ben / Jonson*, who sung this of him," immediately rhymes internally upon his discovered monosyllable, as if to reassure the reader of his intention:

> And learn'd Musicians shall, to honour *Herricks*
> Fame, and his Name, both set, and sing his Lyricks.

Or take Marvell's celebrated four lines from "To His Coy Mistress":

> Thy beauty shall no more be found,
> Nor in thy marble Vault shall sound
> My ecchoing Song: then worms shall try
> That long preserved Virginity.

The movement of these lines is extremely characteristic of Marvell, showing the balanced swing from a somewhat hard, open line ending of one couplet back to closure which, in four stresses, anticipates Pope in five. But the force of "sound / My ecchoing Song" is in the discovered subject of "sound." If the first couplet were closed, "sound" would be uninverted, with "beauty" as its subject, and figurative (beauty being silent); but although it is not, our false surmise lingers on for a bit after the continuation.

In other cases, the rhyme merely gives a final stamp to a closure made in other ways. The famous "imitative effect" of the refrain of

Marvell's "The Mower's Song," supposedly so suggestive of the motion of scything

> For Juliana comes, and she
> What I do to the grass, does to my thoughts and me.

comes from the inverted clausal pattern, and its postponed predicate. Aided by the tendency of the English Alexandrine to break into trimeter fragments, the completion of the main clause, as if in a reciprocal return: "do to the grass"—"does to my thoughts" (the architectonic chiasmus of ["I do to . . . does to me"] also helps) makes us fancy we "hear" the swaying, reciprocating motion of the scythe. In a taxonomic classification of enjambment, this might represent a species in which the *contre-rejet* reveals an almost pathological syntactic inversion or deferment.

In other instances, a rhyme occurring after the discovery may work to reinforce, in a strange, brief kind of restrospect, the discarded initial syntactic reading of the first line. Thus, in Frost's couplet from "After Apple Picking":

> But I was well
> Upon my way to sleep before it fell

there is the effect of the discorded semantic unit's being confirmed by the very revised one to which it gives way as "well" is reread adverbially, not so much in Milton's manner, but by a kind of general implication—if p stands for "But I was well," and q for "But I was well upon my way to sleep," then p *implies* q is true. But notice, for example, how much less total poetic force accompanies the syntactically harder cut in the otherwise similar dummy (from a hypothetical "After Cucumber Picking"?)—"But it was ill / Fitted for pickling without thyme or dill." It is not only because the covert associations of sleep and death in Frost's poem are absent from the ludicrous dummy that it has little power, and it should be hardly necessary to invoke such instances to show that the prominence of verse patterning and its effectiveness do not necessarily generate poetic or even rhetorical power.

But whether or not a strong effect of alliteration or enjambment will startle, reassure, tire, or redirect the reading attention is surely a function of the role of that device in the total poetic style.[23] When enjambment is systematic, as in *Paradise Lost* or some of William Carlos Williams's free verse, a wide range of effects ensures that even strong, pointed cuts at line breaks will never startle by their mere occurrence but, if at all, for what they reveal—about language, about the world, or because of when and where, in the course of the poem, they show it. But when the style avoids strong enjambment, the effect may be to shock per se: T. S. Eliot's "Entertains Sir Ferdinand / Klein" occurs in a context of archly rhymed and stopped Gautier-like quatrains.[24]

But where, in twentieth-century verse, an enjambment can occur without interest in shock or abruptness as a mimetic effect by itself, the Miltonic operations on the lexical level can occur. A paradigmatic case is from William Carlos Williams in a well-known poem which uses the device almost as if in a manifesto:

> so much depends
> upon
>
> a red wheel
> barrow
>
> glazed with rain
> water

23. Allen Mandelbaum has pointed out to me that whereas Dante presents a brilliant and subtle range of enjambments across particles like *quando*, it is not until Canto 17 of the *Purgatory* that a strong cut appears, where it is quickly tempered by the eventual rhyme. Thus

> Questi è divino spirito, che ne la
> Via d'andar su ne drizza senza prego
> E col suo lume sè medesmo cela
> (II.17, 55-57)

24. Or, even more abrupt a case, from *The Waste Land* (ll. 253-54), "When lovely woman stoops to folly and/Paces about her room again, alone," where the surprise is reversed when we discover that the famous Goldsmith quotation will not end the line, and the "and" is promoted metrically and syntactically both. Such a joke of promotion may stem from Lewis Carroll's "And when I found the door was shut, /I tried to turn the handle but."

>   beside the white
>   chickens[25]

The rigorous metrical convention of the poem demands simply three words in the first line of each couplet and a disyllable in the second. But the line termini cut the words "wheelbarrow" and "rainwater" into their constituents, without the use of hyphenation to warn that the first noun is to be part of a compound, *with the implication that they are phenomenological constituents as well.* The wheel plus the barrow equals the wheelbarrow, and in the freshness of light after the rain (it is this kind of light which the poem is *about,* although never mentioned directly), things seem to lose their compounded properties. Instead of Milton's shifting back and forth from original to derived meanings of words, Williams "etymologizes" his compounds into their prior phenomena, and his verbal act represents, and makes the reader carry out, a meditative one. The formal device is no surface trick. But in an even more famous poem from the same group, Williams employs an enjambment which is directly in the line of Milton's type of revisionary disclosure:

>   By the road to the contagious hospital
>   under the surge of the blue
>   mottled clouds driven from the
>
>   northeast—a cold wind. Beyond, the
>   waste of broad, muddy fields
>   brown with dried weeds, standing and fallen[26]

"Blue" in the second line might be nominal, and the surge of azure sky might be a too-easily gained sign of spring; the enjambment pulls it back into adjectival status, paired with, and half-modifying, "mottled." The fairly hard but merely systematic enjambments of "the" in the next two lines tend to soften, in retrospect, the modulation of "blue," as if to suggest, perhaps, that closure is no norm, that linearity has no marked integrity other than the rough typographical width of somewhere around thirty ems.

25. "Spring and All," 22 (1923).
26. "Spring and All," 1. Also see below, pp. 285-87.

Almost at the edge of whimsy is Elizabeth Bishop's startling effect in "Arrival at Santos"; in loose accentual rhymed quatrains she develops a momentary nervous chattiness while describing an awkward descent from a steamer to a tender:

> Please, boy, do be more careful with that boat hook!
> Watch out! Oh! It has caught Miss Breen's
>
> skirt! There! Miss Breen is about seventy,
> a retired police lieutenant, six feet tall,
> with beautiful bright blue eyes and a kind expression.
> Her home, when she is at home, is in Glens Fall
>
> s, New York. There. We are settled. . . .

This enjambment is no merely figurative straddling: a gunwale is indeed being traversed, and the e. e. cummings sort of fracture across "Fall / s" is modulated by rhyme, tone, subject and narrative moment at once. It is no cheap effect.

In all the variations of verse system which twentieth-century poetry has produced, the role of enjambment has expanded considerably: in many kinds of free verse, the mere modulation of degrees of hardness or softness along the spectrum is a more fundamental means of maintaining pace and dramatic build, of controlling the motion of attention along the flow of language, than modulation of line length itself. But this legacy from Milton descended in no closed line of succession. Indeed, Milton's functional, rather than merely rhythmic "music" in his "variety of pauses" seems to have gone largely unheard in the eighteenth century. Even in bald stylistic parody, where perceptions of structure are mechanically heightened and gears creak where, in the original, energy flowed, there is no sense of it. In "The Splendid Shilling," John Philips can only broadly mock an inverted syntax which an Augustan ear could take but as delayed, even tardy complement. Invariably a sinking or mock-heroic descent occurs when the reader is dropped into, rather than discovers, the object of the verb in such cases as

> if he his ample Palm
> Should haply on ill-fated Shoulder lay
> Of Debtor
>
> (11.60-62)

In Philips's parody, the wit moves in a direction opposite to that of usual mock heroic, in that the honest substance of Grub Street life ridicules the high style. At its best, the repeated effect is very funny, as at the first appearance of the dun:

> What should I do? or wither turn? amaz'd,
> Confounded, to the dark recess I fly
> Of woodhole
>
> (11.42-44)

The "dark recess" is made of no embrowning shades, as only the hypallage underlined by the line break reveals. This is one of the few instances in the poem of that form of discovered incompleteness of the previous line. When Philips continues with "strait my bristling hairs erect / Through sudden fear" he cannot take advantage, as Milton would, of the hypothetical adjectival status of "erect" simply because his periods are un-Miltonically short, and because he has not prepared for the effect in the texture of the insufficiently Latinate lines.

Throughout the eighteenth century, Miltonic blank verse tended to neglect the poetic effects of syntactic modulation which degrees of enjambment might achieve. Young and the Wartons wrote what was the next thing to unrhymed couplets, in this respect. Cowper's line endings in *The Task* show a "variety of pauses," but they are ineffective for anything more than control of pace. Thomson occasionally generates an expressive effect, but only of the variety which can either call attention to the terminal word, or act mimetically through pacing. Thus, in the latter instance, the sounds of the hunt in *Autumn* are recapitulated:

> O'er a wild, harmless, flying Creature, all
> Mix'd in sad Tumult, and discordant Joy.[27]
>
> (11.428-29)

27. Or, in the former mode, "Immortal Peter! First of Monarchs! He/His stubborn country tam'd" (*Winter*, ll. 965-66).

The young William Blake, in the flagrantly experimental blank-verse poems of *Poetical Sketches*, would show himself to be as attentive a reader of the verse of *Paradise Lost* as he was responsive to its dialectic. The systematic variation of iambic pentameter lines in the poems to the seasons, and "To the Evening Star," for example, distort accentual-syllabic patternings both in the direction of pure syllabism ("Thy soft kisses on her bosom; and put") and the strange accentualism that occasionally operates in the adapted fourteeners of the long poems later on (as in this Alexandrine from "To Winter" functioning as a pentameter: "Is driv'n yelling to his caves beneath mount Hecla"). This kind of systematic variation may have been part of the young poet's war with eighteenth-century pseudo-Miltonic blank verse. But the "variety of pauses" in these five poems is even more considerable.[28]

In "To Spring" the line endings suggest those of Cowper or Thomson, the cuts being made frequently between monosyllabic verb and object: "turn/Thine angel eyes"; "taste/Thy morn"; "put/Thy golden crown," etc. But "To Summer" starts out with a more forceful breaking:

> O Thou, who passest thro' our vallies in
> Thy strength, curb thy fierce steeds, allay the heat
> (11.1-2)

The *contre-rejet* reveals an unexpected power of word and designation —the "fierce steeds" come hard upon the shock of discovery that summer will assault, rather than caress, and that the second line terminus is iambic, "the heat" being reinforced by its assonance with "fierce steeds." Several such cuts accumulate in the second stanza, where terminal words, normally unstressed in their phrases, receive syllabic attention at the line break

> Sit down; and in our mossy vallies, on
> Some bank beside a river clear, throw thy
> Silk draperies off, and rush into the stream
> (11.10-12)

---

28. Alicia M. Ostriker discusses the meter of the *Poetical Sketches* and the enjambments in particular (*Vision and Verse in William Blake*, Madison, 1965, pp. 36-40); her definition of enjambment as "run-on or absence of pause at the end of the line" prevents her from realizing the syntactic possibilities of the Miltonic type, and she has nothing of interest to say about specific cases.

whereas in the final strophe, the line endings are cut at clausal or parallel phrasal breaks, giving a strong, resolved, declamatory cast to the individual lines.

It is in "To the Evening Star," however, that Blake makes his most sophisticated and truly Miltonic use of "sense variously drawn out":

> Smile on our loves, and, while thou drawest the
> Blue curtains of the sky, scatter thy silver dew
> On every flower that shuts its sweet eyes
> In timely sleep. Let thy west wind sleep on
> The lake; speak silence with thy glimmering eyes
>   (11.5-9)

The cut at "the / Blue curtains" initiates an accentual Alexandrine, bracketed by the *contre-rejet* "Blue" and its rhyming "dew"; its architectonic plan is not allowed to remain frozen, however, as "scatter" is modified and made more specific. But it is the "sleep on / The lake" which represents a response to Milton's most complex enjambments. It is of the type we have been examining, which forces a reinterpretation of the syntax when the opening words of the run-over line are indeed discovered to be a true *contre-rejet*—"sleep on" could be closed, and mean "continue sleeping undisturbed," a reading enforced by the terminal stress position of "on." But this reading (the complete verb phrase, call it *A*) gives way to *B*, a truncated prepositional phrase, whose stress pattern would be "sleep on" (as in "sleep on the floor," for example). As we read, we expect *A*, discover that *B* is meant, and are left with the blurred superposition of the two syntactic alternatives, "keep on sleeping (because?) on the lake" being the resulting phantom image.

Blake's sensitivity to Milton's device is understandable, as is his eventual lack of interest in developing its use in the long poems,[29] where it might have seemed to function more as Blake's hated color or harmony, than as his beloved line or melody. Perhaps, too, he saw Milton's use of it as an attempted substitute for the ultimate intransi-

---

29. Ostriker comments usefully on this, pp. 134-36.

gence of English word-order syntax. Latin verse can produce phantom images by nonsyntactic adjacency alone, as in

> sed nox atra caput tristi circumvolat umbra
> (*Aeneid,* VI.866)

where "head" is surrounded by "black" and "sad," neither of which actually modifies it, but *seems to,* or modifies metaphorically. Milton was to see that the *simultaneous* variousness of the drawing-out of sense from one verse to another could produce such hovering effects, which would vanish in the paraphrase of prose as totally as those of their Latin counterparts would do in translation. Milton's English iambic pentameter was better able to produce such effects, utilizing the underlinings and emphases given by iambic stress maxima, by cutting into its own syntax—producing scholia of and on itself—than even his Latin predecessors could. What Donald Davie has called "syntax as music" certainly claimed the youthful Milton's ear when he was working on his brilliant and experimental translation of Horace: "What slender youth," etc., some years before he encountered the enjambments of the sonnets of Della Casa.[30] But he was able, by plying that most remarkable instrument of English meter, seeming to work midway in the mind between eye and ear, to invent a new mode of image-making in English poetry. Even as lexical diachrony could function in *Paradise Lost* as an emblem of fall or rise, so, at a higher (or deeper, as recent linguistic theory would suggest) level, he could work with syntax (or at least, the experience of scanning it) as image. His invention proved so subtle as well as so powerful that with few exceptions (some instances in Keats and G. M. Hopkins, for example) it would go unused until the syllabic and accentual integrity of the poetic line broke down in twentieth-century improvised metrical styles.

30. The discussion of this in F. T. Prince, *The Italian Element in Milton's Verse* (Oxford, 1954), pp. 14-33, remains the most authoritative one.

VI
RHYME AND THE TRUE CALLING OF WORDS

> Wresting words from their true calling;
> Propping verse for fear of falling
>   To the ground . . .
>
> Ben Jonson, "A Fit of Rhyme Against Rhyme"

In the last chapter, there arose the question of the role of rhyme in enforcing closure at line endings, and of the metaphoric extension of that role to one of restraint upon the poem as a whole, and, ultimately, to the bridling of Pegasus. Certainly the links of words by common ending may be considered to constitute chains, and even bonds and, as I remarked earlier, Milton allowed that those bonds, in a simple rhetorical step, might manacle the poet himself. "The troublesome and modern bondage of rhyming" is his phrase, but the resonances of it suggest "bondage *to* rhyming" as well. Blake went a step further, declaring that "Poetry Fetter'd Fetters the Human Race." In general, rhyme has been made, in post-Renaissance poetic theory, to stand for verse structure itself, and even, ultimately, poetic convention of any distinguishing sort. Such is the implication of Valéry's marvelous aphorism, followed by its more ironic ancillary epigram:

> Rhyme has the great advantage of infuriating the simple people who naively think there is something under the sun more important than a convention. They have an innocent belief that an idea may be "deeper," more durable than any convention.
> This is not the least of the charms of rhyme, nor thereby does it caress the ear less sweetly.[1]

1. Paul Valéry, *Analects*, tr. Stuart Gilbert (Princeton, 1970), p. 102.

The final turn, of course, is against the archaic, purely "musical" notion of rhyme as an instrumentalization of the tonal properties of vowels, nicely encased in consonantal packages. Or again, Valéry invests rhyme with a similar generality: "Rhyme establishes a law independent of the poem's theme and might be compared to a clock outside of it." This is all the more effective when one realizes that in a language without word stress, like French (and with a consequent metrical tradition which is purely syllabic), terminal rhyme plays an even greater part in marking closure—indeed, in the absence of stressed syllables, in "marking time" in general—than it does in English. The crucial relation between the effects of word stress and the quality of rhyme in English has not to my knowledge been adequately considered. The rhetorical powers of end rhyme in English[2]—the ability to command and manipulate the attention of the reading eye and the following ear—depend in good measure on the necessity of the rhyming syllable's being an accented one. An immediate and obvious consequence of this, for example, is that in French or even in Chaucer, the *rime très riche* or total homonymic rhyme is indeed an occasion of plenitude, whereas in modern English (consider, for example, "They are such a charming pair! / Give them an apple, or a pear") it always must fall ridiculously flat, underlined as the like syllables are by their stressed position. In English, *rime très riche* is always in a sense, *rime pauvre*.

The marking, bounding, limiting function of rhyme (and indeed, of all strict metrical commitments) can be seen, in the neatly paradoxical light first cast by Wordsworth's "Nuns fret not at their convent's narrow room" sonnet, to engender thereby a kind of freedom. Valéry, throughout his scattered remarks on poetic form, holds this view almost as an emblem of his Neoclassicism. But there is another way of viewing the linkages of rhyme as helping to form a positive structure for the poetic act. In "Merlin" Emerson snarls at "Efficacious rhymes," by which he means the texts themselves, marked by the sounds and pretty effects of rhyming's "trivial harp." But in a remarkable passage from his Journal of 1839, he proposes an alternative "music":

2. But, see below, for F. T. Prince's slightly different use of the concept of rhyme's rhetoric.

Rhyme; not tinkling rhyme but grand Pindaric strokes as firm as the tread of a horse. Rhyme that vindicates itself as an art, the stroke of the bell of a cathedral. Rhyme which knocks at prose & dulness with the stroke of a cannon ball. Rhyme which builds out of Chaos & Old night a splendid architecture to bridge the impassable, & call aloud on all the children of morning that the Creation is recommencing. I wish to write such rhymes as shall not suggest a restraint but contrariwise the wildest freedom.[3]

The "tinkling" is an attribute of the old "mere" musicality of well-tuned verse, and the "grand Pindaric strokes" the measures of a more generalized sense of verse form (Emerson was probably also thinking of the kinds of irregular spacing of rhymes in large, paragraph-like English "Pindaric" ode strophes, as opposed to the lighter "tinkling" of adjacent rhyming lines in monostichic meters). But the sense of structure, or architecture, of bridging, with its Miltonic allusion to an energetic vision of structures like bridges as augmenting, rather than cramping, human extension—this is another matter. In his last sentence, Emerson returns to the synecdochic use of "rhyme" for form but with a characteristic retention of the literal as well.

The bridging, associating, linking function of rhyme is a dialectical turn upon its ability to handcuff. Rhyme links syllables, and thereby words, and thereby lines, and thereby larger versified structures, and at each level of linkage, it performs another sort of "musical" or "rhetorical" work. F. T. Prince has written forcefully and sensitively about one aspect of this "rhetoric of rhyme"[4] as he calls it, in his discussion of the ways in which the distribution of rhymes among the long and short lines of *Lycidas* control the pace of the scanning process and the effects of the remembered and the echoic, by "a type of rhyme that looks both back and forward." By and large, he was concerned with the patterning of blocks of lines with respect to syntactic and thematic units. W. K. Wimsatt's brilliant and crucial "One Relation of Rhyme to

3. Journal entry for 27 June 1839. In *Journals and Miscellaneous Notebooks*, Vol. VII, ed. A. W. Plumstead and Harrison Hayford (Cambridge, Mass., 1969), p. 219.
4. F. T. Prince, *The Italian Element in Milton's Verse* (Oxford, 1954), pp. 86-88.

Reason" (1944)[5] established once and for all the need to take account of the metaphoric power of rhyming. In respect to rhyming words in accentual-syllabic English verse, at least, he demonstrated that the likeness of sound enforced a juxtaposition of senses in the syllables (and, when monosyllables, the words) involved, whether for comparison, contrast, or both. The significance of his point can perhaps be generalized by suggesting that likeness of word sound (and this is surely to be extended to alliterating adjective-noun pairs, etc.) purports to imitate a likeness of meaning and frequently, especially in the rhymes of wit investigated by Professor Wimsatt, effects a metonymic displacement or disjuncture with a rather sharp force. There is an implicit ratio here: sound is to word as word (or more properly, name) is to thing.[6] By continually manipulating word sounds in lexical contexts, their suggestive quality is forever enhanced, it being remembered that—and this is a cardinal rule for the discussion of the effects of sound in any poetic environment—*words can only "sound like" other words, and it is thereby that they sound like nature if at all.* In tight pairs of rhymes, a "fictional" or hypothetical morpheme, the rhyming VC or CVC, is invoked, and if possible a linguistic field of other carefully selected rhyming words welling up in the reader's consciousness from the corpus of possibles. Thus, for example, the pair *quick:trick* may be so framed, semantically and rhetorically, in the lines and sentence structures which bring them together, that all of the [ick]s of *slick, lick, nick, flick, tick, prick, kick,* and so forth, may fall into place in an ad hoc semantic field, as it were, in which [ick] means something sharp and instantaneous. The hypothetical morpheme (I shall not follow linguists in calling it a "phonestheme"), the as-if-by-virtue-of-meaning-in-English is like the unstated basis of comparison in simile, the "in that . . ." which gives point, whether explicitly or not, to the "A is like B." Similarly, when the rhyme seems to be disjunctive, the analogous or parallel relation is metonymic, e.g. *tall:small*. Between the likeness

5. W. K. Wimsatt, "One Relation of Rhyme to Reason," in *The Verbal Icon* (Louisville, 1954), pp. 153-66.
6. Hence the force of G. C. Lichtenberg's aphorism about a small town where all the people's faces rhyme with one another.

of sound which bridges, and the likeness of sound which divides, there lies a wide variety of structures (consider, for example, *dark:spark*, where the bridging structure implies, when the words occur in this order, an unstated "nevertheless").

Indeed, one might be tempted to arrange this variety of structures along a spectrum, ranging from the enforcing of likeness to the pointing up of dissimilarity. But this analogy between the relation of sound and word and the relation of name and that which is named—a crucial matter ever since its subject was broached in Plato's *Cratylus*—points up only one of rhyme's image-making functions. A whole string of rhymes, identical or interlocking, can itself connect image to image in a transumptive or metaleptic process, for example; and the intricacies of such patterns—those of Dante's *terza rima*, of some of Shakespeare's sonnets, and of moments in Spenser—have been of recent critical concern.

There is, then, a group of interestingly related concepts of the function and effect of rhyme. From the most primitive to the most complex, they might be ranged as follows:

1. mnemonic

2. schematic: serving to delineate and control patterns of versification, both corresponding to and, in more complex structures, playing against, syntactic periods

3. "musical": the chime of rhyme considered as an accompaniment of pure sound to the sense of the text, Valéry's sweet caresses, Emerson's "tinkling," Pope's "echo to the sense"

4. semantic: the dimension first charted by Wimsatt

It should be the task of any sophisticated formalistic treatment of rhyming's effects to analyze out any claims made for category 3 in terms of 2 and 4 and their interrelations. Take, for example, the other kind of rhetorical power of rhyming mentioned earlier—as distinguished from F. T. Prince's "rhetoric," itself an effect of 2—the ability of variation in rhyme to manipulate the attention per se, to calm, startle, speed up, slow down the scanning eye and ear, the power so frequently and carelessly called "musical" which was always distinguished from the more usual sense of category 3. With respect to such a function, a simple phenomenological category like strength vs. weakness becomes useful. It was implicitly invoked above, for example, with regard to the ineffectuality of *rime très riche* in English; in Pope's virtuoso passage in *An Essay on Criticism* about the "sure returns of still expected rhymes"; and in Gerard Manley Hopkins's remark to the effect that the beauty or power of rhyming is "lessensed by any likeness the words may have beyond that of sound."[7]

"Sound" is, of course, a problematic question here, particularly in English poetry. Because of the peculiarities of English spelling, the preservation of the linguistic past in the spelling of the present, the extraordinary generosity of English toward the spelling conventions of other languages in the loan words it has accepted—all of the phenomena which make English spelling so exasperating and so rich—the realm of what is usually called "eye rhyme" or "sight rhyme" (e.g. the *love:prove* of Shakespeare's sonnet, *fly:revelry*, etc.) is more complex than has been suspected. Such rhyme frequently results from a sound shift away from an original true rhyme (e.g. Pope's *obey:tea*), or from what may have been a conventional graphic rhyming almost from the beginning. In any event, the visual similarity of a pair of rhyming words, the degree to which their full vowel-consonant similarity is mirrored in the like spelling of the syllable, must be considered, both for twentieth-century poetry and for twentieth-century readings of poetry of the past, a significant parameter. Such a criterion vanishes, of course, in a language like Czech where there is perfect phonemic-graphemic fit; it remains potential but unrealized in Yiddish poetry, for example, where there are two sets of spelling conventions in the language itself, depending upon whether the word is Hebrew or not. Demotic Greek has some of the same diachronic richness as modern

7. Hopkins's remarks on rhyme in his lecture notes on verse form (*Journals and Papers*, ed. Humphry House and Graham Storey, Oxford, 1959, pp. 284-88), are most interesting, particularly in view of the way in which he generalizes rhyme as a basic phenomenon of association of sound, and for his idiosyncratic ascription of musicality in verse to "tonic accent, or pitch"—more usefully reductive than vowel-tune theory, at any rate.

English, preserving in its spelling the classical word which might be unrecognizable were the writing system to constitute an adequate transcription of speech. But in English, the modulations of this sound-spelling relation are almost limitless.

Two rhyming words, for example, may seem more distant from each other precisely because of the way in which the divergent spellings remind us of the history of languages, of word sounds changing, living a life of their own while yet entombed in the spellings of their youth, and, beyond that, of such matters as the way in which foreign words and spellings enter the complex net of spoken and written English. One has only to realize that

> A classical cacophonist named Beebe
> Called his wife Hebe and his daughter, Phoebe

is possible in modern American English to see that, in the right context, the very possibility of such rhymes can be made to point up ironies of inconsistency.[8] And in modern American English, in particular, there is a reciprocal ambiguity which arises from the implicit assumption that written English spells a kind of neutral, cover dialect. In general American, for example, the following are perfect rhymes, while in my own New York speech, only the first is, the other two representing the flexibilities of near-rhyme which can be so beautifully modulated as a tonal device in themselves:

1. The pail is frozen: go get Mary;
   Shivering cats besiege the dairy.
2. My nose is redder than a berry,
   Shivering cats besiege the dairy.
3. The bucket is too cold to carry,
   Shivering cats besiege the dairy.

One should, in discussing the tonal qualities of a poem which appeared to employ such delicately tinged off-rhymes, whether the poet himself

---

8. This becomes trivialized joking in the modern sub-genre of limerick which points up the eccentricities of English spelling by normalizing all the strict rhymes to the most incongruous of the spellings.

heard them as such. We should also take account of where some of the richness and possibility arising from ambiguities in spelling have been used before. Spenser leaps to mind here: he even managed to employ the conventional sixteenth-century alternation of u/v (the first character used for both letters in medial, the second for both in initial position) for the purposes of a deliberate sight-sound spelling, enabling him to rhyme syllables with the medial u vocalically and consonantally.

Given this other dimension where the ear and the eye intersect, then, we might even allow for a full transitivity along it. Just as a whole sequence of what we could call Wimsattian rhymes might promote a shifting associative pattern of evolving images, the metalepsis I mentioned earlier, so a corresponding, formal metalepsis might be seen at work in the following sequences of end rhyme:

. . . grove
. . . wove
. . . love
. . . move
. . . groove

or

. . . off
. . . cough
. . . rough
. . . slough
. . . bough
. . . dough
. . . row

In both cases, the movement from initial to final "rhyming" word proceeds like a chain of associations, and in the second instance, there is the pivotal ambiguity of *slough:* it might be /slaf/ or /slau/, forming a perfect rhyme with either the preceding or the following word, functioning, in fact, like an enharmonic pivot in a musical modulation. (Or, indeed, given the richness—or, for the plain man, the lunacies—of this particular graphic cluster, it might have gone, in the American pronunciation, /sluw/, to rhyme along another route with *true*.)

The consciousness, of course, of like sound covering an original etymological connection, has been exploited in many ways since Milton. I am thinking more of interior rhyming than of terminal here; the effect lies somewhere midway between the heavy Miltonic etymological irony—in which "original" and "derived" senses of Latinate English words will be made, in *Paradise Lost,* to reflect fallen and unfallen states—and the Joycean pun. This consciousness can be extremely subtle, almost liminal. In A. E. Housman's lines

> The chestnut casts his flambeaux, and the flowers
> Stream from the hawthorn on the wind away . . .

the alliteration of the metaphoric name for the blossoms and their more proper one (albeit divided among two different trees, the metaphor being appropriate only to the chestnut) seems almost coarse when compared to the resonances of the first verb. "Cast" is a weak off-rhyme for "chest—" but it is there to whisper *"castanea,"* the Latin word for "chestnut," as well as *"castus"* ("chaste")—for the Latinist Housman, the *chastenut* tree was being gustily but not lustily deflowered in the rough winds. One may venture further, perhaps, to the degree of wondering whether Pope wrote his great lines with the tiniest surge of rejoicing which a modern might feel at

> Another age shall see the golden ear
> Embrown the slope, and nod on the parterre . . .

The "golden ear" only puns, chimes, and connects across the Latin-English border: the English *"ear"* of grain (from the Indo-European root meaning "pointed") is not the Latin word for "ear," *"auris,"* but the latter does indeed pun on *"aurum"* ("gold"). But this is more properly part of the general question of poetic echo, in which rhyme plays a prominent but limited part.

Rhyme, then, is hardly in modern English and American poetry a matter purely of likeness of sound. What makes jokes out of the pairs *Chloe:showy* and *crikey!:Psyche* is an effect that lights up the diachronic axis. Contrariwise, the contortions of Ogden Nash rhymes joke in another way: after rhyming "leopard" with "peppered," he closes his little verse with "But best of all, when called by a panther / Don't anther"—a style which can handle the first pair needs neither to distort a word for the rhyme nor not to scan; doing so has a kind of inverted panache. In general, vers de société finds complex, polysyllabic rhyming funny per se, but the usual ascriptions of their effects to mere surprise or incongruity overlook one important aspect of the way in which they can work most effectively. The tradition of comic rhyming that runs from Byron through Praed, Gilbert, Swinburne in his great self-parodies, etc., ends up in Cole Porter and Lorenz Hart, and one of the latter's famous polysyllabic rhymes is an excellent example of yet another kind of fiction about words that rhyming can generate. In "To Keep My Love Alive," written for a 1944 revival of *A Connecticut Yankee*, a serially polyandrous lady recounts how, among others, Sir Paul appeared "a wreck to me," and was "a horse's neck to me," until she rhymingly "performed an appendectomy" upon him.

Here the comic device of rhyming polysyllabic word with phrase is underlined by the augmented distance occasioned by the Greco-Latin word. Its constituent morphemes *append(ix)* + *ectomy* give way to the notional or fictive morphemes *dec* + *to* + *my* which match up with those in the phrase. This kind of ghostly presence is frequently embodied in modern spellings resulting from analogic change in English—the place names *Chelsea, Battersea*, etc., should more properly have remained "Chelsey," "Battersey" (cf. *Anglesey*), for the [s] is a genitive inflection, and the [ev] means "island," and the [Batter] + [sea] composition is fictional (metanalytic). Funny polysyllabic rhymes, then, can make jokes about the structure of words, as well as about their diverse sources. And, as always, the rhetorical quality of English rhyme is at work in cases like this, the sharp, emphatic prominence given end rhyme by its association with the accentual-syllabic system. The fact, mentioned earlier, that rhymes occur there only in positions of maximum stress points up their operation even more. Just as *rime riche* is perfectly strong in French, polysyllabic rhymes which implicitly analyze morphology are not in the least funny, save in the insane, long strings of the *Grands Rhétoriqueurs* of the fifteenth century,⁹ in schoolboy tongue-twisters, and in such Dadaist games as Marcel Duchamp's *"Rrose Sélavy."*

All of these features of rhyming in modern English, then, from those which can make for the sort of surface wit which calls attention to its own mechanics (the polysyllabics) to the subtle gradations of off-rhyming (whether used systematically, as by Wilfred Owen to flatten, deliberately, a lyrical tone into an ironic one, or as a kind of occasional shading)—all of these features of rhyming are always turned on the reader, contributing to a total effect. This over-all strength or weakness mentioned earlier might be seen as an aspect of generalized *distance* between rhyming elements: that is, the question should not be whether two elements rhyme or not, but how close they are. A spectrum immediately suggests itself, analogous in some ways to the enjambment spectrum I proposed earlier (p. 100), along which a possible rhyming string would be arrayed according to the total or composite distance between them. Such matters as lexical form, actual morphophonemic elements in common, sharp contrast of meaning, sharper contrast of conceptual category, treated directly or implicitly by Wimsatt, would enter the picture at the same level as some of the visual-aural problems sketched out above. Consider, for example, the spectrum below, where the array of rhymes on *meet* (verb, transitive) from left to right moves from closeness to distance. The trivial cases have been excluded, as serving only to bracket. Thus, the case of mere repetition of the verb in, say, third person plural form (as opposed to *I meet:they meet* which embodies, albeit hidden in the same form, at least one element of grammatical contrast) is missing from the extreme left of this picture. Similarly, one might frame the array on the right with an inscription of no prima facie relevance, say "ψʃʃ" (to be read as some syllable possible in Slavic but not English:/pšchit/)—a limiting case because both graphically and phonetically out of the English

---

9. E.g. Jean Molinet's Justice in *"La Resource du petit peuple"*: Ma voix avoit la force de Sampson/Par son/Reson/Baritonnant tonnoye./Hélas! Mon Dieu, sans tourner à bas ton,/Par ton/Baton/Les basteurs bastonnoye *etc. etc.* See M. E. Langlois, *Receuil d'arts de séconde rhétorique* (Paris, 1902). I am grateful to Michel Beaujour for this example.

picture, as it were. But starting with the contrast between *meet* and *meet*₂ (the archaic adjective meaning "fitting"), we might move as follows:

Meet/meet₂/mete/meat/greet/treat/cheat/heat/sleet/concrete/gleet/Lafite/zieht

A few observations: the relative role of differences in grammatical form, visual appearance, meaning (in the sense that *greet* lies closer to *meet* than does *treat* for two of these reasons), etc., cannot be agreed upon as generally as the hierarchy of cuts in syntax in the enjambment model proposed earlier. In fact, the poetic environment of the particular pair of rhymes would serve to give prominence to one or another of these features. Second, the diachronic or historical dimension enters in an unexpected way: notice that a French word of ancient borrowing, like *quite, polite,* etc., would rhyme with *night,* having gone through the Great Sound Shift, while only a more recent or specialized borrowing, like the term from the dialect of the English-speaking gourmet, retain their characteristic undiphthongized Indo-European vowel. Finally, the difference between the French loan word and the "quoted" German verb is clearly a matter of reaching outside English, instead of to one of its edges.

Such a spectrum, of course, ignores a number of crucial matters. The first of these, the most basic, perhaps, is the role of accentual-syllabic meter in enforcing the power of English rhyme. In purely syllabic verse, like Marianne Moore's, for example, the rhymes are almost encoded in their unstressed syllables. Thus, from "In Distrust of Merits":

> And we devour
> ourselves? The enemy could not
> have made a greater breach in our
> defenses. One pilot-
>
> ing a blind man . . .

Were these lines in fact accentual-syllabic (iambic tetrameter in this instance), the *"our"* would have been forced into an emphatic position by the terminal position and the rhyme, rather like the "things that are not" of Donne's "Nocturnal Upon St. Lucy's Day" (see above, p. 53), and a contrastive stress (*our* defenses, not *theirs*") created by the metrical situation. But this is not the case here, and the rhyme of *not: pilot*, problematic enough as it would be, is suppressed even further into inaudibility by the hyphenation of the word, à la Ben Jonson in the Cary and Morison ode, across a stanzaic boundary. To say that these unstressed rhymes are for the eye alone is only part of the matter; their weakness involves grammatical matters as well. The rhyme on *wing:burying*, for example, works because the dependent morpheme "-ing," unable to take stress-maximum position in an iambic line when part of a disyllable, pivotal in a trisyllabic word, here rhymes with a monosyllabic noun whose meaning provides an obvious contrast to the verb stem bearing the participial syllable. Not so, of course, with *playing:splashing*. All this only underlines once again the necessity of considering accentual phenomena in dealing with English rhyme. They are much more significant than the so-called harmonies of vowels, which are largely a non-accentual French concept in any case.

Another question is that of sequential order. The rhetoric of rhyming depends not merely upon a word pair, but a word pair occurring in a particular order, almost outlining in itself the syntactic and logical relation between the lines/sentences/assertions terminating in them. From another point of view, the dynamics of closure are involved: poets who use near or off-rhymes seem to develop intuitive mystiques—analogous to those of nineteenth-century composers about the absolute ethos of a particular key—about the effects of sequence. Thus *narrow:borrow* might be considered more closing than the reverse, as would the lowering of "merely a mirror/Whose image was in error"—this is undoubtedly a matter of a front vowel followed by a back vowel, an alternation built deep into the *Sprachefühl*, as the Germans call it, the language sense, of English. The repeated *tick-tick-tick-tick* of clocks is conventionally rendered *tick-tock-tick-tock*, even though there is no phonetic difference between either pendulum strokes or the clicks of escapement. It is simply that the back vowel, with its possible general connotations of greater weight, mass, darkness, depth as compared to the front one, seems more the appropriate sound of the returning stroke.[10] Thus an off-rhyme sequence which followed the back vowel with the more frontal one might have less of a quality of closing a sequence, and more of leading to a pause, or underlining a trivialization of what was given in the first element.

This question of sequence, of whether the sound of the second word or syllable augments or derives from the first, operates in the realm of strict and relatively rich rhyming as well. George Herbert's "Paradise" makes typically brilliant use of metonymic rhyming sequences to stand for the conceptual sequences they describe, the central device being one of seeming to extract each rhyme of a tercet from its preceding one, the corresponding trope in the poem being one of pruning. The sequences GROW:ROW:OW(e), CHARM:HARM:ARM, etc., are made to embody conceptual, as well as phonetic "derivations" (and, certainly with CHARM:HARM, where one cannot audibly chop c from a ch cluster any more than he can prune w down into v by removing half of it, graphemic or scribal ones as well).

There is, finally, also the matter of occasional rhyme, occurring in various ways and modes in the unrhymed context to work in an echoic way, or to do the work that other devices might perform in a rhymed situation. While the blank verse of *The Ring and the Book* ultimately traces back, like so much else in English verse, to that of *Paradise Lost*, it is clear that the frequent occasional rhymes in the latter, and the scrupulously avoided ones in the former, represent the operation of different systematic rhythmic criteria for shaping line endings in the two styles.[11] The off-rhymes of poets like Wilfred Owen, mentioned before, were paralleled by their use of the stanza form *abax*, with its delib-

---

10. See Otto Jespersen, "Symbolic Value of the Vowel *I*," *Linguistica* (Copenhagen, 1933), pp. 283-303, for a discussion of the connotations of littleness here. Also, on a possibility of the same effect in French (*"tic-tac"* vs. *"antique"*), R. A. Sayce, "Language and Literature," *Essays in Criticism*, VII (1957), 125.

11. Robert Abernathy, "Rhymes, Non-rhymes and Antirhymes," in *To Honor Roman Jakobson* (The Hague, 1967), Vol. I, pp. 1-14, discusses *P.L.* and part of *The Ring and the Book* with this in mind. But he appears to know nothing of Milton's control of line terminus, his substitution of a lexical and a semantic "rhyme" for a phonetic one, etc. The article is full of the blunders that a non-reader of poetry might make.

erate, but conventionalized letdown: this, too, was a stylistic device taken up by W. H. Auden's generation. What appears to be a sudden, expressive letdown of this type is used brilliantly by George Herbert in "Denial." The unrhyming final line of the first stanza is self-descriptive not only in its rhymelessness, but in its accentual-syllabic amorphousness—

> When my devotions could not pierce
>   Thy silent ears;
> Then was my heart broken, as was my verse:
>   My breast was full of fears
>   And disorder:

—an amorphousness that echoes the expressive displacements of stress in the third line. But in subsequent stanzas, the *ababx* pattern is confirmed; it is as if the reader were expected to share a rueful hopelessness about the prayer's ever being answered. At the conclusion, the final appeal is for a spiritual integration,

> That so thy favours granting my request,
>   They and my mind may chime,
>   And mend my rhyme.

The mended line is metrical as well, being "healed" accentually by the exigencies of the stressed, rhymed terminus, and the phrase echo: "*mind may chime*":"*mend my rhyme.*" The whole poem (in the more extended sense of "rhyme" as verse and *verses*) is thereby healed, and all the sunderings in the poem are brought together at, and *by* the conclusion—the parable is certainly eschatological, in a small way, as well.

The occasional non-rhyme can have an expressive effect of gentle letdown, as well as of the assault of disorder. Instead of startling, the evasion of an expected or half-expected rhyme can have a deadening effect and, in the right circumstances, a lulling one. Tennyson's avowed choice of non-rhyme to evoke languor at the very opening of "The Lotos-Eaters" is a master-stroke:

> "Courage!" he said, and pointed toward the land,
> "This mounting wave will roll us shoreward soon."
> In the afternoon, they came unto a land
> In which it seemèd always afternoon. . . .

It is not only what Tennyson himself called the "no rhyme" of *land* and *land* which sounded "lazier,"[12] but the added and interwoven repetition of *afternoon* as well, which conjures up the gentle imprisonment in one's own perceptions which helps define the narcotized state: a world in which all rhymes are repetitions.

The modern master of occasional rhyme is Wallace Stevens; from the electric uses of it in the blank verse of "Le Monocle de Mon Oncle" as a momentary introduction of melody, as it were, in speech, as a way of opening up what had been a closed period (the sixth and seventh lines of the first stanza, for example), he began to use it in the blank verse which became his general mode. The in-and-out movement from rhymed couplet to blank couplet in "The Man with the Blue Guitar" represents a whole subgenre of the partial rhyme scheme. More typical is the flexible use of the occasional rhyme, corresponding to the plangent modulations of repetition and of the syntactic periodicities of the qualifying, dependent clauses of the long, later poems. The fourth section of Part III of *Notes Toward a Supreme Fiction*, for example, celebrates the marriage of the "great captain" of red sun and earthiness, and the "maiden Bawda" of blue and moon, in a consecrated, high place that chimes with the raw-spelled vowel of her name:

> There was a mystic marriage in Catawba,
> At noon it was on the mid-day of the year
> Between a great captain and the maiden Bawda,
>
> This was their ceremonial hymn: Anon
> We loved but would no marriage make. Anon
> The one refused the other one to take . . .

The epithalamium embedded in the firm stanzas is the rhyming couplet, pentameter to Alexandrine, concluding the Spenserian stanza:

---

12. See Christopher Ricks's note on these lines in his excellent edition of Tennyson's poems (London, 1969), p. 430.

"Anon we loved but would no marriage make./Anon the one refused the other one to take," where the inversion is part of the Spenserian echo. The brilliantly framing and bracketing "Anon"s, the rhyming of the internal, but marked "make" with the line-and-tercet terminal "take" typify Stevens's magnificent control over the structures of his verse. Notice, too, how the section continues:

> Foreswore the sipping of the marriage wine.
> Each must the other take not for his high,
> His puissant front nor for her subtle sound,
>
> The shoo-shoo-shoo of secret cymbals round.
> Each must the other take as sign, short sign
> To stop the whirlwind, balk the elements.
>
> The great captain loved the ever-hill Catawba
> And therefore married Bawda, whom he found there,
> And Bawda loved the captain as she loved the sun.

Her music, the music of the spheres long since vanished into silence and secret sound and whisperings of nature (the "secret cymbals round" line, aside from the secret tinkle of "symbols," does seem to echo "That the birds there in all the garden round" of Frost's "Never Again Would Birds' Song Be the Same") is present, unsecretly rhyming in a conventional couplet wedding two stanzas. But it is not to be the contractual basis for the union, which will be underlined in the "sign, short sign" and the way it makes more subtle song with the more distant "marriage wine" (only the repetition of "sign" would have underlined the effect). At the end of such controlled underscoring, the "therefore" of the penultimate line only confirms what, at the outset, we had taken as a capricious gusto of naming—a South Carolina Arlo-Hill and a lusty heavenly body—as a rhyme of profound simile. Rhyming for the later Stevens does the imagination's work and not the jingling and tinkling of evasions; it occurs as "the luminous melody of proper sound."

Despite its inability to deal with such questions as that of sequence and structure, however, the rhyme spectrum may yet remain useful in marking out a range of closeness and distance which corresponds to a scale of purely rhetorical strength, of the power to compel notice, to attune and even orchestrate, as it were, the attention of the scanning and listening reader as it moves over the totality of the text, sometimes displaying its inner linguistic workings on its surface, sometimes submerging them, echoing in the memory, or lighting up expectation and hope.[13] This, if any, is a sophisticated basis for ascribing a musicality to rhyme in major poetry, and, as has been observed in an earlier essay, it can at least be appreciated by critics for whom music itself possesses structure and even dialectic, rather than that baneful British cliché of tunefulness. Indeed, the "tinkling" of the rhyme despised by Emerson, the jingle of Ben Jonson "Spoiling senses of their treasure,/Cozening judgment with a measure,/But false weight," resides only in the bad poetry for which, until Milton and in the shorter lyric thereafter, rhyme was a necessary but sadly insufficient condition. Perhaps, too, its tinkle was merely an echo of the brass and cymbals of inept critical praise of its function.

13. Barbara Herrnstein Smith in *Poetic Closure* (Chicago, 1968) handles matters involving the schematic consequences of rhyming groups, and the larger patternings they enforce, with great skill and sophistication. Her book is, generally, a pleasure to read and to contemplate. See particularly pp. 38-70, 109-50.

VII
THE METRICAL FRAME

Fifty years ago, I. A. Richards distinguished between two functions of poetic meter. After acknowledging its primary domain of interest for poets from Wordsworth and Coleridge on ("The fact that we appropriately use such words as 'lulling,' 'stirring,' 'solemn,' 'pensive,' 'gay,' in describing metres is an indication of their power more directly to control emotion.") he turned away from this formulation of the "music" of verse to "more general effects," as he called them. "Through its very appearance of artificiality metre produces in the highest degree the 'frame' effect, isolating the poetic experience from the accidents and irrelevancies of everyday existence."[1] The relation between the music, as it were, and the frame, as it were: the way the second affects us both independently and by the ways in which the first of them is contingent upon it—this is the subject of the study of form that has proved most tantalizing in recent decades.

Aside from their use in Classical and Modern musical theory, the words "meter" and "rhythm" might be conveniently applied along the line of demarcation drawn by Richards so long ago. The word of flow, "rhythm," characterizes the series of actual effects upon our consciousness of a line or passage of verse: it is the road along which we read. The meter, then would apply to whatever it was that might constitute

1. I. A. Richards, *Principles of Literary Criticism* (London, 1925), p. 145.

the framing, the isolating; its presence we infer from our scanning. The distinction is rather useful because so many other sets of opposed linguistic and literary dimensions seem to be comprehended by it: design and particular; norm and instance; spatial, or at least schematic and temporal; singing or speaking and writing; and ultimately, in the matter of the angles of vision of linguistic theory itself, synchronic and diachronic, phenomenological and historical.

These distinctions have come to be disregarded in recent work on prosody not because the terms "meter" and "rhythm" continue to be used interchangeably, but largely because of the primarily synchronic orientation of most linguists who have turned their attention to problems of poetic structure. Whether concerned with the phonemic actualities of the poem as an act of speech, or, more recently, with the idea of a metrical scheme as a set of rules for generating lines of verse (each, be it said, with its unique set of characteristics which might be called rhythmic), most linguistic models of the production or the reading of English verse seem to have propounded a maker or a reader with no memory and no range of reading, a world of poetic language sacred to motherless Muses. Nevertheless, their contributions have been of great use and interest, both in sweeping away useless and inoperative critical apparatus, and in lighting up some dusty corners.

2

"Meaning," "significance," "function," "relevance," on the one hand, then; on the other, "meter," "prosody," "music," "form." To connect the terms of the first group with those of the second; to distinguish between the terms in each group and to account for and prevent their frequent confusion; and, finally, to justify the lines along which these distinctions are drawn, have come more and more in recent years to engage the fullest concerns of poetics. The more specifically instrumental roles played by structural linguistics in this engagement were considerable. Many of its basic principles were brought to bear by Richards upon the clichés and mystiques that, accumulating over two centuries of poetic theory, had blurred the boundaries and overlappings of these analytic concepts. In addressing itself to the problem of sound, pattern, and sense, recent inquiry has been particularly successful in clearing away a compost heap of conflicting, often self-inconsistent traditional prosodical theory, increased in the past hundred years by ritually sustained errors and, even more, by an inability to confront what it actually was that contemporary poets were doing. Thomas Hardy was possibly the last major poet to write in a long tradition of English versifying whose founding we might assign to Ben Jonson on the grounds that he confessed to writing all his verses "first in prose." And yet one of Hardy's chief difficulties as a poet resided in his latent uneasiness with a tradition for which he invokes the authority of Wordsworth: "It is supposed that by the act of writing in verse an author makes a formal engagement that he will gratify certain known habits of association." It is possible, that is, to speak of Hardy's *choice of meter* in a way that we would be reluctant to do in the case of Hopkins, Eliot, Pound, or Yeats, and, even more, to pass judgment on that choice by designating it an arbitrary one. For it is the poet's own sense of the function of the verse itself which changes from one literary epoch to another, and recent critical methods which treat poems like objects, like artifacts such as vases or sculptures, or even like organisms with souls, all answer in some measure the requests of modern poems to be treated as just that.

Traditional prosodical analysis, whether carried on for polemical or avowedly speculative reasons, was still a little too much like cataloguing styles in clothing to be able to deal effectively with a body of new poetry with the form of cloth puppets or sea animals whose garments were their bodies or shells themselves. In such a world of organistic, post-symbolist poetry and criticism it was the particular utility of structural linguistics to take us back to taxonomy, to encourage us in the use of biological categories that help us to classify, sort, dissect, and anatomize the natural history of verse. English poetry since Hardy has cried out for such murder, if murder it be. The study of literary history itself may be seen to have profited from it, if only because it revealed the long record of prosodical inquiry itself as a history of ideology and of taste in analytic methods.

The uses of linguistics as a tool have actually extended beyond the clearing away of traditional confusions, and the resolving of questions like that of quantitative verse in English by undermining the bases of traditional arguments about them. A general program of making more public, of verifying, the private insights of the ear of a sensitive reader, for example, has proved a hopeful one. Particularly in the case of those poets, such as Wyatt, Shakespeare, the Jacobean tragedians, Donne, Yeats, and Frost, whose formal diction is always informed by the syntactic and emphatic stress patterns of colloquial speech, have the suppositions, if not the methods, of modern linguistics been helpful.

By an examination of contemporary poetry in which a purely graphic scheme of line arrangement can operate in open conflict with equally prominent phonemic ones, almost any reader can come to understand how aural and visual entities merge in status when they operate as metrical segments. And here a more general application of linguistic theory to poetics presents itself. For just as the conceptual distinction between the phonetic and the phonemic is crucial if one is to talk about the elements of a particular language, so is a clear distinction between the phonetic and the metric basic to a consideration of the role of sound in the game of poetic sense. In short, it is as a heuristic model that phonemics might have been most useful to poetic theory, rather than merely as an implement for the treatment of a poem as a spoken utterance.

There is good reason, I think, in the light of recent work and old warnings both, for drawing this distinction. In the first place, although poems are neither purely spoken utterances nor inscriptions, their peculiar status, straddling the two, seems to lose itself under certain kinds of analysis that start out with putting the poem into phonemic transcription. The poem becomes the phonetic parts of its texture, really, while metrical conventions, the whole substance of traditional prosodic theory, are ignored or treated at best as an unexamined *donnée,* a given condition rather like the fact that the poem is in English, but in no way as binding on the interpretation of discrete signals. It may be that the influence of recent statistical approaches has generated the view that signals with a low probability of occurrence must necessarily have an increased *importance.* Within the framework of information theory, it is certainly true that the more surprising event is the more significant one, for the only kind of significance is defined as a function of the reciprocal of the probability of occurrence. But to equate "information" with "significance" in a non-rigorous sense may not be possible. In many cases, something like the opposite would appear to be true. The extremely high redundancy of capital letters at the beginning of lines of printed verse, for example, renders their informative value, in the above sense, trivial. But their actual role is of considerable importance, being one of definition, or of labeling the utterance in question as a poem. Its significance for the statistical analyst lies in the fact that it sets up prior expectation that will itself affect the relationship between the "surprise value" (for the reader) and the probability of occurrence (for the post-mortem analyst). Information theory must necessarily take the highly probable event more or less for granted. But in the analysis of a poem as a work of literature, these conventional events are of major importance.[2]

It has been rather to the structure of self-contained poetic texts, than to the metrical conventions governing many such texts, that linguistic analysis has been devoted. But the literary critic, or even the well-informed reader, tends to think in terms of both what he is reading and how what he is reading resembles other things that he has read, of the poem as a thing in itself, and as an example of a literary form. The reader of any subtlety at all will often talk about a poem as if he felt that there were two sequences of events going on at once. The literary critic (who may have helped train the reader to talk in this way) will distinguish "meter" from "rhythm," assumed norm from actual instance, and perhaps resort to Gerard Manley Hopkins's rich, but misleading notion of "counterpoint" to describe their relation. The greatest temptation to employ this notion arises when one occurrence

2. When this essay was originally conceived, information theory appeared to be of some interest for formalist poetics; see the statements by René Wellek and myself in *Style and Language*, ed. Thomas A. Sebeok (Cambridge, Mass., 1960), pp. 396-419. The relation between critical and linguistic approaches to problems of form has been rather complex, even during the past two decades. For a sophisticated and most useful account of this with an excellent selected bibliography, see Seymour Chatman and Samuel R. Levin, "Linguistics and Literature," in *Current Trends in Linguistics*, 10 (The Hague, 1973), 250-94.

in a poem seems to be part of two different schemes simultaneously. We have already considered the nature of enjambment in a previous chapter. It will serve here again as an excellent case in point.

In the most general sense, an enjambment is any lack of alignment between syntax and line structure, but it is usually considered in the cases where a normal correspondence between the two is violated. Textual analysis treats enjambments not only in terms of their effects upon the poem's "flow of movement," but for their direct semantic operation. The most obvious cases of this occur when a compound is broken up between two lines, suddenly revealing, in a startling way, that the whole, rather than the separable part, is to be employed:

> And one can have a savory or a sweet
> Potato after dinner, if he chooses.

Another example might be that of the covert allusion for which only a line division seems to provide optimum syntactic ambiguity:

> Under a soupy tree
> Mopes Daphnis, joined by all
> The brown, surrounding landscape:
>
> Even in Arcady
> Ego must needs spoil
> Such a beautiful friendship!

Here the rhymes and the sense (depending on a modern colloquial use of "ego" or *amour propre*) as well as the line structure force a separation of the two words which, when juxtaposed, recall the famous *memento mori* in the paintings of Guercino and Poussin, *Et in Arcadia Ego*, with the exception here that vanity, rather than death as the speaker, is made the ubiquitous subject. T. S. Eliot's notorious

> Princess Volupine extends
> A meagre, blue-nailed, phthisic hand
> To climb the waterstair. Lights, lights,
> She entertains Sir Ferdinand
>
> Klein. Who clipped the lion's wings
> And flea'd his rump and pared his paws?

makes the name straddle two stanzas as well as two lines, but the abruptly turned-to question nevertheless claims, by its alliterating "clipped," a line kinship with what is nastily being treated as the offending patronymic particle.

It is to a case which may have actually influenced Eliot in this poem which I should now like to turn. Ben Jonson's ode *To the Memory and Friendship of that Noble Pair, Sir Lucius Cary and Sir H. Morison* is, from the point of view of metrical conventions, not only an extremely programmatic poem, but a didactic one as well. It is the second purported but first actually imitative "Pindaric" ode in English, written in couplets of varying line length to suggest Pindaric irregularity, pedantically labeling each triad strophe, antistrophe, and epode as "The Turne," "The Counter-Turne," and "The Stand," respectively.[3] The poem mourns and moralizes upon, in an appropriately public way, the separation of a pair of close friends brought about by the death of the younger of them. Cary and Morison were both public men as well as members of Jonson's coterie. Jonson's stanzaic form keeps to the pattern of the Pindaric ode, *aab*, with two stanzas identical in structure, the third slightly different in its pattern of line length and rhyme. Although the stanza headings serve more as glosses than as discrete titles, the stanzas are self-contained and end-stopped. When an occasional enjambment does occur, it is of the common type that realigns itself in the very next line, creating no effect of surprise. But in Jonson's eighth stanza an enjambment even more startling in some ways than Eliot's occurs:[4]

> The Counter-Turne
> Call, noble *Lucius*, then for wine,
> And let thy lookes with gladnesse shine:

---

3. Carol Madison, *Apollo and the Nine* (Baltimore, 1960), p. 301, suggests that Jonson may have borrowed the terms from Antonio Sebastiano Minturno's *volta, rivolta,* and *stanza* in two odes published in 1535.
4. The less dramatic and more subtle modulations of enjambment are discussed on pages 91-116. There the context is explicitly syntactical, and concerns the kinds of effect not treated here, as at, for example, "Of which we *Priests* and *Poets* say/ Such truths . . ." and "Or taste a part of that full joy he meant/To have exprest . . . ," both below.

> Accept this garland, plant it on thy head,
> And thinke, now know, thy Morison's not dead.
> Hee leap'd the present age,
> Possesst with holy rage,
> To see that bright eternall Day:
> Of which we *Priests* and *Poets* say
> Such truths, as we expect for happy men,
> And there he lives with memories; and *Ben*
>
> The Stand
>
> *Jonson,* who sung this of him, e're he went
> Himselfe to rest.

This is again a kind of pun by discovery. Just as "Sir Ferdinand" is a perfectly proper appellation, abruptly qualified by the enjambed remainder, the *contre-rejet,* so the line

> And there he lives with memories; and *Ben*

is complete in itself, ending its stanza like the others on a full stop (the seventeenth-century punctuation often uses colons and semicolons where we would employ commas). Just "Ben" may appear overfamiliar; but for the living Cary and the late Morison, as well as the close-knit coterie of friends who called themselves "The Tribe of Ben," "Ben" alone was as frequently employed in dedicatory poems as in conversation. The line ending *"Ben,"* then, is for a coterie reader; with the addition of the *contre-rejet,* it becomes more properly public. But Jonson continues his ninth stanza through an even more grotesque example:

> Or taste a part of that full joy he meant
> To have exprest,
> In this bright *Asterisme*:
> Where it were friendships schisme,
> (Were not his *Lucius* long with us to tarry)
> To separate these twi-
> Lights, the *Dioscuri;*
> And keepe the one halfe from his *Harry.*

Even more grotesque, perhaps, although some readers might rush through the hyphenation unperturbed, and with some reason to which I shall turn in a moment. But those readers who do dwell over the hyphenation will be following Jonson's conceit of the Greek twins Castor and Pollux being separated by death (this grows into the splitting of the constellation Gemini); they will read the "twi-" of "twi-/lights" as both root and prefix. "To separate these two (or twin) lights" is itself "separated" quite literally; the name, in an almost schematic logical trick, is treated *qua* object in the same way that its metaphorical bearer (the pair of Cary and Morison) is thereby reported to be treated. An effective device, this is not an unusual sort of thing in the Renaissance, being commonly used in polyphonic songs (*cf*. John Wilbye's madrigal "Sweet Honey-Sucking Bees": "For if one flaming dart come from her eye,/Was never dart so sharp, ah, then you die!," where on the last line, the upper soprano part moves to an *f#* on the word "sharp").[5]

But the impulse of many readers to carry along through the break, to treat this as the common kind of flowing, non-ironic enjambment, is also of interest. The hyphenated enjambment is rare, but not in the least capricious, in the poetry of Jonson's age; it was used in English verse that was consciously attempting to model itself on certain Greek meters. Thomas Campion's polemical *Observations in the Art of English Poesie* (1602), a metrical study that urges the abandonment of all rhyme and stressed scansion by English verse in favor of an adopted quantitative system making even less phonemic sense than it may have for Latin, contains an example of hyphenation in one of the model poems therein set forth, and quoted (above, p. 80) in its entirety:

> Like cleare springs renu'd by flowing,
> Ever perfet, ever in them-
> selves eternall.

---

5. There is a further complication with the Dioscuri, though; Jonson knows well the etymology of the word from *dios* + *kouroi* ("two boys"), but because of his pun on the "twi-lights," he seems to pretend that the etymology is Italianate (*di* or *duo* + *oscuro*)—the twin darks, the setting suns, stars, or Sons, of a world made less perfect by their setting. See also below, pp. 176-78.

The *locus classicus* for this is in Greek choric meters, in Pindar, and in Sappho; Catullus and Horace (I think only once) so hyphenate in their Latin Sapphics. Its justification in Jonson's ode must be ascribed to a purpose akin in some ways to Campion's, and although he eschewed the latter's prosodic theories, his commitment to Classical models was very strong. Any reader in any way aware of the models, either through direct knowledge or through other adaptations, will to some degree recognize the device. Like Campion's and others' quantitative experiments it is a purely graphic convention (it was on the basis of letters, rather than phonemes, that syllables were assigned their weight); but in the case of both of Jonson's enjambments the separation engages the phonemic junctures of English.

I should like to cite a final case in which a less startling but equally effective enjambment produces the quasi-metaphorical kind of effect which we saw in Pope's careful use of rhythm. The second stanza of Keats's ode *To Autumn* invokes the personified season in an idle moment, after the images of harvest in the first stanza, and proceeds through indolent play, winnowing, and reaping. Keats says of her

> And sometimes like a gleaner thou dost keep
> Steady thy laden head across a brook;

F. R. Leavis remarks of these lines that "As we pass the line-division from 'keep' to 'steady' we are made to enact, analogically, the upright steadying carriage from one stone to the next. And such an enactment seems to me properly brought under the head of 'image.'"[6] I dislike intensely this way of putting it. Such a notion of analogical enactment is being used in a kind of magical way; this is really nothing more than a little poem of Dr. Leavis's about what is going on in Keats's lines. Actually, all we are made to enact here is all that lines of poetry ever make us enact: an act of speech. But to say this is not so trivial as one might think. Certainly the enjambment is an effective one, especially in a poem whose norm is more in the direction of being endstopped. And certainly we do have a feeling of a heavy bale of grain

6. F. R. Leavis, *Revaluation* (New York, 1947), pp. 263-64.

balanced on Autumn's head as she picks her way through the waters of a stream or across stepping stones.

But there need be no mystery in explaining the way that Keats's metrical device works. In ordinary speech the English phrase "keep steady" is accented [keep *steady*]. That is, the first monosyllable abandoning principle stress to the first syllable of the second word. But here, the word "keep" is in a stressed position in the first line, as if it were to be followed by something like

> And sometimes like a gleaner thou dost keep
> A bale of grain against the winter's blast . . .

Here there is no surprise at the enjambment, for "keep" is both transitive and primary, and the line break follows a subject-predicate boundary. But Keats's "keep" is tinged with an auxiliary quality—it is almost as if it were a Greek middle, say; the verb is "keep steady," and the cut between the words points this up. Again,

> And sometimes like a gleaner thou dost keep
> Thy laden head steady across a brook

would remove the effect, while setting up a more Miltonic ambiguity of reference of the "steady." The Keatsian arrangement forces us to read a stress pattern of " ′ / ′ ·", which in ordinary speech would be given to the phrase used in a musical way to assist verbally someone who was indeed balancing something and nervous about it. In short, it is quasi-imperative, something uttered by an onlooker who tries to assist with verbal magic, with incantatory body english.

But it is to Ben Jonson's enjambments, and particularly to his second one, that I should like to return. There seem to be two different *sorts* of significance at work here. The first is semantic; the second, more purely formal, in this case, graphic or what we might call *literal*. We have already observed that Jonson's intention throughout the ode seems to be referential; it might be suggested that the overhangs, and particularly the hyphenated one, were consonant, if not actually cooperative, with the strophic titles. It is the fact of their appearance, however, and their role once they have appeared in the texture of the poem, that I wish to contrast here. The significance of the elements of Neoclassic "form" in Jonson's ode is quite simply a historical significance; while the ironic and quasi-self-descriptive effects of the two might more properly be considered as showing up under the application of some poetic analogue of a synchronic analysis. (Of course, our knowledge about the "tribe of Ben," the frequent use of the Christian name alone in verse, etc., are historical facts themselves. But in invoking them, one is simply giving the meaning of the word "Ben" in Jacobean and Caroline poems.)

Now even if we want to reject the notion that either or both of these effects of the enjambments are, properly speaking, significances; and especially if we wish to follow a by now proverbial philosopher's guide, "Don't look for the meaning; look for the use," we may observe that their *functions* are clearly different, the uses to which they are put are as divergent as any verbal acts, such as admonishing, deceiving or requesting, can be. The workings of the formal, *metrical* effect are somehow prior to those of *rhythmic* (and since English has phonemic stress, hence *semantic*) processes; the former set up contingencies affecting the latter. The problem of accounting for and charting these contingencies actually underlies some of the most dubious enterprises of traditional prosody, placing much weight on graphic conventions or choices of form, perhaps (as if there were several possible outfits for the same poem, albeit one proper one) without really knowing why they might be important.

3

Let us look at some of the operations of poetic rhythm as it works within the contingencies established by the poet's chosen, normative meter. I say "chosen" not because I wish to imply that the actual effects of linguistic sound which occur within the poem itself are forced upon the poet; or necessarily unconsciously selected; or revealed to him by an incontrovertible muse. Even in the case of the most complicated and apparently "free" rhythmic schemes, the actual composition of lines within the pattern seems to result from a different order of decision-making than does the selection of the scheme to begin with. Whether willing or not, poets are capable of discussing their choice of meter, while rarely would we trust their analyses of their rhythmic invention. It seems possible to show that in some cases the over-all poetic form, metrical scheme, etc., may result from a bit of *"donnée,"* given, material, whether a phrase, an image, a word, a rhythmic effect of some kind. In this case, the metrical choice will depend on finding the meter in which a rhythmic event will be utilized, as well as on the possibilities afforded by convention. The famous so-called *vers donné* from Racine's *Phèdre*, for example, has for generations been held out to French schoolboys as the triumph of pure poetry over the absence of rhythmic effect, imagery, and poetic diction. Bloch, in *Swann's Way*, introduces it to Marcel, with an air of hermetic confidence, as a line which "says absolutely nothing": "*La fille de Minos et de Pasiphaë.*" The line was praised because only a great poet could have characterized his heroine in so bare a way, the truest poetry, according to this doctrine at least, being the least feigning. It appears that Racine may have taken the line from a handbook of mythology; here we have a case of the poetic act consisting not of writing the line, but of seeing it (1) as an Alexandrine, (2) as the conclusion of the couplet, and (3) as being able to carry the weight of a meaning of monstrosity, born by historical reference alone. A similar example in English is Yeats's great line in "A Long-Legged Fly":

> There on that scaffolding reclines
> Michael Angelo.

Here it is a matter, again, of seeing the name as one of the three-beat lines of the poem; of the name carrying great weight after the subject of the first stanza of the poem (Caesar) has been mentioned in epithet ("Our master Caesar"), of the second only by "she"; and finally of the fragmentation of the name into what looks like a name and an epithet again.

The choices governing rhythmic execution are as complex and elusive of analysis as are the elements of our response to rhythmic events. There exists a celebrated pyrotechnical display of such execution that is all the more of a triumph because it sets out to brandish its machinery, and must stand or fall by how well it really works. It is even more interesting for our purposes because, as a rhythmic display, it is set off within the confines of a meter so formal and confining that Matthew Arnold could think of it only as a kind of mechanical jingle which was overlaid on prose. In Book II of Pope's *An Essay on Criticism*, he puts forth the thoroughly Hobbesian notion that "Imagination is the dress of thought"; that the relation of poetic invention to poetic *sentence* or meaning is like the relation of clothes to a body, a mechanistic version of the Platonistic relation of body to soul. The passage I wish to discuss starts out with an attack on those bad critics who reject the true notion that *le style*, so to speak, *c'est l'homme*, in favor of the fashionable error that, figuratively speaking, clothes make the man:

> But most by Numbers judge a Poet's song;
> And smooth or rough, with them, is right or wrong:
> In the bright Muse tho' thousand charms conspire,
> Her Voice is all these tuneful fools admire;
> Who haunt Parnassus but to please their ear,
> Not mend their minds; as some to Church repair,
> Not for the doctrine, but the music there.
> These equal syllables alone require,
> Tho' oft the ear the open vowels tire;
> While expletives their feeble aid do join;
> And ten low words oft creep in one dull line:
> While they ring round the same unvary'd chimes,
> With sure returns of still expected rhymes.
> Where-e'er you find "the cooling western breeze,"
> In the next line, it "whispers thro' the trees";
> If crystal streams "with pleasing murmurs creep,"
> The reader's threaten'd (not in vain) with "sleep."
> Then, at the last and only couplet fraught
> With some unmeaning thing they call a thought,
> A needless Alexandrine ends the song,
> That, like a wounded snake, drags its slow length along.
>
> (*An Essay on Criticism* II, 337-57)

The denunciation here is of what Empson once called the "cult of pure sound," which, he remarked, always struck him as being rather like Darwin playing the trombone to his French beans. Dryden had voiced the basic sentiment earlier, when he wrote of John Oldham, "But satire needs not these and wit will shine / Through the harsh cadence of a rugged line" but he was helping to initiate the metrical form in which Pope was to succeed so brilliantly, and he could not go so far with it as could his successor, particularly in playing tricks with it. The eighteenth-century metricians who demanded that accentual weight be equalized were ruling out the possibility of effective rhythmic writing by loving unwisely and too well what they thought to be a basis of musical rhythm itself. Yet Pope puts them down by a stroke of syntactic genius: the line about the open syllables would not work so well if the word order were "Though oft the open vowels tire the ear"—it depends on the triad of "Tho' oft," "the ear" "the open," and, of course, on neglecting the elision rules which Pope himself normally uses but which, if employed here, would give a tetrameter line "Tho' oft th'ear th'open vowels tire." Again, the line with all the monosyllables in it is a dull one because (1) he tells us it is and (2) he makes it dull by repeating the rhythmic pattern "ten low words"—"one dull line": the two phrases have the identical stress contour in speech. In addition, he makes things harder by following up "And ten low words" with a great density of prominent syllables. Were he to have written "And ten low words are all a man can bear," there would have been a dip in prominence of the following syllables: a stickler for *phonetic* rather than metrical stress here would say that in Pope's line there were eight stresses rather than five, whereas in my revision there were at any rate only five, although grouped [·′′′···′·′].

As we go on through the lines, we find that all the effects are accountable for along two axes, the phonetic and the contextually semantic. These lines are aimed at those who prefer sound to sense, and the lines themselves are all self-descriptive. In formal logic, self-descriptiveness leads to pure and empty paradox; here, they lead to a kind of poetic meaninglessness. What they are about is how bad they are. The ways in which they are bad result from the manipulation of phonetic and morphophonemic material in patterns that are too regular at one level, while they strain and distort the regularity of another kind that constitutes the essence of smoothness for Pope.

The joke about the rhymes, for example, momentarily aligns these two axes. The alliteration in the line centers on the "ring-round" nucleus. After we have been put off by not getting the word "rhymes" but instead a non-alliterating word that makes us realize our loss by rhyming with the withheld word, the additional /r/ sounds in "unvary'd," "sure," and "returns" make us realize that not only have we not been expecting the word when it does come in the second couplet, but that we have, like Pavlov's dog, been slavering for it. And finally, we realize that the trouble with rhyming can be that the word which names a unit of it rhymes, itself, with "chimes." There is, of course, the logical play here with a thing and its name. A full-blown use of the logical trap of confusing use and mention (such as, for example, in the innocent remark that "there's spaghetti on the menu") comes in the line about the sleep that crowns the short list of clichés that also rhyme.

In the lines about the Alexandrine, we get a much subtler use of the phonetic-semantic interplay. In the first two lines, the same progression is repeated: [some unmeaning thing thought] and [needless Alexandrine ends]. In each case, the subject ("thing" and "Alexandrine") is connected to an epithet and a logical predicate by means of some sound association. And the Alexandrine itself, conventional in a closed-couplet style when used at the end of some kind of rhetorical period (although its use in triads was much abused between the stylistic peaks of Dryden and Pope), commits all the faults of a bad one. Its split in the middle into two trimeters is underlined by the unusually sharp syntactic break of the caesura. The second half-line seems even slower than the first, because the consonantal clusters and piled-up stresses of "drags its slow length" end up with a pun on "along," conditioned by the noun preceding it.

But after this demolition job, Pope goes on to reconstruct, and, like Amphion playing on his lyre and causing the walls of Thebes to build themselves, he sings the elements of a style back into their proper place.

> Leave such to tune their own dull rhymes, and know
> What's roundly smooth, or languishingly slow;
> And praise the easy vigour of a line,
> Where Denham's strength, and Waller's sweetness join.
> True ease in writing comes from art, not chance,
> As those move easiest who have learn'd to dance.
> 'Tis not enough no harshness gives offence,
> The sound must seem an Echo to the sense:
> Soft is the strain when Zephyr gently blows,
> And the smooth stream in smoother numbers flows;
> But when loud surges lash the sounding shore,
> The hoarse, rough verse should like the torrent roar:
> When Ajax strives some rock's vast weight to throw,
> The line too labours, and the words move slow;
> Not so, when swift Camilla scours the plain,
> Flies o'er th' unbending corn, and skims along the main.

The sound effects here differ from those in the first part of the passage by reason of the fact that these are "good" lines, rather than examples of "bad" ones, and that they all have a fine, straightforward, pseudo-Classical subject matter. They are all about the great, model subject, rather than, as in the earlier ones, about their own ineptitude.

The couplet about the smoothness, for example, employs not only the device of phonetic linking which connects the core attributive word, "soft," with "strain" and eventually with "Zephyr gently," which two words finally give us the /f/ and /t/ phonemes of "soft" in the proper order. In the second line of the couplet, the image which gives the line its weight of content engages a powerful allusion to the canonical emblem of the kind of style which Pope's age takes for granted. The idea that lines of verse should move like flowing water is embodied in a text that was almost scriptural for the Augustan age. In Denham's *Cooper's Hill* the poet, surveying the beneficent prospect of the Thames from his visionary eminence, concludes a passage of moralized topography with the proto-Augustan hope, couched in full-blown Augustan sincerity, neatness, and aptness of thought:

> O could I flow like thee, and make thy stream
> My great example, as it is my theme!
> Though deep, yet clear, though gentle, yet not dull,
> Strong without rage, without o'erflowing, full.[7]

What Pope referred to a few lines earlier as "Denham's strength" was thought to be expressed here as a program for the Augustan use of the heroic couplet. The "smooth stream" in Pope's line is, of course, some stream being described in the line, not improbably Skamander; but by a conventional image, it is also the line itself. There is the further implementation of the phonetic linkings of [*smooth-stream*] and [*smoother-numbers*]. Then again, there is the final clinching of the implicit argument that art often more obviously conforms to the mechanical rules of created order than does nature (although, with Pope, "to copy nature" was "to copy them"). This is done by the rhythmic contrast between the first half-line [··′′] ("And the smooth stream") and the second, which is absolutely canonical in its distribution of stresses: "in smoother numbers flows" [·′·′·′], where the phonetic linkings of the subjects and the smoothness attributed to them are disposed first in a less, then in a more regular way.

"When Ajax strives," we strive, too, not to produce a string of words like "When Ajax drives": the enunciation forced upon us by the consonantal cluster, and the realization that it is intentional is forced upon us by the growing realization that his rock is, symbolically, the remainder of the line. In a trivial phonetic sense, *the words move slow*, despite the tendency in spoken English time units in actual utterances to dispose themselves into syntactic paradigms. Thus, in the following sequence of utterances, the durations of enunciation increase much less rapidly than the increasing amount of linguistic material crowded into the same sentence matrix would lead one to conclude:

7. See also Dr. Johnson's comment on these lines, p. 281 n.

"I'm going on Tuesday"
"I'm going home on Tuesday"
"I'm going home to Indianapolis on Tuesday"

Pope must slow up his words by setting up a parallel rhythmic package at the beginning and end of this line, reinforced by the syntax of "the line, too, labours" as well as by the symmetry of the assonance of "too" and "move," which pins the rhythmic structure together: phonetically, we have a pattern like this

    •   /   /   /   •   •   •   /   /   /
The line, too, labours   and the words move slow

syntax forces a juncture   *parallelism dictates one here*
rhyme (assonance)
enforces parallelism

Here, as always, it is a sound pattern working with semantic and syntactic ones which gains the desired effect.

So, too, in the case of the quickly moving lines. Notice that swift Camilla flies along in an Alexandrine, but by no means a slow one; this is an added bit of virtuosity, for in the context of the previous section, Pope has almost made us feel that it is the essence of Alexandrines to be too long. Here again, too, it is Camilla who is chosen to be the swift one, because of the linking assonance, and here too, we have the association of [*scours the plain*] (′ ∙ ′) and (*skims along the main*) [′(∙ ∙)∙ ′]: the extra two syllables in the second line become less prominent when we view the phrase in the rhythmic matrix set up by the first, and the Alexandrine seems to contract.

This is indeed a virtuoso rhythmic performance. It is conducted within the confines of a rigorous metrical scheme, one which allows less displacement of alternation of stressed syllables, on the whole, than Milton's iambic pentameter, or Keats's or Wordsworth's. And yet the effects are profound, and the moral pointed. We cannot, in studying the effects of rhythm or of its associated phenomena, ignore the interaction of the rhythmic groupings and patterns with lexical and syntactic elements. Any general theory of metaphor in poetry must deal with the notion of non-literalness of meaning, with transfer, or distortion or reshaping of reference. But the way in which, as Pope puts it, the sound can "seem an Echo to the sense" is effected only by means of associations between words which rub off, somehow, onto their designata: it is something like the metaphorical process, but it operates somehow at a different level. By and large, the so-called imitative effects of poetic rhythm will be seen to work in two ways: through those devices which associate words or parts of words, and through those which enforce re-groupings of them by more subtle means than simply those of connection. Of the associative or linking devices we have already seen a few: The use in Latin poetry of *intralinear juxtaposition* as allowed by flexible syntax, for example, allows us to discern discrete semantic packets within the line, where the sense of a word is transferred to an adjacent one without being syntactically connected with it at all. Rhyme links not only lines, but words; whether used as end rhymes or as interior ones, rhyming syllables have an increased prominence, no matter what their metrical role, and play an important part in associating the words that contain them. Assonance and alliteration link parts of words, as well as syllables, and their operation is through what a linguist would call a morphophonemic medium, creating momentary fictions about the association of sound and sense in the language. The effects of onomatopoeia in general can all be traced to these devices.

All of these methods may be employed either metrically or rhythmically. They may play only a structural role in defining the schematic form of the poem or its lines. Or they may be used for the kind of expressive effects we have been considering. For example, alliteration occurs prominently in Old Germanic verse, in Spenser, in the Shakespeare *Sonnets*, and in Hopkins. And yet we would want to characterize its roles very differently in the four cases. In the first instance, the alliteration is a necessary feature of the meter, and while it tends to produce a little poetic package in the first half-line consisting of two words linked by the alliteration, its frequency of occurrence tends to depress its significance for expressive purposes. Not so in Spenser, where its relatively high frequency of occurrence in *The Faerie Queene* is nevertheless a matter of rhythmic texture rather than of metrical form. Still, Spenser's alliterations tend to produce a decorative surface rather than a metaphoric connection. In the opening line of *F.Q.* "A gentle knight was pricking on the plain" we have a typical instance of its use to link parts of a predicate, although the noun-adjective pair is even more common. At times, the rate of alliteration per line will go up in passages describing an excited encounter or a lush display, but the higher rate will simply add up to a slightly more ornate linguistic surface. In the Shakespeare sonnets, however, the alliteration functions in several ways. Occasionally it will be in the Elizabethan, Spenserian "decorative manner," but often it will be used expressively, to echo sense.

For example, sonnet 116:

> Love's not Time's fool, though rosy lips and cheeks
> Within his bending sickle's compass come.

The naïve observation would be that we seem to hear the sound of the blade mowing the grass to which the implicitly invoked scriptural text likens all flesh. The effect depends upon several rhythmic events. In the first place, there is, as Empson has observed, the grammatical ambiguity of *bending:* it means both "bent" and "causing to bend," and these two meanings help to establish a frame within which we recall the lines we have just heard. Then there is the core word for the alliterating sequence, "sickle." Its first syllable suggests words like "Click," "pick," "flick," "nick," etc.; we half expect the following sequence "compass," "come" to finish up with "cut." The iteration of the hard /k/ sound carries through the core association to "sickle" and suggests the repeating blows that we know a reaping blade to give.

A similar analysis of the associative effects of expressive alliteration might be given for the more famous "When to the sessions of sweet, silent thought / I summon up remembrance of things past," where the two core words are "sessions" and "silent," both employing initial /s/ and final nasal, but with only the latter containing a /t/. They are further distinguished by the fact that "sessions" manifestly establishes the vehicle of the law court conceit and "silent" the tenor of it, the mood of moral meditation. Only the final phrase, "things past" contains both nasal and /t/ elements and encompasses both levels of the conceit.

As with alliteration, so with assonance. We can have purely decorative patternings, as in the phonetic chiasmus of Coleridge's "In Xanadu did Kubla Khan." It is more frequently used expressively, often with reinforcing alliteration, as, again from Pope, this time of unrelenting old harridans: "A fop their passion, but their prize a sot; / Alive, ridiculous, and dead, forgot."

The assimilation of these devices into generalized onomatopoeic musicality is frequent in Spenser, Keats, and Tennyson.[8] Onomatopoeia, as I. A. Richards has observed, must be divided into two sorts, which we might differentiate by applying the distinction that Greek philosophers used, illusory as it was, when considering etymology: *physei*, or natural, and *nomo*, or by convention. Certain primary onomatopoetic representations of non-linguistic sounds, such as the characteristic noises of animals, become morphemes of a language quite early in its development; the result is that they seem "natural" to it. Thus, "meeow," "tick-tock," "ding-dong," "baa-baa," "cock-a-doodle-doo" are common English patterns, showing either reduplication or a front-back alternation of vowel. Secondary, or conventional onomatopoeia is the kind we find used in verse, or in jokes like the proverbial "The pig is rightly so-called." In it, words are made to sound not like the noises of nature or of physical processes, but like other words. Some core word, often itself designating something about sound, may be associated with others. Occasionally a word not itself specified may be echoed by other ones: the classic case is the song about fancy in *The Merchant of Venice*, where the rhymes on "bred," "head," "nourishëd" all call to mind the lead casket which we know must be chosen if all is to end well.

8. One would, for example, analyze the "mimetic" effectiveness of the wonderful line from Keats's "The Eve of St. Agnes"—"The hare limped trembling through the frozen grass" in the same manner as Pope's line about Ajax. The common ground is the iambic metrical framework and the role of the consonantal clusters. On the other hand, the celebrated mimetic lines from Tennyson's *Idylls of the King* (e.g., "First as in fear, step after step she stole/Down the long tower-stairs hesitating"—a kind of scazon) depend, as one might expect in a more Miltonic poetry, upon syntactical as well as accentual arrangements.

There are also the famous, lush lines from Tennyson that are always extolled to school children:

> The moan of doves in immemorial elms
> And murmuring of innumerable bees

In cases like this, we must first rule out the operation of those minimal sound clusters which seem to act like ghosts of morphemes: on the surface, it would appear that words like "slide," "slip," "slick," "slink," "slim," "slop," "slope," and others are associated, through their initial cluster, with a general connotation of smoothness. But such cases are too rare to allow us to assume that onomatopoeia operates in any other way than to associate words already given us with others having common sounds. Assonance, alliteration, and even rhyme do some of the work of metaphor by associating words through their sounds alone, and by thus juxtaposing them with some of the same strength as an actual image. Thus, in the lines from Tennyson, the alliterating words are "moan," "immemorial," "elms," "murmuring," and "innumerable" with "bees" being related to the last syllable of "innumerable" and the phrase "of doves" being linked by a rhyme. Clearly the *core word* for these alliterations is "murmuring," and we associate with it all the connected words. But it is flatly misleading to tell a student that the "m" sounds have any meaning or evocative power, apart from words they connect. I realize that such assertions are frequent, and some appreciators of poetry like Dame Edith Sitwell carried this method to a comical extreme. Clearly Tennyson's lines have a suggestive musical richness. But just as clearly, this is a music of words, not of extrapolated sounds.

"Imitative movement" of words can, of course, really only imitate the sounds of other words or sounds. Some of the finest examples of it occur when a semantic relation is reinforced by a rhythmic parallel between words or phrases, and when we are almost tempted to say that the designatum of the phrase is being represented by that movement rather than the phrase itself. Thus in Florizel's great speech to Perdita in *The Winter's Tale* (IV, iv):

> When you do dance, I wish you
> A wave o' the sea, that you might ever do
> Nothing but that; move still still so . . .

Here the description of the girl's imitative dance doesn't "sound like the sea," but rather follows the rhythm of the phrase "a wave o' the sea." Also, in Yeats's *Sailing to Byzantium*, the "Monuments of unaging intellect" at the end of stanza I are echoed in a later line invoking singing schools that all study "Monuments of their own magnificence." Here, again, the repetition of the word "monuments" is reinforced by the symmetrical alliterating rhythm of the final word in the line: the whole line, so to speak, looks into a mirror and gazes at itself.

Something more might be said here about echoic patterns in general. There are echoes which operate beyond the boundaries of the poem itself, and those which work purely within it. Examples of the first abound, whether in open or hidden form. There is no difficulty with the relation between (again, from "Sailing to Byzantium") "Those dying generations" and Keats's hungry ones in the Nightingale ode. Sir Richard Fanshawe's translation of the famous chorus on the golden age from Guarini's *Il Pastor Fido*, which is itself full of material from Tasso, Ovid, and Horace, works in a specific little Catullan allusion of his own, by echoing Ben Jonson's adaptation of *"Vivamus mea Lesbia, atque amemus"* ("'Tis no sin love's fruit to steal, / But the sweet theft to reveal") in his own heroic couplet: "Nor think'st it any fault love's sweets to steal, / So from the world thou canst the theft reveal." Less public, avowed, or even, perhaps, conscious are echoes which allude to words, structures, rhythms, rather than quoting or re-framing, like the above. Thus, for example, there is the delicate echo of Spenser at the end of Milton's *On the Morning of Christ's Nativity:* "And all about the Courtly Stable / Bright harnest Angels sit in order serviceable." In this most Spenserian poem, Milton sinks at the end into a cushion of borrowed music; in Calidore's vision of the ring of damsels in *FQ*, VI.x, the thirteenth stanza concludes with the setting into heaven of the constellation Corona: "And is unto the stars an ornament, / Which round about her move in order excellent." It is not merely the specific phrase inverted pattern of "—in order (adjective)" which came to mind (or should we say, to ear?). It occurs in Spenser in a terminal position in a stanza, in the propounding of a complex and central image in what is hardly an obscure region of *The Faerie Queene,* and ends in an Alexandrine. Milton was echoing a whole movement.

Again, Wallace Stevens can echo Milton in equally subtle ways. There is the allusive Miltonic movement, transmuted from one kind of blank verse, through Wordsworth's, to another in the flight of the Canon Aspirin in *Notes Toward a Supreme Fiction:* "Descending to the children's bed, on which // They lay. Forth then with huge pathetic force / Straight to the utmost crown of night he flew." But the echo of *Il Penseroso,* ll. 73-75, in "Moving across wide water, without sound" from "Sunday Morning" is more like the Milton-Spenser case mentioned above. The source goes:

> I hear the far-off Curfew sound,
> Over some wide-water'd shore . . .

Stevens's *La Penserosa,* turning away from one sort of conventional meditation (in church) toward her own questionings, heeds but rejects the call not of a curfew, but a Sunday church bell.[9] This sort of echoing is not allusive, is not a public signal but rather a kind of private one for the poet himself.

So, I should think, would be the internal echo, the muted half-refrain in Keats's Grecian Urn ode, save that here it sets up an interesting grammatical ambiguity. The relation is between the second line: "Thou foster-child of silence and slow time" and the much later one: "Pipe to the spirit ditties of no tone," the echo being located in the final spondee. The problem is that, once heard, the echo tends to make "spirit" in the second line adjectival, so that instead of meaning "pipe toneless ditties to the spirit" it suggests "pipe to the tune of those spiritual, silent ditties." It is not so much that the second reading is probably incorrect,

---

9. But see the discussion of other Stevensian echoes, and the claim that the source is Tennysonian, in Robert Buttel, *The Making of* Harmonium (Princeton, 1967), p. 223. If there is indeed a Tennysonian echo in "Sunday Morning," it is probably of "The earliest pipe of half-awakened birds" from "Tears, Idle Tears."

but that Keats's metrical, rhythmical, and grammatical styles do indeed allow for it.

We have been examining a wide range of "musical" or attention-shaping effects of poetic rhythms operating within, in these instances, accentual-syllabic English verse. It is clear that many of them depend upon the very contingencies set up by the metrical choice for their ability to function. But the framing, defining, conventional aspect of the metrical choice with which this essay commenced must not in any sense be thought of as submerged or effaced by the occasionally prominent ways in which they can affect the ear. Let us return for a moment to this title or rubric-like function of metrical form, to the way in which style and genre are intertwined, to the ways in which a verse form may set up referential or allusive ground-rules for the poem and the reader, as well as serving to mark, diagram, underline, or gloss the language organized within it.

4

Behind so much Western aesthetics since Classical antiquity lies a nostalgia for what was believed quite naïvely to have been a perfect, mystical marriage, in Attic times, of musical mode and ethos, of form and the effect upon human behavior proper to that form; a nostalgia for what was thought to have been a perfect music-poetry that made of human sense an instrument whose own sound was human feeling. The myth of such a golden age in which communication was immediate, and guided only by the channel of suitable form, became in the Renaissance a myth of literature itself. Like the musical modality that many Greek writers themselves appear to us to misunderstand, meters and verse schemes have seemed to widely differing ages to possess inherent, psychologically affective qualities, and seemed to be measurable by decorum, in that any breach of this in their use would reveal itself upon comparing the nature and function of a mode, form, or style. This is a little like the way we *feel*, and have been rightly chastized for thinking, about onomatopoeia, sound symbolism and the like. (It may be worth noting here that the important classic parables of decorum for Neoclassic ages included that of Terpander, who was punished for adding an extra string to his lyre, and of Marsyas, who was flayed for playing the wild, passionate *aulos* which the goddess of reason had disgustedly cast aside—in both cases, the breach consisted in strengthening or widening the effectiveness of the music.)

This musical metaphor that underlies the history of literary notions about literary form was such a convenient one for poetic theory, and for so long, precisely because it could accommodate both the notions of formal significance under consideration here. In the whole Classical doctrine of form and ethos there lay resolved what later ages came to feel as a dialectic of conventional and instant form, revealed in the struggle for authority of schematic and pathetic accounts of the workings of music and poetry. In antiquity, the only "formal" elements were of the first type, the *metrical* type (although *meter* and *rhythm* had clearly opposed and also several confused sets of meanings in Greek times;[10] any particular work was distinguishable only cognitively ("rationally") from other works in the same convention. The rationalistic treatment of music by Greek theorists made this possible by ignoring all textless music for theoretical purposes; *song* was always the subject under discussion. A conceptual distinction between "music" and "poetry" of the kind that has been made since the Renaissance was impossible; and there was no need to create musical metaphors to aid in describing the ethos of any particular poetic utterance.

This whole paradise of communication was originally a quasi-mythical account of the power of literature (as opposed to persuasive speech: it was only the later Renaissance that sought metaphorically to identify music and rhetoric). But its power as an ideal account of the less obvious workings of carefully planned utterances held poetic theory in subjection for ages. For an empirical world view that demands much more of its accounts of things, such a myth is hardly even heuristically useful. The ethos of a passage of poetry or of a segment of that passage is to be understood as operating linguistically, that is, in that domain of shared experience of sound that connects a speaker and his hearer. And if there were no such thing as *literature*, but only *poetry;* that is, if all poems were utterances whose structure was as

10. See Chapter I, pp. 13-14.

significant as their assertions, making no attempt to share or imitate structures, but only to generate novel ones, then the whole problem of the two kinds of significance would vanish. There would remain only the "rhythm" of poems; there would be no such thing as "meter," for there would be no common scheme, no redundant elements, nothing "given."

But this is not the case. Poets continue to believe in modal myths long after they abandon other creeds. They continue to think in terms of "choosing" a meter even though, in stylistically eclectic ages like our own, they may resurrect, adapt, or newly forge their stylistic patterns. And poems continue to be literary events, which is also to say that it may be misleading to consider them as existing in any but a rather peculiar dialect of the language in which they are written. Their literary status in no way obliterates their linguistic status; it qualifies it only. Neither does the classification of a shouted "Go to the devil!" as a curse prevent it from remaining an utterance nevertheless; it merely specifies a rhetorical context. Now "meter" traditionally considered as arising from the literary classification and analysis of poems, jumps into prominence as a result of the historical mapping of several kinds of utterances in their historical contexts. The "rhythm," the flow of the poem in passage (aural or visual), the stream of effect upon the reader are all just as much the special concern, it is true, of the linguistically oriented poetic analyst as is the "meter" the concern of the historian or of the apologist for a style. To analyze the meter of a poem is not so much to scan it as to show with what other poems its less significant (linguistically speaking) formal elements associate it; to chart out its mode; to trace its family tree by appeal to those resemblances which connect it, in some ways with one, in some ways with another kind of poem that may, historically, precede or follow it.

But we have seen how in one case metrical qualities may coincide, coexist in the same element, with rhythmical ones. This may occur with respect to rhymes, stress patterns, syllabic arrangements, or even larger forms. The sonnet form functions, apparently, in two ways at once. By setting up certain canons of line length, rhyme scheme, etc., and by tending to limit larger syntactical patterns (in the case of a Shakespearean sonnet, by tending to set up an arrangement of a clause with two dependent clauses and a final sentence) the sonnet is spoken of as demanding a certain kind of logical form. On the other hand, the sonnet form itself is like a title, in that it serves to set up a literary context around the utterance, directing the reader to give to it a certain kind of attention just as the frame around a picture can urge a viewer to look at the picture in a particular way. Thus, to talk about the sonnet form of any poem may be to comment on either its "rhythm" or "meter" or both; about the particular role that it announces for itself, on the one hand, or about its actual movements on stage, so to speak, on the other.

Now this titling, framing, (or, as we might call it, *emblematic* or *badge-like*) function of meter is no less a linguistic operation than are those of smaller elements of the poem. To qualify the study of that function as macro-linguistic, or to confine it to a diachronic domain, may be a strategy necessary to the organization of a whole empirical pursuit. But there seems to be no reason for trying to separate the literary from the over-all linguistic in any metaphysical way (perhaps by insisting that there is "something more" to works of literature than the language they are composed of).

Whatever may have been accomplished by traditional metrical studies in the way of dissecting out and displaying this emblematic function of meter may have to be done over again without recourse to beliefs that poems were somehow beyond language, or to methods of analysis that barely hid their function of stylistic prescription. It has always been literary critics per se, arbiters, stylistic apologists, and makers of judgments who have directed most attention to the metrical emblem and its framing, self-titling function. In connection with this, it should also be observed that the metrical emblem operates differently under different stylistic climates: an epoch like the Augustan age in England, for example, marked by a canonical style like that of the heroic couplet; or a "pre-literary" or "folk" period in which there may be single authoritative styles, not strictly canonical in the sense that they are ruled into usage so as to exclude certain others, but retaining status because there is little or no contact with foreign or past forms and styles; and finally, an eclectic, history-ridden age like the present one in which such stylistic anarchy prevails that one almost feels that a poem need be defined as any utterance that purports to be one. In the first two cases, the badge of meter has the fundamental work of *defining* the utterance as a literary event (Dr. Johnson could hardly consider Christopher Smart's rich, mad *Jubilate Agno* as a poem; but an age that includes *The Cantos* among its monuments must surely value highly the fragments that Smart in the eighteenth century "shored against his ruin"). But in the last case, that of the eclectic age in which competing styles war for a lost authority, the meter becomes more than Wordsworth's "formal engagement"; it becomes almost a stipulation of what a poem ought to be. The frame begins to recommend, so to speak. And the emblem starts to take on a moral.

But the urging of a work of literature, perhaps accomplished by its formal frame, is no less an act of urging than any other kind of exhortation. The analysis of urging and exhorting can no longer be properly linguistic. And, finally, it is *as such* that it lies outside the realm of poetics.

VIII
BEN JONSON
AND THE MODALITY OF VERSE

Considering that they are the work of a literary genius, Ben Jonson's poems have had a curious critical fate. The epoch that most intimately responded to their virtues never singled them out for special praise, while our own age, so acutely conscious of history, acknowledges their importance and success and at the same time retains a fundamentally unsympathetic view toward them, seldom praising without apologizing. It is true that the importance of Jonson's non-dramatic works as a source for the whole current of poetic style during the course of the seventeenth century has only been adequately assessed during the past several decades. But even at the height of the Augustan style whose origins must be traced to Jonson's influence, the fame of his poems lagged behind that of his plays, and even further behind that of his personality.

There is perhaps some irony in this. In the audaciously entitled *Works* that the poet himself, in 1616, collected in the folio format until then reserved for editions of the great writers of antiquity, it was the lyric and epigrammatic portions that were popularly neglected in favor of the plays that at the time seemed to have even less right to publication under the presumptuous rubric of "dramatic literature." Jonson was, in every sense, a man of letters. He always devoted great attention and care to the cultivation of an organized *oeuvre* or corpus of literary creation. To be fair to him, one should include in a balanced selection of his "poems" examples of all the verse and prose, dramatic and non-dramatic, lyrical, satiric, critical, didactic, and occasional, that he left behind him. Poetry, Jonson knew, meant "making," and the senses of "things," "actions," or "deeds" are partially conveyed in his translation of "*opera.*" On the other hand, what we would today call "poems" he would consider a misleading category, lumping together and blurring distinctions between the sub-species populating his literary world. A lack of sympathy with Jonson's attachment to just these distinctions between literary genres has led to the peculiar judgment and appreciation of his poetry characterized by the critical attitudes of the present age. That peculiar judgment has crystallized about a rival for Jonson's laurels: for if his greatness as a dramatist has always had to contend with often inappropriate comparisons of his plays to Shakespeare's, it is only recently that his poems have seemed to lurk behind the obliquely cast shadow of those of John Donne.

It was the rediscovery of Jonson's contemporary, and Donne's critical canonization in the past forty years, that have helped to establish the very criteria by which, three hundred years after his death, a poem is considered to be a poem. In the narrowest view of these criteria, Jonson does seem a strange sort of poet, perhaps. He informs us (through the offices of the obliging William Drummond of Hawthornden in his *Conversations*) that he wrote his poems out in prose before versifying them. It is only the Romantic belief that poetry is somehow inspired and mysteriously spontaneous, or the post-symbolist insistence that a poem must *be* its own meaning, scheme, and purpose, rather than have separable skeleton, flesh, and organs, that can make us blush for Jonson at such a remark. Donne's poems, far from having been formalized out of prose statement, resist even our own efforts at prose paraphrase; and Donne is, or at any rate until very recently has been, a model English poet.

It must always be remembered that Jonson often writes in the metaphysical style, and that in one mode of writing, at least, the two poets are almost indistinguishable, as continued scholarly argument about the authorship of one of the elegies in *The Underwood* would suggest.

But in general, we may oppose them to each other. Where Donne is grotesquely original, Jonson strikes us as being overly imitative. Jonson, moreover, seems at once to brandish his Classical learning like a weapon, and to depend upon it for guidance and support, as if he were momentarily both halt and blind. Donne, conversely, subtly inoculates his rhetorically violent arguments with doses of sacred and profane lore. Donne is an ironist with no stage for which to write, and his poems seem as a consequence to condense the complicated structures of dramatic irony into a dramaturgy of image and tone: in a sense, Donne's poems are all dramatic monologues. Jonson, on the other hand, is a moralist with no pulpit. He makes of his theater a kind of complicated moral machine for projecting human behavior onto a screen so constituted as to reveal the true nature of that behavior, a nature always kept hidden by the distorted perspectives of mundane interests and commitments. For Jonson all of literature has this same moral purpose, and the poet is a secular priest.

But there are even greater differences between the two. Jonson, a schematic and devoted prosodist, declared that "Donne, for not keeping of accent, deserved hanging"; it is in just this metrical roughness of Donne's, however, that so much modern interest lies. Jonson writes in what look to be many styles, but all of Donne's verses, sacred or secular, amatory or satirical, songs or letters, are very much the same sort of intellectual ceremony, synthesizing the occasional and the spontaneous. It is this spontaneity of the dramatic rather than the inspirational sort that we miss in Jonson. Donne's wit often constructs a public or even a universal occasion from the most intimate and private ones, and "makes one little roome, an every where." But Jonson's occasional poems are frankly public, and it is significant that he makes pioneer attempts to adapt to English the Pindaric ode, that most ceremonial of forms.

A rewarding contrast might be drawn between two typical "occasional" poems: Donne's pair of "Anniversary" poems, in which the death of a patron's little daughter becomes the occasion for a lament over the passing of an epoch in the West's intellectual history, and Jonson's uncompleted elegy on the wife of Sir Kenelm Digby. In "Eupheme," Jonson commits himself to eulogistic extravagances, but struggles against them:

> What's left a *Poet*, when his *Muse* is gone?
> Sure, I am dead, and know it not! I feele
> Nothing I doe; but like a heavie wheele,
> Am turned with an others powers. My Passion
> Whoorles me about and to blaspheme in fashion.![1]

Aside from a punning reference to the lady's heroic name in "blaspheme," it was just the charge of blasphemy that Jonson leveled at Donne's first "Anniversary," perhaps having taken much of it far too literally. But in "Eupheme," Jonson's own literalness often leaves him breathlessly hyperbolic.

Although Jonson indeed esteemed "John Donne the first poet in the world in some things," he added later on that Donne "for not being understood, would perish." The irony here is that our day, which understands Donne so well as to have resurrected and animated his remains, should still misunderstand Jonson in some basic ways. The same influential judgment of T. S. Eliot that praised Donne as one who "knew the anguish of the marrow/The ague of the skeleton" could not approve of Jonson without insisting that "His poetry is of the surface." This, I feel, lies close to the heart of the question of Jonson's reputation as a poet today. Modern poetic taste distrusts surfaces because they seem too detachable, and demands the extrusion of the core of a poem, so to speak, onto its outside. For us, the meaning of a poem consists in its imagery and elaboration as much as in its "subject," and the separation of "sense" from expressive content in poetry is the arch-heresy of orthodox reading today. Yet Jonson insists on in theory, and demonstrates often enough in practice, a view of the nature of poetry depending on the notion of a "core" of prose sense or even moral purpose, surrounded by an exterior added by art, rather than secreted by the poem's soul within. Similarly, his widespread use of Classical sources

---

1. All quotations are from the text, based on that of Herford and Simpson, of my own Laurel Poetry Series *Selected Poems* of Jonson.

as models, texts, and themes, as well as for direct translation, seems to modern sensibilities somehow *inauthentic*. Indeed, the Classic poetry upon which he most frequently draws—Horace, Catullus, Juvenal, Martial, the corpus of Greek verse called the Anacreontea—itself tends to buckle under the same analysis of structure and texture that college students are today taught to apply to English poetry as a test of its very essence.

Beyond all these things, however, modern poetic theory requires of a poet a consistently recognizable language of his own, a characteristic voice sounding through any masks he may choose to wear, and overriding the accents of any style or manner he may elect to use. For a true poet, we feel today, all occasions, subjects, forms, and conventions must come under the absolute command of one governing style, and a major poet like W. H. Auden was often treated suspiciously by many otherwise sympathetic readers precisely because of his *use* of so many voices and techniques. But here again, Donne serves as textual authority, and here again, Jonson resists automatic commendation. With Donne, lyric, epigram, longer satire, and prayer are all, as I have already observed, the same kind of poem. With one or two dubious exceptions, none of the *Songs and Sonnets* are primarily lyrical, affecting us as being, first and foremost, song texts. Jonson's most celebrated lyrics, however, such as the too-heavily anthologized "Drinke to me, onely, with thine eyes," or the "Hymn to Diana" from *Cynthia's Revels*, have accumulated about them modern critical clichés concerning their "purely" lyrical character primarily because of their radical difference in manner from his odes, and even greater difference from his satires and epigrams. Jonson's lyrics seem "lighter" than his other poems; it is certainly true that, in contrast with Donne's, they are more properly "songs."

If we look through the body of Jonson's non-dramatic poetry, we come across his own schematic arrangement of various types of poem, both in the 1616 folio edition and in the larger posthumous publication of 1640. The epigrams form a collection of their own. Then follows *The Forrest*, a short selection of pieces of many sorts that he considered at the time to be his very best accomplishments. In the 1640 folio, Jonson prefaced his volume called *The Underwood* with the explanation that

> With the same leave as the Ancients call'd that kind of body *Sylva* or *Hule*, in which there were workes of divers nature, and matter congested; as the multitude call Timber-trees, promiscuously growing, a Wood, or Forrest: so am I bold to entitle these lesser Poems, of later growth, by this of Under-Wood, out of the Analogie they hold to the *Forrest*, . . .

It is not surprising, incidentally, to find him carrying through this "analogie" in the naming of his prose miscellany, *Timber: or Discoveries Made Upon Men and Matter*. . . . But with the exception of the separate compilation of epigrams, Jonson's categories are based upon the departments of a literary *oeuvre*, and arranged with respect to relative importance, rather than to distinctions between literary genres as such and as represented in the poems themselves.

The fact that Jonson took these modes or forms utterly for granted is quite significant for any clear understanding of what he meant by poetry, or for that matter, by literature in general. One of the most overpowering myths of Classical antiquity was that of the power of music at the hands of heroes like the poet-musician Orpheus. Of all the lore about ancient music that was transmitted through the Middle Ages down to Jonson's time, the notion of what I shall call modality most fascinated Renaissance thinkers and writers who sought to understand that fabled power. The modes or keys of ancient music, called Dorian, Lydian, Phrygian, etc., were all held to affect the hearer's feelings and actions, each in its prescribed way. (Thus the Dorian had a manly and martial character, the Lydian was held to be voluptuous and relaxing, the Phrygian, frenzied, and so forth. The modern musician may think in terms of a whole species of distinctions corresponding to that drawn by the Romantic imagination between a "happy" major key and a "sad" minor one.) Great importance was attached to these modes, to the kinds of poetic texts conventionally sung to their melodies, the occasions appropriate to the use of each, and their respective characters. Socrates, it will be remembered, carefully indicates which modes are to be permitted in Plato's Just City. In general, the idea of modality in the music of the ancient world becomes a kind of standard or model of the relation of musical or poetic form to content or purpose.

Now for a Neoclassicist like Jonson, the music-poetry of antiquity is the unfallen ancestor of all literature, and Orpheus' lyre a heraldic bearing. The idea of musical modality thus expands into a general literary principle, analogous to the Greeks' purely musical one, in an age whose literary program aimed at the achievements, if not at the actual forms, of Classical literature. And thus, for a writer like Jonson who believed in a vital tradition embracing the poetry of the ancient and modern worlds, never use styles, forms, and conventions to be thought of as spontaneous channels of expression, shaped by the unique identity of the poet, his experience, and his voice. Only a Romantic writer would insist on that triumph of feeling over form. Rather would the Neoclassicist employ forms and styles of modes of discourse having certain quasi-musical effects upon the reader, perhaps, but more clearly serving as a proper vehicle or designation of an occasion, a subject, or an attitude. Granted the notion that art is to be a mirror of life, the relationship between poetic form and poetic purpose, between the public or private occasion of a literary utterance and the mode or style proper to it, becomes a moral one.

In praising a sentence of Demosthenes, the Hellenistic Pseudo-Longinus accounts for its power not only by allusion to its *dianoia*, "thought," but because of its *harmonia*, "melody": "Its delivery depends wholly on the dactyls, which are the noblest of rhythms and make for grandeur—and that is why the most beautiful of all known meters, the heroic, is composed of dactyls.[2] Here is a beautifully framed example of what would become a dogma of Classicism: a form or mode is seen to possess an ethos or attribute of its own by nature, rather than because of an association with certain kinds and occasions of utterance. A modern formalist critic would say just the opposite about the dactyls, namely, that they acquired an aura of grandeur because of their conventional use in heroic, epical poetry. Jonson, like many good

---

2. Pseudo-Longinus, *On the Sublime*, XXXIX, tr. W. Hamilton Fyfe, Loeb edition, pp. 236-37.

Renaissance scholars, knew something of the arguments in antiquity about whether powers of language and music were to be ascribed to nature, or to convention. But like all Renaissance poets who drew on antiquity for anything more than stylistic models, he grasped the force of the idea of the naturalness of stylistic effects, and lived with that idea as with a most useful fiction.

He retained always a vigorous and healthy attitude toward the relation between the modern and the antique. He castigated Spenser who, he felt, "in affecting the Ancients, writ no language," although we may suspect that other aspects of *The Faerie Queene* may have troubled him as well, and that by concentrating on the language, he was anticipating the strategy of twentieth-century Moderns like Eliot and Pound in rejecting Milton, Spenser, and much more poetry of the past that posed aesthetic and moral problems far deeper than stylistic ones.

Jonson took no part in the attempt to employ Classical quantitative meters in English. He seemed firmly committed to the English iambic pentameter line from the outset. Drummond of Hawthornden reminds us that Jonson distrusted longer lines, denouncing the translations of Homer and Virgil "in long alexandrines as but prose," and having no patience for the twelve-syllabled line of Drayton's *Poly-Olbion*. With his knowledge of the ancients, Jonson must have understood well that the accentual decasyllabic that descended (although his generation did not yet know this) from Chaucer would have to do a variety of jobs in English poetry. In Classical verse, the modalities, or generic associations, of various meters are sharply differentiated. Thus, Classical iambics (usually an iambic trimeter of six feet because iambs and anapests were always doubled up as two to a foot) was a conversational meter, used on the stage and hence for some of Catullus' invective, for example. The heroic hexameter was the line of epic and, in the tradition that Theocritus inaugurated and Virgil confirmed, of pastoral eclogue. The couplet was the meter of inscription, epigram, and, later, satire and epistle. A modulation from one to another could constitute a revision of a genre. Thus Ovid's joke, in the first two lines of the *Amores*, about how he had originally planned to write of high heroic doings, but Cupid, the naughty thing, came along and filched a foot from his second line (thus, it went without saying, transforming the hexameters into elegiac couplets of alternating hexameter and pentameter lines). A modern analogue of this might be an improvising pianist who muttered as he played about how he had meant to play a rousing march in C major, but Sorrow came along and sadly draped three blue flats on his melody.

Jonson realized early that the English-stressed decasyllabic would have to serve as iambics when unrhymed on the stage, as hexameters and as elegiacs both when indented;[3] similarly, he would translate iambics of the Catullan sort by a shorter English line, usually tetrameter. The iambic pentameter line, he knew, would have to do, on and off the stage, for high and low matters. His brilliant translation of Petronius' epigram about sadness after sex that begins "Doing a filthy pleasure is, and short" maintains that wonderful balance between the schematic written grammar and the spoken force that we associate with Milton (the Latin original goes *"Foeda est in coitu et brevis voluptas"*) —the sequential build from one of the paired modifiers of "pleasure" to the second, last, and most telling being the inner "narrative" of the line and the moral it embodies. It is no wonder that Jonson had written a (now lost) "discourse of poesie both against Campion and Daniel, especially the last, where he [proved] couplets to be the bravest sort of verses, especially when they are broken like hexameters." Here was Dryden's, and Pope's, direct ancestor.

Jonson thus seems to follow directly upon Sidney in his understanding of the relation between form and genre, and of the necessity of building a new world of expression, wielding style in the purposes of truth and right, upon the ruins of the ancient one. "He cursed Petrarch," Drummond tells us, "for redacting verses to sonnets which he said were like the tyrant's bed," by which he meant that of Procrustes; but as we shall see a bit further on, his one sonnet is an anti-sonnet, not merely because of distaste for the format, but out of revulsion against the institutionalized Petrarchan convention. (This did not prevent him, in "Eupheme" or, brilliantly, in the masques, from wrench-

3. See Chapter XII, pp. 268-69.

ing the rituals out of their normal molds, and reapplying the rhetorical and mythological strategies of celebration.)

Jonson's interest in form, then, is by no means superficial. The brilliance and permanence of many of his achievements in a purely technical direction lie close to the foundations of what he considered to be the fundamental problems of the man of letters. For him, poetry was the same mirror of life that it was for his contemporaries. It exercised a moral function by *illuminating* on the stage the hiding place of folly and vice, by calling down in satire nasty self-interest for what it is, celebrating the knowledge and generosity of individuals in commendatory poems, etc. But for Johnson in particular, the glass of poetry presented in addition a view of what might be. He flourished in a spiritual climate too close to the miasmas of medieval despair over nature, and was of too fierce and loathing a temper himself, to partake of any optimism for the economic, social, and religious consequences of the sixteenth century. Neither is his Neoclassicism to be considered a historical nostalgia for golden days: the virtues he responded to in Augustan Rome concerned what he felt to be a model relationship of literature to life, while life was as petty and vile, he knew, as ever. But without necessarily apologizing for any old order, he made his task as a poet the representation of the ideals of what he felt to be the most important Establishments of his day: aristocracy, order, and a kind of humanist orthodoxy. Prior to all these, perhaps, lay a notion of courtesy, no hodgepodge of chivalric ideology and scraps from medieval writers, but a more universal idea of civilization involving knowledge and enlightenment allied with power and effectiveness. Literature was for Jonson the language of that courtesy. The understanders of that language were the various aristocracies of enlightened courts, literate theatrical audiences, university intellectuals in public service, and a learned reading public. When eventually the playgoers proved too fickle, the court unappreciative of his greatest efforts in the form of the masque, and readers in general too unsubstantial an entity, he must have turned, in his later years, for more than consolation to the group of surrogate sons calling itself the "Tribe of Ben," and including in its numbers most of the distinguished poets of the Caroline age. The coterie of such younger men of letters as Herrick, Carew, and James Howell, such public men as Sir Lucius Cary, Sir Kenelm Digby, the Earl of Newcastle, and others, turned exclusively about "St. Ben," its unwobbling pivot in a mad world. It is perhaps as much as anything else the doing of this "cult of personality" of Jonson's later years that Jonson's public figure seemed for so long to eclipse the light of his works.

But the idea of a civilized society as well as its microcosm in the literary cabala of the Tribe of Ben were both modern versions, for Jonson, of the idea of a literate community that emerges from even a cursory reading of Classical writers. The sense of Augustan Rome that we get from its poets, for example, suggests the paradoxical condition of a tight coterie upon which, nevertheless, no sun could ever set. Jonson knew that of all the aristocratic Establishments, the most carefully preserved, pruned, cultivated, and revered is The Past. His Neoclassicism was the one element in his poetic program that brought together questions of purpose, theory, and actual practice. It is no wonder that his basic notion of what poetic language is by nature, and of how and when it was to be used, was so strongly conditioned by his self-adopted kinship with Latin writers.

The many modes of Jonson's poetry, then, betoken no superficiality or inconsistency. Although there may be recognized everywhere in his range of accomplishment the combination of toughness of wit and vigorous delicacy of control that characterize Jonson's unique poetic elegance, to list his very best poems is to include an astonishing variety of successes. From the half-wry, post-pastoral lyric of the "Celebration of Charis" or "The Musicall Strife," for example, is a considerable stylistic distance to the dramatic climax of the magnificent "Elegie on the Lady Jane Pawlet":

>What Nature, Fortune, Institution, Fact
>Could summe to a perfection, was her Act!
>How did she leave the world? with what contempt?
>Just as she in it liv'd! and so exempt
>From all affection! when they urg'd the Cure
>Of her disease, how did her soule assure

> Her suffrings, as the body had beene away!
> And to the Torturers (her Doctors) say,
> Stick on your Cupping-glasses, feare not, put
> Your hottest Causticks to, burne, lance or cut:
> 'Tis but a body which you can torment,
> And I, into the world, all Soule, was sent! . . .

Then there is the dual brilliance of the famous "Come my Celia, let us prove": in its original context in the superb seduction scene in *Volpone*, it is no mere Classically imitated *carpe diem* lyric, but rather an expression as well of the whole play's themes of acquisition and deceit. But as printed with a companion piece in *The Forrest*, it presents itself to us as a Catullan adaptation made with an almost gnomic concision. Different again is the extreme Mandarin elegance of "To Penshurst," whose authoritative couplets frame a poetry of statement rather than of gesture or indirection:

> The earely cherry, with the later plum,
> Fig, grape, and quince, each in his time doth come:
> The blushing apricot, and woolly peach
> Hang on thy walls, that every child may reach.
> And thou thy walls be of the countrey stone,
> They'are rear'd with no means ruine, no mans grone, . . .

Even the complimentary conceits woven into the splendid tribute not only to the ancestral home of the Sidney family, but to a whole way of life as well, look ahead to the near-Augustan tone of Andrew Marvell: the "ripe daughters," a few lines further on, have baskets that "beare/ An embleme of themselves, in plum, or peare." The tone of the closing lines might be said to resound at the tonal center of Jonson's highest commendatory mode:

> Now, *Penshurst*, they that will proportion thee
> With other edifices, when they see
> Those proud, ambitious heaps, and nothing else,
> May say, their lords have built, but thy lord dwells.

Jonson is perfectly capable of using the resources of metaphysical poetry, however, as in the great Pindaric ode, "To the Immortall Memorie, and Friendship of that Noble Paire, Sir Lucius Cary, and Sir H. Morison." At the very opening image, based, it is true, upon an obscure incident mentioned in Pliny, the wretchedness of a world that cuts off virtuous lives is figured forth in a conceit that makes one think of the wilder excesses of an extreme poet like John Cleveland:

> Brave Infant of *Saguntum,* cleare
> Thy comming forth in that great yeare,
> When the Prodigious *Hannibal* did crowne
> His rage, with razing your immortall Towne.
> Thou, looking then about,
> E're thou wert halfe got out,
> Wise child, did'st hastily returne,
> And mad'st thy Mothers wombe thine urne.
> How summ'd a circle didst thou leave man-kind
> Of deepest lore, could we the Center find!

In the antistrophe immediately following, however, Jonson employs a more Classically expository language to clarify that "deepest lore":

> Did wiser Nature draw thee back,
> From out the horrour of that sack,
> Where shame, faith, honour, and regard of right
> Lay trampled on; the deeds of death, and night,
> Urg'd, hurried forth, and horld
> Upon th'affrighted world:
> Sword, fire and famine, with fell fury met;
> And all on utmost ruine set;
> As, could they but lifes miseries fore-see,
> No doubt all Infants would returne like thee?

And then, again, Jonson is capable in the same frequently underrated poem of violent grammatical tricks, such as when he expresses the shock of the breach of friendship occasioned by Morison's death through a likening of the two men to the constellation of the Gemini ("this bright *Asterisme*" he calls it), and then writing

> To separate these twi-
> Lights, the *Dioscuri* . . .

whereby, as already mentioned (pp. 143), the "twin lights" are separated, by the enjambment of the line, from the unified word "twilights" in which they were joined. Here the meter imitates the action of death by cutting the word apart even as death divided the two men. In the previous stanza, Jonson has also employed a striking enjambment, where Morison leaps "the present age,/Possest with holy rage," into eternity. The strophe ends: "And there he lives with memorie: and *Ben*," and there one tends to come to a full stop. But the next strophe begins "*Jonson*, who sung this of him, e're he went/Himselfe to rest." This is no arbitrary shock, but is again a kind of pun-by-discovery. Just "*Ben*" may appear over-familiar; with the addition of the enjambed line, the poet, as he would have been known by the living Cary, the late Morison, and the whole "Tribe of Ben" becomes the public figure, the author of the *Works*. Thus is the poem labeled with the poet's dual name, expressing his private and public roles and duties.[4]

But Jonson has countless other modes of performance. Even in satire, he can be as personal as in the account of the burning of some of his writings in the "Execration upon Vulcan," or in his attacks upon Inigo Jones. He can adopt the traditional genre of mock-epic for the magnificently Rabelaisian "Voyage" (which was apparently too scatalogical for Swinburne, incidentally, whom one would have thought barely capable of shock). He can adopt the varying tones of "Ben" the critic, in epigrams addressed to his fellow writers like Donne, Selden, and Drayton, and of the public "Ben Jonson," in occasional pieces on broader subjects.

Aside from the public theater itself, the "loathed stage" which he could never quite leave, perhaps the one poetic mode which Jonson found most congenial was that of the court masque. This peculiar form, for Jonson almost a miniature world of humane letters, is lost to us as

---

4. There is an additional discussion of these lines in Chapter VII. Jonson's one other truly startling enjambment is in ll. 20-21 of his translation of Horace's *Ars Poetica* (Folio edition). It is the part about the purple passages, when he talks of "A Scarlet peece, or two, stich'd in: when or/*Diana's* Grove, or Altar, with the bor-/Dring Circles of swift waters that intwine/The pleasant grounds . . ." It looks to be most ingenious, along with the possible pun on "stitch-*stiche*." For a systematic treatment of enjambment, see Chapter V.

dramatic literature today for it is impossible to resurrect the theater in which it occurred. The most devoted archaeology and technology might reproduce some of the brilliant scenic and mechanical effects of Jonson's great collaborator and eventual rival, Inigo Jones, or allow us to hear the music of such composers as Alfonso Ferrabosco. But nothing could ever really duplicate the total milieu relating author, musician, performer, and audience. Masques were more than merely festival pageants full of singing and mythological figures and clever stage machinery. The Jacobean masque was an elaborate kind of dramatized court dance, in which some courtiers themselves participated, while others observed, with the monarch, from the vantage point known as "The State." The masque in Jonson's hands became, over a period of more than thirty years, a unique poetic instrument. With the sovereign, his court, and "The State" in a Hall on Twelfth Night, say, and the world enclosed, so to speak, in a more ideally compacted microcosm than the "wooden O" of the public theater, the poet could lead his nobility through a series of allegorical dances. The texts of the songs surrounding and accompanying them explained and moralized the very patterns, often, of the intricate series of dance figures, just as their melodies and rhythms provided the proper measures to govern them. In Jonson's masque *Pleasure Reconciled to Virtue*, for example, the masquers, costumed as pleasures and virtues, are led through a "laborinth of love" by Daedalus, the fabulous artificer of antiquity. As they "put themselves in forme" for the various dances, he sings

> Come on, come on; and where you go,
>   So interweave the curious knot,
> As ev'n th'observer scarce may know
>   Which lines are Pleasures, and which not.
> First figure out the doubtfull way
>   At which, a while all youth should stay,
>   Where she and Vertue did contend
>   Which should have Hercules to frend.
> Then as all actions of mankind
>   Are but a Laborinth, or maze:
>   So let your Daunces be entwin'd,

> Yet not perplex men unto gaze.
> But measur'd, and so numerous too,
>   As men may read each act you doo.
> And when they see the Graces meet,
>   Admire the wisdom of your feet.
> For Dauncing is an exercise
>   Not onely shews the movers wit,
> As he hath powre to rise to it.

Here is the perfect combination of "pleasure and profit," that Renaissance cliché about the purpose of art to which Jonson did not hesitate to give assent. But in this masque, moral subject, poetic figure and dramatic action are all unified. (Is the first stanza actually *metaphorical*, by the way, or rather a literal injunction to embodied abstractions about the structure and value of their imminent dance?) The animated moral emblem of the masque, moreover, might be said itself to approach most closely to Jonson's ideal of the proper role of poetry in the real world, involving the principals of The State not as spectators only, but as amused, amusing, and profitable participants, instructed both in and by allegorical roles by the poet himself. Such songs as these (and, of course, the masques include almost every type of dramatic and non-dramatic lyric as well) are supreme cases of the lyric doing the work of dramatic, speculative, and didactic poetry as well. But they can do so only because of the perfect, artificial literary milieu in which they are conceived. As the work of such scholars as Stephen Orgel has shown us, the masque remains in some senses the form of Jonson's most original poetic achievement.

Yet the range of his technical accomplishments is quite broad. Among its high points must be mentioned the establishment of the couplet in form and purpose as it was to continue through the century, and the extremely original and personal tone, texture, and form of the odes. For lyrics Jonson employs a variety of forms extending from the tetrameter couplet (analogous to the meters of the Anacreontea?) to the complicated stanza forms taken by pastoral madrigals. Certain forms he eschews utterly. His sole sonnet is almost a joke; "To the Noble Lady, the Lady Mary Wroth" at once casts aspersions on the form as a kind of Sunday painting, and manages to celebrate most delicately the Lady's own accomplishments in just that form.

> I that have beene a lover, and could shew it,
>   Though not in these, in rithmes not wholly dumbe,
>   Since I exscribe your Sonnets, am become
> A bitter lover, and much better Poet.
> Nor is my Muse, or I asham'd to owe it,
>   To those true numerous Graces; whereof some
>   But charme the Senses, others over-come
> Both braines and hearts; and mine now best doe know it. . . .

It is the same impulse operating here that accounts for the "Fit of Rime against Rime," in which he can choose no other instrument to launch his complaint about the necessary barbarisms incidental to the carving of literature out of the living, rather than the dead, language. Jonson uses all the attacks on the debased state of modern languages and their need for rhyming that were employed in the turn-of-the-century debates over prosody. At the end of the poem, he condemns the imaginary inventor of rhyming to a fate no worse than what must have been the endemic agony of a conscience-ridden Classicist who, unlike Thomas Campion, for example, refused to write quantitative poetry for polemical purposes alone, while hewing to the line of rhyme in all the rest of his work:

> May his joynts tormented bee,
>   Cramp'd forever;
> Still may Syllabes jarre with time,
> Still may reason warre with rime,
>   Resting never. . . .

Jonson's mastery of the short poem led him to avoid, in all but satires, the kind of drawn-out, dialectical elaboration which Donne delighted in producing. Consider the perfection of the little poem on the hourglass, from *The Underwood:*

> Doe but consider this small dust,
>   Here running in the Glasse,

>   By Atomes mov'd;
>   Could you beleeve, that this
>   The body ever was
>   Of one that lov'd?
>   And in his Mistris' flame, playing like a flye,
>   Turn'd to cinders by her eye?
>   Yes; and in death, as life, unblest,
>   To have exprest,
>   Ev'n ashes of lovers find no rest.

This is like a collapsed version of a Donne song, starting with a formal reading of the emblem of the hourglass (what does it mean? here is the signification: etc.) and ending up where Donne might have after several stanzas and much brilliant digression. It is brilliantly, and tactfully, compressed, and calls to mind several lines from Herbert's "Church-Monuments"; a Latin original on which it is based is three elegiac couplets, but Jonson modulates with line length and half-rhyming (the opening "dust" never rhymes with "this" or "was," and comes to an uneasy rest of closure in the triple-rhymed, final "rest"). Similarly, "My Picture Left in Scotland," with its opening casual paradox "I now thinke, Love is rather deafe, then blind" closes in a bluster of material from the opening of Donne's "The Canonization":

>   My hundred of gray haires,
>   Told seven and fortie years,
>   Read so much wast, as she cannot imbrace
>   My mountaine belly, and my rockie face,
> And all these through her eyes, have stopt her eares.

Between the intimately private and the didactically public, there are many modes, and Jonson played in them all.

But even Jonson's most personal triumphs of technical skill and concern cannot put off post-Romantic objections to his imitativeness. Originality and novelty are recent virtues, and the Renaissance did not demand of "making" or "feigning" as poetry was frequently called in English, that it work out of whole cloth. But even against such a background, Jonson seems often to be doing patchwork. Translations, adaptations, and borrowings appear almost everywhere in his poetry. A particular poem may echo several different sources, while the same classic text may show up in several poems. His "translations" proper never aim at preserving a particular poem, however, but at carrying over a method, a style, a way of writing, thought, and life.

But Jonson's adaptations betoken no failure of imagination; rather they reveal a particular kind of mind. Edmund Wilson, in an extremely provocative essay in literary psychology, likened Jonson to James Joyce, and the similarities he draws between the two writers apply to the question of their use of literary reference and allusion as well. Both Joyce's and Jonson's learning is like a kind of hoarding. Lines, phrases, patterns, shapes (as, with Joyce, sounds, fractions of syllables, rhymes, puns) become the objects amassed in the store of knowledge—in his feelings for language, Jonson seems much like one of his own stage misers. Learning is for him not so much a play of light upon, or elevation of, the self, or a metamorphosis in the inner life, but rather an accumulation of treasure which cannot help but overflow.

Moreover, Jonson, like Joyce, aims at the creation of language itself. The latter sought in his later writing to make the One Great Statement that, once made, would render all other assertions tautological or trivial, and he tried to cast that Statement in a Universal Language, assembled from all the tongues of men and of angels. But Jonson makes no attempt to go beyond English. Rather, he attempts to mark off a literary dialect within it, manipulating larger instead of smaller linguistic elements. He selects building blocks from Classic writers in much the same way that Modern poets will come to choose forms or styles in this eclectic age. Today, times past and places distant are raided for metrical and rhetorical schemes, or even for the very notions of what a poem *is*, in an attempt to find an authority broader and more compelling than that given by the uses of the previous generation. Jonson's tags, phrases, and comparisons become the counters in no universal language, but rather in a particular civilized one. It is the language of poetry whose ultimate constituents are not so much words, but rather combinations of and ways of using them.

And finally it must be said that Jonson's very way of being derivative was in itself original. F. R. Leavis has pointed out that if Jonson's followers in the seventeenth century seem to derive more from his own Classical sources than from Jonson himself, it is because "the indebtedness to Jonson's models is of a kind that it took Jonson's genius in the first place to incur; if the later poets learnt from these models, they had learnt from Jonson how to do so."[5] This is undoubtedly true; but it should be added that Jonson's own pioneer concerns were for creating discourse in an ideal community, within which the literary dialect would be as speech. His Classical allusions and quotations are not covert tricks hiding cosmic jokes, as in Joyce, just as his poems, unlike those of Donne, Herbert, and Vaughan, for example, are not modeled on difficult texts for study, contemplation, and close reading, rather than upon songs, letters, dialogues. Their allusions aim at being recognizable accents, recognizable not only to a coterie of poets and gentlemen-scholars, but to a whole culture as well. If the notion of a civilization seems today to demand something larger, and the idea of humanistic literacy to be something smaller, perhaps, than it was for Jonson, his poetry nevertheless remains a monument of a literature that sought to engage life, but on its own terms. This is surely at once the oldest and the most urgently modern demand made upon the poetic virtue.

For the student of poetic form, Jonson's contribution to literary history is immense. In his grasp of the modality of verse, of the inevitable "choice of meter" which must be made, he advances the original contribution of Sidney. The latter's myriad attempts at all sorts of lyric forms were in the main, experimental: whether in the variety of meters in which he versified the Psalter, or the quantitative poems in the *Arcadia*, sheer compositional exuberance, and the exigencies of a particular moment seem to be at work. It is either a matter of trying on a form for its own sake, or casting about for a structural idea. But there is no sense of metrical genre about Sidney's shorter poems. With George Herbert, we have a radical extension of Sidney's practice in one direction, that of expressiveness. The overflowing variety of invention in *The*

5. F. R. Leavis, *Revaluation* (New York, 1947), p. 20.

Temple, the scores and scores of unique through-composed and strophic patterns—all these seem directed not at a modal or generic variation, but at an internalized array of states. The form is frequently "read" tropically or figuratively by the language of the poem cast in it. Each form, as each poem for Wallace Stevens, is "the cry of its occasion."

Another Sidneyan experimentalist is Coleridge, using an array of meters but so enmeshed in the Romantic struggle to evolve new genres that although he is keenly aware of Classical and Neoclassical modality, he is torn between theorizing about it and practicing in a more expressive tradition as far as metrical "choice" is concerned. An extreme of non- or even anti-modal variation of style in the short poem is presented by Thomas Hardy, who makes us feel uncomfortable, often, at a decision about form which seems to have been taken in caprice, and then stuck to at all costs. Indeed, it is just out of such a sense of difficulty overcome that he is frequently able to generate formal, rhetorical, and structural force. But Hardy is almost the textbook case of want of modality; perhaps it is traceable to his having started a serious poetic career so late in life, and bursting into the blossom of verse so frenziedly because his poems, although written since his twenties, had been more a matter of the left hand until he gave up novels in the 1890's. It was not a matter for Hardy of finding a voice by searching for style and form, but of singing as many songs as possible.

Hardy's vast formal and structural repertoire exerted, as by his own frequent admission, a considerable formal influence on the young W. H. Auden, who was also absorbing Edward Thomas, Frost, Hopkins, early Germanic verse structures, and, later on, Rilke and Brecht. But after an early, self-consciously experimental approach to form, Auden developed a keen modal sense, and he became in the twentieth century the epitome of the master craftsman of verse.[6] Modern poets can take one of two directions, it seems, in moving toward a characteristic use of form, in seeking to "learn a style from a despair" of be-

---

6. Consider, for example, the use of a wide array of conventional forms in *The Sea and the Mirror* for almost emblematic purposes, as opposed to the casually irrelevant use of particular lyric forms throughout *The Dynasts*.

lated arrival in a world where forms are not given, where style is not canonical. One of these is that of American Modernism, following the Emersonian injunction to "mount to Paradise / By the stairway of surprise"—in short, to seize early enough upon a poetic tessitura of one's own, to frame a mode of singing, as it were, that would make any other formal style impossible. The effect is to dissolve genre: it is not that the poet wishes to make distinguishable, say, "a short, ironic meditation on landscape by Poet X," but rather only "a Poet X poem." The other tradition is best exemplified by Auden, and in this he was Ben Jonson's heir in our age. His grasp of the competing necessities of the public and private realms were mirrored not only in his poetic morals but in his stylistic practice; using a vast array of forms, styles, systems, differentiating between private messages, songs, sermons, inscriptions, pronouncements, and so forth, he made of his technical brilliance more than merely a matter of his own delight. In craft began, for him as well as for his predecessor Jonson, responsibilities.

IX
ROMANTIC VERSE FORM
AND THE METRICAL CONTRACT

The fascination of Romantic literary thought with the interplay of nature and convention has at least one infrequently studied aspect in some questions of metrical theory. This lies close to the problems about the framing of poetic utterance that so occupied, from time to time, the utterance itself, and, in fact, comes as near to the heart of the poem as some of the more specific studies of the actual poetic rhythms of particular poets and texts. It would be absurd to suggest that all Romantic poetry falls along one line of prosodic tradition, or even along one line of approach: while the first generation of poets was more concerned with freeing poetry from the institution of eighteenth-century literature, the second was seeking new affirmations in re-engagements, stylistically speaking, with older voices. Keats, Shelley, and Byron contribute virtually nothing to any continuing discussion of formal theory. Leigh Hunt, aided by the most sophisticated knowledge of music of all the English Romantics, has left a few trenchant observations of the subject of what, following Coleridge, he calls "variety in uniformity" as being the basis of verse, but his concern is primarily with "metrical excitement" or actual rhythmic effects. Had he been able to expand adequately upon his opening remark to a discussion of versification, "Poetry stands between nature and convention, keeping alive among us the enjoyment of the external and the physical world,"[1] he might have led straight to the heart of the problem I should like to raise.

For this problem has some interesting repercussions for the whole idea of what a literary program is. That even Romantic poetry is doomed to become literature, as antinomian heroes become locked into the laws of their eventual worship, seems inevitable. But the poets who knew this all too well wished to exercise their control over the ways in which this would happen, and in the following remarks I should like to try to set out some of the formal mechanisms of this control. But first, a few words about the whole matter of metrical theory and practice.

In recent years, the most illuminating studies of prosody in general have been devoted to showing the relation of patterned sound and semantic sense in particular poems. This concern with the music of poetry, with the expressive function of rhythm, has centered primarily on the analysis of how the poem's sound structure, formed within the limits of a particular metrical scheme, amplifies from moment to moment what is being said. This is an important matter, of course, and for lyric poetry in particular; since the fundamental separation between the lyric poem and the actual text for music early in the seventeenth century, the expressive rhythms of language have come to permit the lyric poem to sing its own song.

But by and large, prosodists since Saintsbury have been less concerned with another dimension along which the problems of poetic meter may be viewed. This dimension I should call purely conventional, or formal, rather than expressive, and its function is rather like a definitive or axiomatic one for the whole literary work. It involves the element of convention which link a metrical style or type to a whole poetic genre and, hence, a poet's choice of meter to a larger intention. In an age of canonical metrical styles like the Augustan period, the

1. Leigh Hunt, "An Answer to the Question What Is Poetry Including Remarks on Versification," in *Imagination and Fancy* (London, 1891), p. 1. The discussion of "variety in uniformity" occurs on pp. 31 ff. and 43 ff. The relevant passage from Coleridge is one from *Anima Poetae* quoted by Shawcross in his edition of *Biographia Literaria* (Oxford, 1967), Vol. II, p. 278, although Hunt's application of it to meter is his own. Cf. also Wordsworth's "preception of similitude and dissimilitude."

relation between meter and intention is very clear. In the nineteenth century it is less so, and in our own day the *sine qua non* of originality has led to an almost obsessive concern, in American poetry in particular, with metrical format.

As Northrop Frye has suggested,[2] the Age of Sensibility represents an interesting period of transition in the history of English meter as well as in the history of the literary imagination. In very different ways and for very different reasons, Smart, Ossian, Chatterton, and, finally, Blake, all seem to threaten the very basis of English literary meter— the accentual-syllabic system that is normal from Chaucer through Tennyson—in outbursts of self-made song. This threat may be brought about as the result of the influence of the English Bible, as in the case of Ossian; or it may result from the completely graphic reality of Chatterton's fake dialect, a speech that his heart may have heard but his ears, never. In any event, the major Romantic poets' extremely sophisticated sense of literary history and of their own various relationships to the past gave them to understand that iambic verse, official though it may have been, was by no means necessarily the strained, cruel voice of an enemy. But this *rapprochement* had to be accomplished, I feel, only after an expense of some awkwardness, and I think that the whole problem of metrical choice may be usefully reconsidered for a moment.

The stylistic choices (which I am calling *metrical,* rather than *rhythmic*)[3] occur at a different level of decision-making from those of mysterious choices which must occur in actual composition. (This remains true, I think, even though the poet himself could not or would not differentiate between the types of choice.) The metrical choice provides a basic schematic fabric of contingencies governing the range of expressive effect. But it also establishes a kind of frame around the work as a whole. Like a title, it indicates how it is to be taken, what sort of thing the poem is supposed to be, and, perhaps, taken in historical context, what the poet thought he was doing by calling his curious bit of language a poem at all.

2. Northrop Frye, "Toward Defining an Age of Sensibility," in *Fables of Identity* (New York, 1963), pp. 132-34.
3. I have discussed this at greater length in Chapter VII.

But there are some cases in English literary history where a poet does seem to acknowledge the importance of metrical choice. One with which we are probably all familiar is that of the prose apology prefaced to *Paradise Lost*. In it, Milton defends his choice of blank verse as a measure for the poem, and seems to allow his selected meter to stand emblematically for the entire mode of language of his epic. He never touches upon his Latinate syntax, reinterpretation of the use and structure of epic simile and so forth, and only in the poem itself does he deal with his choice of subject or his myth of the poem's origins. The metrical mode is there, we are told, both a fabric and a frame for what will be worked within it.

Now we know that Milton, even more than most learned writers of the seventeenth century, was acutely aware of the Classical notion of musical modality. Although unable to understand its empirical bases, Renaissance and later Neoclassicism often took as a modal notion of style this canonical correspondence in Greek music between each type of musical scale and its particular *ethos* or persuasive quality. One knew from Plato alone, who admitted to or excluded from his Just City certain scales because of their necessary effects upon a listener, that the Dorian scale was considered vigorous and manly, the Lydian, relaxing, the Phrygian, wild, etc.

The relation of a mode or scale to its particular *ethos* was held to be as fixed as that of a word to its meaning. Thinkers since the Renaissance have looked in vain for some necessary, unwavering connection between melodic contours and feelings generated by their perception; the association between musical mode and human mood remained one that was maintained by convention alone. The words of the poetic text to which the melody was sung, we must remember, gave to the melody's succession of intervals its duration and accent: the meter gave to the pitches half of what we would call its melodic quality. The meaning of the text, its form and poetic occasion seem to have been the decisive factors in maintaining the convention of *ethos*.[4]

There are good grounds for suspecting that Greek thinkers them-

---

4. Also see my *The Untuning of the Sky* (Princeton, 1961), pp. 206-20, and the remarks on modality in the previous chapter.

selves believed that modality had its affective consequences for human behavior because of connections established by nature rather than by convention. In any event, successive ages would conclude, from their experience of Classical theoretic and mythological writings only, that music and poetry in antiquity had been mysteriously wed, and that subsequent literary history was a record of their divorce. Moreover, it was easy to move from the close connection of mode and mood in music to an analogical correspondence, longingly pursued by the Renaissance, of meter, diction, image, subject, presentation or performance style, and occasion. Certainly Alexandrian literature contained the modern notion of the literary occasion per se (rather than the public ones of the theater, ritual ceremony, games, formal inscription, etc.). And in any event, what had been for Classical Greek poets canonical metrical uses became for Roman ones a matter of choice, a choice personal and in its own way expressive.

The very idea of literature is in some senses based upon an extension of this notion of modality. Even in Latin poetry, where we see the beginning of the dislocation of stylistic genre from its original context in Greek life, there emerges the phenomenon of metrical forms beginning to take on a life of their own, and something very like a kind of *ethos* developing for them. As early as Longinus, we see hexameters being praised as the proper meter for epic because of their stirring manly qualities, rather than the other way around.[5] A Roman poet will imitate a Greek metrical form, sometimes for an analogous type of poem and sometimes not; but in any case the form constitutes a kind of badge of literary authenticity. We are faced, quite early in the history of Western literature, with the problem of metrical genre and its relation to individual intention and the history of style in general.

Of the genres of Greek poetry, all clearly differentiated by form, occasion, musical accompaniment, and presentation style, as well as by context, only comedy, tragedy, epic, and lyric have in any way been transmitted to successive cultural epochs. Distinctions among various types of solo and choral lyric, dithyrambic, iambic, and elegiac poetry

5. Pseudo-Longinus, *On the Sublime,* tr. W. Hamilton Fyfe, XXXIX, Loeb edition, 4. See also Chapter VIII.

became blurred even in Latin poetry, and traditional forms began to be used for different purposes. The modern theories of genre propounded by literary historians tend, as René Wellek has observed, to treat literary types as something very like political or social institutions, preserving either form or content, but not both, throughout changing historical contexts.[6] Studies of genre may concentrate upon form or underlying strand of content; their classification may be modeled either on taxonomy or on embryology, or, as we might say, on either a synchronic or diachronic linguistic approach. Hobbes's famous tripartite distinction in his letter to Davenant divided the world of human affairs into three realms, court, city, and country, and suggested that to each of these there corresponded tragedy and epic (courtly), comedy and satire (urban), and pastoral (rural);[7] this association is full of historical mistakes (about pastoral, for example) if taken as a genetic approach. But it seems to anticipate certain strains in modern criticism both by taking very seriously the concept of literary occasion and by establishing a kind of central mythic pattern within which genres may be said to have a kind of analogically general significance (as in the critical theory of Northrop Frye).

Meter has always remained a curiously strong indication or emblem of genre. Whether or not a seventeenth-century writer like Milton might choose to use the names of the Greek musical modes metaphorically to describe a general shift of poetic style (or even use the word "monody" in such an extended sense in the subtitle of "Lycidas"), he would certainly tend to think of the meter of a particular poem in a frame of previous ancient and modern use. And although the stylistic connotations of certain metrical schemes from the early sixteenth through the late eighteenth centuries in England may be seen, from a historical point of view, to have been rather grotesquely acquired, it nevertheless remains true that during that period, English poetry is written in a framework of canonical metrical style; innovation and in-

---

6. See René Wellek and Austin Warren, *Theory of Literature* (New York, 1949), pp. 235-47.
7. In *Critical Essays of the XVIIth Century*, ed. J. E. Spingarn (New York, 1908), Vol. I, pp. 54-55.

dividual invention tend usually to consist of a unique rhythmic style, using and interpreting the underlying formal fabric of the meter.

Milton's defense of his blank verse, against the expectation, for example, that he might, like Sylvester in his translation of Du Bartas, use couplets, is addressed then to those who might feel he was inventing the *use of* a meter, a subject and genre and occasion for a particular formal pattern so wrenched away from previous traditions of use that it might be said to be actually a new meter. But let us look for a moment at some particularly perceptive remarks on meter, also produced in the course of stylistic polemic, nearly 150 years after Milton. They represent at the same time an unusually clear understanding about just this question of genre being entailed by meter, and an eventual refusal to consider meter as being too important in itself.

"It is supposed that by the act of writing in verse an author makes a formal engagement that he will gratify certain known habits of association; that he not only thus apprises the reader that certain classes of ideas and expressions will be found in his book, but that others will be carefully excluded. This exponent or symbol held forth by metrical language must in different eras of literature have excited very different expectations: for example in the age of Catullus, Terence and Lucretius, and that of Statius or Claudian; and in our own country, in the Age of Shakespeare and Beaumont and Fletcher, and that of Donne and Cowley, or Dryden, or Pope. I will not take upon me to determine the exact import of the promise which, by the act of writing in verse, an author in the present day makes to his reader; but it will undoubtedly appear to many persons that I have not fulfilled the terms of an engagement thus voluntarily contracted."

This is Wordsworth, writing in the 1800 Preface to *Lyrical Ballads*.[8] In the 1802 Appendix to the Preface, he again says of the "unusual" language of poetry: "In process of time metre became a symbol or promise of this unusual language." Wordsworth's concern here, of course, is not with type or style of meter, just as he gives no indication of even a trivial Neoclassical interest in poetic genre. His problem was

8. Text from *Wordsworth's Literary Criticism*, ed. Nowell C. Smith (London, 1905), pp. 12-13.

to defend an attitude about poetic diction, and his discussion of poetic language comes down to that matter almost immediately. Still, the sense that a meter as distinguished from a prose format does represent a kind of contract, involving "certain known habits of association," is a keen and sure one. It is interesting to find a poet dealing with the question of meter from the point of view of a choice conditioned by variables of expectation on the part of an audience—a modern literary-historical concept, in short, of convention.

Coleridge, in his revision of Wordsworth's remarks in *Biographia Literaria*, goes on to assert the contractual basis of metrical choice quite unequivocally, albeit in connection with some additional concerns of his own. Discussing "the interpenetration of passion and will, of *spontaneous* impulse and *voluntary* purpose" (in which, incidentally, our two domains of the metrical and the rhythmic might be said to operate), he remarks of the union of the two: "It not only dictates, but of itself tends to produce, a more frequent employment of picturesque and vivifying language, than would be natural in any other case, in which there did not exist, as there does in the present, a previous and well-understood, though tacit, *compact* between the poet and his reader, that the latter is entitled to expect, and the former bound to supply, this species and degree of pleasurable excitement."[9]

Insofar as the early Romantics considered the question of the effect of rhythm at all, it was a matter eliciting feeling or giving pleasure; here is Wordsworth again, from the 1800 Preface: "Now the music of harmonious metrical language, the sense of difficulty overcome, and the blind association of pleasure which has been previously received from works of rhyme or meter of the same or similar construction, an indistinct perception perpetually renewed of language closely resembling that of real life, and yet, in the circumstance of meter differing from it so widely—all these imperceptibles make up a complex feeling of delight, which is of the most important use in tempering the painful feeling always found intermingled with powerful descriptions of the deeper passions." "The sense of difficulty overcome," of course, is more that of the poet than of the reader, who in a sense shares the poet's

9. *B.L.*, ed. Shawcross, Vol. II, p. 50.

feeling through sympathy if he has it at all. This is a theme which becomes more and more important in the informal metrical remarks of twentieth-century poets; we can see it in Frost's likening free verse to playing tennis without a net, or in Valéry's famous prescription: "The exigencies of a strict prosody constitute the artifice which bestows upon natural speech the qualities of an unyielding material, foreign to our spirit, and almost deaf to our desires. If they were not a bit mad, and if they did not encourage our rebellion, they would be basically absurd."[10] Again, we can see a touch of this notion in Coleridge's remark on the origin of meter (although "origin" is used in an extremely peculiar sense): "This I would trace to the balance in the mind effected by that spontaneous effort which strives to hold in check the workings of passion. It might be easily explained likewise in what manner this salutary antagonism is assisted by the very state, which it counteracts; and how this balance of antagonists became organized into *metre* (in the usual acceptation of that term) by a supervening act of the will and judgement, consciously and for the foreseen purpose of pleasure."[11] But Coleridge, like Wordsworth, goes on to talk about poetic diction, which is far more important to his concerns at the moment.

Here, then, is the notion of the metrical contract. For Wordsworth it covers only the commitment engendered by writing verse rather than prose; but what I have been pointing out as the framing or defining function of a particular metrical choice extends the idea of the contract to cover the choice among various metrical possibilities. Wordsworth and Coleridge would dismiss meter as a criterion for the poetic character of an utterance. But unless we are judging or being polemical, I think we must take the fact of verse form as an indication that the writer feels he has written a poem—whatever he may mean by that— and expects it to be recognized as such.

In a sense, they are both struggling against "the tendency of metre to divest language, in a certain degree, of its reality," as Wordsworth

10. Paul Valéry, "Au Sujet d'Adonis," in *Varieté* (Paris, 1924), p. 70 (my translation).
11. *B.L.*, ed. cit., Vol. II, p. 50.

put it in the Preface:[12] for both of them, there is a disposition to regard metrical structure as an element *added to* potentially poetic language. Thus Wordsworth, in discussing the process of "selection" from among human utterances in order to distinguish poetic language from mere speech, adds that "if metre be superadded thereto," the distinction will have been made complete. For Coleridge, chemical images presented themselves, whether of "yeast, worthless or disagreeable by itself, but giving vivacity and spirit to the liquor with which it is traditionally combined," or of something more like the modern notion of catalysis for which perhaps he was groping: "Metre therefore having been connected with *poetry* most often and by a peculiar fitness, whatever else is combined with *metre* must, though it be not itself *essentially* poetic, have nevertheless some property in common with poetry, as an intermedium of affinity, a sort (if I may dare borrow a well-known phrase from technical chemistry) of *mordaunt* between it and the super-added metre."[13]

This aspect of the metrical contract, the choice of a particular style, did not interest the Romantics very much. They attended to it at the pragmatic level, and their actual choices and inventions had far-reaching effects. Even so, Wordsworth, in the first of his remarks quoted, realizes that different historical epochs embody various accepted styles of meter, with various modal significances which serve as the unstated terms against which the contract is drawn. (I am ignoring for the moment Blake's marginalia on Wordsworth's remarks: "I do not know who wrote these Prefaces, they are very mischievous & direct contrary to Wordsworth's own practise.") The real difficulty here comes from the fact that every canonical style has evolved from an earlier one, and that the metrical forms take on new modal significances with each new use, and with different sorts of awareness of past ones. Perhaps the test of the canonical status of a metrical mode is the inability of anyone working within its range and age of power to see that it rules not by divine right but, as Milton's Satan said of God, by convention.

Metrical traditions in English have evolved, however. Aside from

12. *Wordsworth's Literary Criticism*, p. 31.
13. *B.L.*, Vol. II, p. 55.

the metrical crises—Whitman, Hopkins, twentieth-century free verse—that underline dramatically the drawing up of a new contract, there remains the long history of the so-called iambic tradition itself. As opposed to these crises, the milder variations of metrical evolution occur within the boundaries of a particular system. Even the briefest sketch of the normative pattern of accentual-syllabic verse in English shows that, time and again, certain formal patterns within the system have become displaced from previous sorts of usage and adapted to new ones. In the centuries before Chaucer, English had replaced the pure accentualism of Germanic verse with the fairly regular tendency, in octosyllabic lines borrowed from the French romance, to alternate stressed and unstressed syllables; it was Chaucer's stroke of invention to see this system as capable of embracing an adaptation of the Italian *endecasillabo*, which, because of the invariable placement of a final /e/ at the end of the line, regularized itself into the pentameter line of English verse. Chaucer's adaptation, it must be remembered, was made not to preserve a form for its own, or for some symbolic sake, but in order to write in a genre that had previously existed only in other languages—Italian and French. The *Canterbury Tales* contain examples of many genres and types of medieval storytelling; most of them usually appeared in English in completely different metrical clothing from Chaucer's pentameter couplets (octosyllabics, for the most part). But his triumph of accomplishment depends in some part on his having seized upon one style for his over-all voice in the poem: such a choice is always basic to the conception of literary, or, as C. S. Lewis called it, *secondary* epic.

In the century after Chaucer, however, we begin to see instances of metrical evolution through utter formal dislocation, occasioned by an interest in practicing a particular form without regard to any of its significance as an emblem of literary type. The extremely complicated stanza forms of the medieval drama in England, of the Wakefield cycle in particular, are derived from lyric poetry, where we expect in the later Middle Ages to see more complication and flexibility in stanza form than in narrative verse. Through the early Tudor morality play we see this use of a lyrical verse form for dramatic poetry continuing, and it is only odd when humanist drama, written with the eye glued to the Senecan and Plautine model, begins to enmesh actual popular theatrical conventions that the Modern use of a unilinear form for poetic drama develops. Perhaps the Modern sense of the peculiar rightness of such an association of unilinear forms with narrative and dramatic verse is the result of unavowed latent neoclassicism: it was only Greek lyric poetry, it will be remembered, which was strophic, while narrative and iambic dramatic verses were always arranged by line.

There are many other examples of metrical evolution or transfer in the sixteenth through the eighteenth centuries in England. They vary in the degree to which the new or adapted use of the metrical pattern wishes to engage prior associations—and which associations in particular—generated by other uses. The history of blank verse in English is obviously a case in point: it moves from the early dramatists, through the later ones, to Milton, through the eighteenth-century speculative poem consciously connected with Milton's spirit, through *The Prelude* and eventually toward the later Romantic lyric. The crisis here occurs with Milton; and yet it is during the eighteenth century that all poetry save for the sung lyric begins to have to confront the growth of prose as an authentic vehicle of imaginative expression. For Milton, blank verse had the virtues of a canonical poetic cadence, but by the middle of the eighteenth century, it was important that it be more like prose in some ways than rhymed verse could ever be.

Then again, there is the case of the preservation of lyric stanza forms over the categorical change in genre from the Elizabethan to the metaphysical lyric. The Elizabethan lyric poem is a song text per se; it may merely extend a popular or courtly convention, or it may, like the songs in Shakespeare's plays, play itself off against those conventions in order to perform the far more intense and exacting work of a kind of summarizing symbolist lyric, catching up and embodying the themes and movements of the whole play. But the metaphysical lyric, starting with Donne, is not in any essential way modeled on the song, but rather on the written text for study. Emblem verses, patristic writings, and other theological disputation, natural philosophy, all lie behind Donne's *Songs and Sonnets,* with the additional complication that each poem generates its own immediate dramatic context. There is always a particular erotic situation behind the rhetorical one of every poem, and the relation behind the lyric ego and the "you" is quite complex. It is as if the stylized Petrarchan lover, the "I" of the sonnet tradition, had suddenly acquired real knowledge instead of lore, and real feelings in place of gesture. But Donne and his followers invariably employ the variety of line and strophe forms used by the Elizabethan lyric, wherein a density of formal texture is compensated for by an attenuation of semantic and iconographic complexity—they can be comprehended upon hearing, or rapid reading, for the most part. The metaphysical lyric is to be read and studied and considered, and the over-all formal shape of the poem is often at ironic odds with the cognitive density of the thought and language. But the effect of the maintenance of the song forms, of the name "song" for poem, is the literary justification for the new departure, and the justification is based, as it is so often, upon the authority supplied by continuity itself.

The Romantic reinterpretation of sonnet form is another case in point. More revealing for literary history than the eighteenth-century restorations of the sonnet by Warton, Thomas Russell, or even by Bowles, is Wordsworth's reconstitution of the form, as a total lyric mode, in the essentiality of its Miltonic type. Wordsworth's sense of the implications of the form as resulting from its being short, binding, and historically complex is well-known through the "sonnets on the sonnet"; the heart of the question, however, lies in the form as representing a fit instrument for the "soul-animating strains" of Milton's strong, self-contained bursts of utterance, an eloquence too complete to display its structure. In a letter to Dyce in 1833, he puts quite clearly the central, pregnant formal difference between the Elizabethan and the Miltonic types: "Instead of looking at this composition as a piece of architecture, making a whole out of three parts, I have been much in the habit of preferring the image of an orbicular body—a sphere—or a dew drop."[14] It is, in fact, by virtue of its providing a

14. See *Poetical Works*, ed. E. de Sélincourt (Oxford, 1946), Vol. III, p. 417, for a letter, also, to Landor, on 20 April 1822. Also for some valuable reminiscences on the sonnet, Christopher Wordsworth, *Memoir of William Wordsworth* (London, 1841), p. 277.

rounded period, not unlike a blank verse paragraph in that the rhymes do not force logical and rhetorical units, that it serves Wordsworth so well. And it is finally, the rhetorical model of Milton's invocations, prophecies, and confessions, rather than that of the more meditative or painterly sonnets in the eighteenth century, that helped him to shape his own. It is almost safe to say that despite his archaeological interests in Shakespeare's sonnets, it was Milton alone whom Wordsworth's sonnet writing was, in a peculiar formal sense, about.

The concept of elegy in English, insofar as it involves purely metrical matters, is an interesting one too. The genre is metrically defined by Neoclassical poetry, and entails a longish poem in couplets, often indistinguishable from the sort of poem called a satire in the seventeenth century, as well as from the verse epistle imitated also from the Latin poets. It is only toward the end of the eighteenth century, when Gray's tranquilly recollected quatrains, or Cowper's hippity-hop anapests in "The Poplar-Field," define for Romanticism and ever after the elegiac tone as a mood rather than as a formal mode:

> Twelve years have elaps'd since I first took a view
> Of my favorite field and the bank where they grew;
> And now in the grass behold they are laid,
> And the tree is my seat that once lent me a shade.

would have served, in the seventeenth century, as the proper meter in which to frame a coyly erotic lyric; in the earlier eighteenth century, they would have violated the voice of seriousness. But for Cowper, the form of these lines stands for the emotional authenticity of the personal. It is the meter alone which is significant here, by the way, for the parallelism of syntactic and rhetorical structure is firmly in the eighteenth-century tradition.

Cowper's "elegiac" use of the anapestic tetrameter, incidentally, has interesting consequences for Romantic prosodic practice. It echoes more than faintly through Blake's distortion of it in the dimeters of "The Echoing Green." Wordsworth employs it, most successfully in "The Reverie of Poor Susan," but also in the overly willed attentiveness to the city fiddler in "The Power of Music"; "The Two Thieves," "A

Character," "The Childless Father," and "The Farmer of Tillsbury Vale," all early, and the later "At Vallambrosa" all use the anapestic elegiac as well, whether in pairs of couplets or *abab* quatrains. "Repentance, A Pastoral Ballad" is more immediately suggestive of Cowper. The contractual effects of Cowper's version of the meter seem to have been not unconnected, for Wordsworth, with a sense of smoothness and evenness of flow, rather than with an equally justifiable sense of the meter's jumpiness and abruptness, which suited it not only to drinking songs and bawdy in earlier times, but to an alternative convention in Romantic verse. Coleridge, as well, seems to have acknowledged this smoothness: in a letter to Wordsworth in which he discusses the meter of *The White Doe of Rylstone*, he makes the distinction between meters that are "in general, rather dramatic than lyric, i.e. not such an arrangement of syllables, not such a metre, as acts a priori and with complete self-subsistence (as the simple anapestic in its smoothest form). . . ."[15]

The subsequent course of the anapestic elegiac mode is easy to trace. The Cowper-Wordsworth tradition is clearly marked in such uses of the form as John Clare's (in Grigson's edition alone, for sixteen poems); William Barnes's (in seven poems in standard English and nine in dialect); the young Shelley's (five times in the Esdaile Notebook); Darley's; and in countless song texts. These last may be as overtly minor-Wordsworthian as the "How dear to my heart are the scenes of my childhood/When found recollection presents them to view" of the grossly familiar "The Old Oaken Bucket." On the other hand, the 6/8 rhythms of the transcribed salon-versions of many Scotch and Irish melodies seemed frequently to call for texts in this meter, such as Burns's words to "Afton Water." The irrepressible Thomas Moore also presents a case in point, with no less than fifty-four elegiac anapestic poems throughout his works, from the *Irish Melodies* to pieces set into *Lalla Rookh*. On the other hand, Moore, who could not be accused of much direct Wordsworthian influence, uses the same anapestic tetrameter almost twice as often in the alternative modality. Ninety-seven of

15. See E. K. Chambers, *Samuel Taylor Coleridge, a Biographical Study* (Oxford, 1938), p. 35.

his satiric and comical poems are written in it; *The Fudge Family*, and comic poems by Hunt and Landor, undoubtedly contribute to the use of the form in subsequent society verse (James Russell Lowell comes immediately to mind here). The two different modalities of the anapestic four-stressed line, in fact, tend to make us forget that the words of "The Star-Spangled Banner," on the one hand (on the model of its originally bibulous eighteenth-century melody), and the blank verses parodying Persian poetry in the standard English translation of *Vathek* (unrhymed so as to give the effect of Oriental translationese verse, perhaps) on the other, share the same verse form.

The specifically discontinuous quality of the rhythm is used by Byron in a lyric like "The Destruction of Sennacherib" for its expressive force; his rhythmic interest in the form points neither toward the elegiac nor the satiric-comic metrical modes, and this sense of expressive vigor is refined even more sharply by the selective ear of Browning for the suggestion of hoofbeats in "How They Carried the Good News from Ghent to Aix." But in general, the smooth flow and the hippity-hop, attainable rhythms in the same metrical schema, provide the bases for reflective lyric and satirical verse respectively.

All of these instances, however, represent what I have called metrical evolution within the limits of a metrical system. The emblematic character of particular forms is employed to cover the shifts in literary milieu, in a kind of eternal struggle to maintain the condition of a poem as a Platonic entity: as if a poem were a poem always, by virtue of some quintessential character which different ages may merely call by different names. Metrical form (and we have, of course, been considering the larger variations in form, line lengths, stanza forms, rhyme patterns, etc.), then, acts to define a type of poem, even a poem itself, as well as to set up formal contingencies within which some linguistic event will become a poetic one, and something literary may be said to have happened.

What, then, of the metrical crisis, where the very conditions of the metrical system seem to be questioned? What looks to be a pathological form emerges, and it appears that the contract of meter has been broken. For example, there is an interesting aspect of Christopher Smart's *Jubilate Agno:* it ought properly never to have been an eighteenth-century poem at all. Written while its author, in his late thirties, was confined in a madhouse with a degenerative psychosis from which he never fully recovered, the poem consists of 32 foolscap sheets covered with 1735 long, unmeasured lines. Lost in Smart's lifetime, it seems to have ceased to exist in its own age and come to life only in the literary bedlam of the twentieth century when the ms. was discovered and first edited in 1939. *Jubilate Agno* could really only be considered a poem in our time, for its methodical madness, prophetic bursts of energy, obsessive learning, and almost symbolist associative coherence could only be read as a realized poem by an audience with the Romantics, Whitman, and Pound's *Cantos* behind it.

Smart's meter in the poem is aggressively Hebraic. Not only is it conditioned by the language of the English Bible, but by the cadences of the actual Hebrew which Smart knew. The verses are all self-contained and end-stopped, and the most recent edition[16] suggests that many of them may have been written antiphonally, in pairs. They all exhibit intralinear or line-to-line parallelism. The actual rhythm of these lines is exceedingly complicated and various, and to describe it would entail an involved analysis of syntax, classical and biblical references, interlingual puns, and the like, as well as some consideration of the rhythmic effects of lists and catalogues, acrostic sections, balancing of symbolic allusion and autobiographical detail, and other rhetorical devices. Representing a complete break with accentual-syllabism in English, Smart's meter had no immediate results. Had the poem been made public in its time, it would have been dismissed as lunatic ravings; by the time it was discovered, it could begin to be read with recognition.

Jubilate Agno, historically speaking, is an encapsulated event. For the modern notion of a personal meter that flows, like rhetoric, like personality, from the source of the self, we must turn to the specialized consequences of Romanticism in Whitman and Hopkins. In both cases,

16. *Jubilate Agno,* ed. W. H. Bond (London, 1954).

a new type of metrical contract is being drawn, in which the commitment is made not to convention, but to the poetic self. For both poets, the terms of the metrical contract become the bases of a whole aesthetic, but in radically different ways. Hopkins's constant allegorization of metrical terms like "stress" and his very clear historical commitment to what he feels are "inner" and underlying prosodic traditions —Old English, Celtic—are in one sense a far cry from the myth of organic form in Whitman. When Whitman says: "I and mine do not convince by arguments, similes, rhymes,/We convince by our presence," he is insisting that readers recognize his attempt to finesse all the framing, formal implications of meter which I have been discussing. In a prose passage,[17] he is even more explicit about his verse: "Its analogy is *the Ocean* . . . the liquid, billowy waves, ever rising and falling, perhaps wild with storm, always moving, always alike in their nature as rolling waves, but hardly any two exactly alike in size or measure, never having the sense of something finished and fixed, always suggesting something beyond." In our terms, it might be said that Whitman is claiming to have made a metrical principle out of the unique shapes of rhythm. The actual constituents of his metrical style are syntactic; his invariably end-stopped lines are connected by parallelisms, expansions of sentence matrices, types of catalogue, and so forth, and the interactions of recognizable stress pattern with these syntactic formulae are frequently reminiscent of the prophetic and lyric sections of the English Bible. But his claim nevertheless remains that expression takes on natural form from the self that releases it.

The study of metrical choice in the eclectic twentieth century must start from these two crucial breaks with tradition. But much of their avowed intention to allow an idiosyncratic meter almost to stand for an aesthetic manifesto is foreshadowed earlier, not by Smart's acsthetically unavowed poem, not by Milton's thundering choice of what had been a dramatic meter for his epic one, but by the very problematic metrical invention of William Blake.

Blake's metrical contract has deceived some of his most sympathetic

---

17. See Horace Traubel, *With Walt Whitman in Camden* (Boston, 1906), Vol. I, p. 414. The whole paragraph is reprinted below, p. 231.

readers.[18] Swinburne, for example, spoke of "an exquisite and lyrical excellence of form, when the subject is well in keeping with the poet's tone of spirit" as characterizing the verse of both Blake and Whitman, and he is constantly treating Blake's long lines as if they were the undulant outpourings of the other poet. In short, he was able to take the meter of, for example, *Jerusalem* and consider it as an example of what I have been calling a crisis. But it surely represents within Blake's own development a carefully and even systematically evolved style. Even the barest outlines of this development reveal an astonishingly consistent attempt to evolve a whole metrical system to serve as an alternative to the normal one, emblematic of the profoundly systematic undertaking of the engraved canon of Blake's works.

In the *Poetical Sketches*, the move toward freer accentualism than one would find in, say, Collins, is perhaps even less significant than the atmosphere of real experimentation that prevails. There seems to be a conscious formal perversity to the Spenserian imitation, for example, in which every stanza is "defective" if taken from one point of view, or "adapted" if from another. There are startling enjambments that quite exceed some of Donne's in his *Satyres*. In the closing strophe of "To Summer," he writes blank verse as perfectly end-stopped as that of the Elizabethan "drab" style, and in the conclusion of "To Winter," he will appear to employ not merely a different mode, but a different system. In any event, the two poems represent considerably different versions of what iambic pentameter is to be. What emerges from this experimentation is, of course, a commitment to a traditional-sounding accentualism. There are overtones of balladry in the freely accentual stanzas of the short poems from the manuscripts and from the *Songs of Innocence and of Experience*, but this is inevitable in such cases. Just as "free verse" in English so often turns out to be a version of the English

---

18. I am grateful to Professor L. C. Knights for calling my attention to Jack Lindsay's sensitive and powerful "The Metric of William Blake," prefaced to the Scholartis Press edition of *Poetical Sketches* (London, 1927). He is sensitive to the essence of Blake's struggle with the Miltonic epic line, but keeps reading undue invention and improvisation into the long line of the so-called prophetic books. Alicia Ostriker's *Vision and Verse in William Blake* (Madison, Wis., 1965) also largely ignores the metrical dimension as opposed to the rhythmic one.

Bible (or, in the twentieth century, to be modeled on line-for-line prose translations of the classics), loosely handled rhymed quatrains will smack of popular poetry, particularly when there is a dactylic flavor to them.

The pure fourteeners of "Holy Thursday" are rhymed and are among the most syllabically regular of all the verses in *Songs of Innocence*. These are probably Blake's first production[19] in a meter which is to become profoundly important for him later on. The unrhymed fourteeners of *The Book of Thel* and *Tiriel*, still quite regular in their alternations of stressed and unstressed syllables, present no problems to the prosodist or to the critic. It is only what Blake was to make of his inherited line that became problematic.

The fourteener in English verse had been the meter of Chapman, Phaer, Golding, and Warner's *Albion's England*. Moreover, fourteeners in couplets are merely an alternate way of notating ballad stanzas, and their use in broadsides, Leveller verses, and other popular and even sub-literary verse continued through Blake's own day. For Blake to use the strict, unrhymed fourteener as the basis for further expansion and modulation of a metrical style is more than merely an unfettering of poetry by enlarging its cell to the size of a long line. It seems to result from a positive attempt to create an anti-meter, as opposed to the norm of blank verse. Just as the iambic pentameter had crowded out the late Elizabethan experiments in seven-stressed lines, consigning them to the sub-literary dungeon of doggerel, so Blake may have thought to resurrect them and some of what they stood for. His attempts to undermine metrical conventions are present everywhere in his shorter poems. The last two lines of "The Garden of Love," for example, break the expected conclusion of what begins like a sentimental song in quatrains, and thunder out in a little sub-quatrain of their own, with the epigrammatic tension of the kind of inscription or motto Blake uses elsewhere. "The Question Answered" is an anti-epigram:

> What is it men in women do require?
> The lineaments of gratified desire.

19. It predates the version in *Songs of Innocence*, appearing first in *An Island in the Moon*.

What is it women do in men require?
The lineaments of gratified desire.

The whole Augustan tradition of the two-couplet epigram is undermined by the unyielding hammered insistence of the repeated line and the ironic absence of wit. The reader is implicitly rebuked for expecting a logical movement toward the discovery of a conclusion—as if all epigrams were merely circular, just as logical proofs produce only new tautologies—and the form plunges us into the identity without remorse. It is not surprising, then, to find one of Blake's most explicit anti-epigrams couched in a couplet of fourteeners: "Her whole Life is an Epigram, smart smooth & neatly pen'd,/Platted quite neat to catch applause with a sliding noose at the end." Epigrammatic tautology, for Blake, seems to be a kind of death.

Blake's subversion of English meter proceeds through his modulation of the strict fourteener in the later long poems. In the puzzling, longer, still early lines of "The French Revolution," an accentual seven-stressed core remains, the number of syllables varying from fifteen to more than twenty-one or twenty-two within a group of five or six lines. After this rather peculiar poem, Blake evidently decided that his modulation of the septenarius lay not in the direction of free-accentual expansion, and in the subsequent longer poems we see him adapting the basic line in forms analogous to those of normative meter. His stanza forms in *Europe*, in Nights 2 and 5 of *Vala*, and various staves of three, four, and five lines in other poems, even the enigmatic short lines in *Ahania*, *Los*, and *Urizen* (where it has been suggested that the engraving called for longer, thinner columns)[20] involve combinations and units of four and three stresses—the relation of Blake's meters to traditional iambic lines of varying length are like that of a duodecimal modulo number system to a decimal one.

The rhythmic possibilities established by the fourteener are interesting, for the tendency of the familiar ballad rhythm to intrude on the ears of the reader allows for frequent syntactic juncture after the

---

20. By George Saintsbury in *A History of English Prosody* (London, 1910), Vol. III, p. 26.

fourth stress. Blake's rhythmic derivations from Ossian and from the English Bible, which have been so frequently commented upon, often involve structural parallelism hung across such a juncture—again, an underground substitute for the balance and antithesis of Augustan verse. But Blake never completely surrenders to the Whitmanesque program of claiming that rhythm is its own meter. At first glance, the metrical apology prefaced to *Jerusalem* suggests this, in terms clearly implying an alternative to the apology to *Paradise Lost:*

> Of the measure in which
> the following poem is written.
>
> . . . When this Verse was first dictated to me, I consider'd a Monotonous Cadence, like that used by Milton & Shakespeare & all writers of English Blank Verse, derived from the modern bondage of Rhyming, to be a necessary and indispensible part of Verse. But I soon found that in the mouth of a true Orator such monotony was not only awkward, but as much a bondage as rhyme itself. I therefore have produced a variety in every line, both of cadences & of number of syllables. Every word and every letter is studied and put into its fit place; the terrific numbers are reserved for the terrific parts, the mild & gentle for the mild & gentle parts, and the prosaic for inferior parts; all are necessary to each other. Poetry Fetter'd Fetters the Human Race. Nations are Destroy'd or Flourish in proportion as Their Poetry, Painting and Music are Destroy'd or Flourish! The Primeval State of Man was Wisdom, Art and Science.

Blake is suggesting here a kind of traditional modality of meter, albeit in the guise of a declaration of rhythmic independence. It would be the expressive rhythms that would be fettered for him in a "Monotonous Cadence." What he in fact does in *Jerusalem* is to extend the loosening of the fourteener in several directions, from regular to loose, from syllabic fourteeners with only five or six major stresses to cluttered ones of eight. He frequently enjambs lines in ways that he had done previously only in the blank verse of the *Poetical Sketches,* allowing a mono- or di-syllabic word at the line break to count for a strong stress, even though the principle of his free accentualism throughout his work has been to let speech stress, in its syntactic and rhetorical context, govern the metrical role of syllables.

As for his rhythmic modes of mild, terrific, and prosaic, it is obvious from the text that the key is provided not by the measure of syllable or stress, nor by some referential rhythmic pattern alone, but by the diction. In some ways, Blake's sense of meter here is closer to the concerns of Wordsworth than one might think. But throughout the poem, the fourteener is never far away, and the poem's meter is most like a transformed equivalent of the freest kind of blank verse. Were the norm to have been five stresses rather than seven, there would never have been as much puzzling about Blake's meter as there has been.

Among all the Romantics, then, Blake's meter is perhaps the most programmatic, and perhaps the most paradigmatically contractual. His evolved metrical style results not from a nihilistic smashing of metrical conventions in order to free an oppressed rhythm (he is not Whitman), but rather to use metrical choices in the way in which certain twentieth-century poets, historically self-conscious, have used them: to engage certain prior conventions, and, rejecting others, to form a new tradition, discontinuous in some ways as it might be. His contract was, in a way, with the Devil's party which, he felt, Milton finally betrayed, "though sublime/In Number, Weight and Measure," as Marvell had put it. But echoing the same text in his *Proverbs of Hell*, Blake was engaging the literal sense of poetic "numbers" as well as conceptual ones: "Bring out number, weight & measure in a year of dearth," he half-snarls, and we can perhaps too easily leap from what we think Blake's intentions might be to the unfetterings of a Whitman, or even beyond, to some kind of transcendence of the very ways in which intense language controls its own shape. But in that realm there is never plenitude. For art, the task is always "What to make of a diminished thing." Blake could no more have abandoned numbers entirely than he could have dispensed with, say, the containing power of line over color in his graphics.

Blake's metrical practice typifies Romantic critical thought generally in its ability to resist the actual linguistic analysis of metrical schemata and rhythmic processes which so plagued eighteenth-century prosodic theorists.[21] At one point, Coleridge accuses Wordsworth of evading this same issue, and yet he is himself able to come up with only one example, and that a crude and obvious one, of the more elementary operations of rhythmic modality: "The discussion on the powers of metre in the preface," he says, "is highly ingenious and touches at all points on truth. But I cannot find any statement of its powers considered absolutely and separately. On the contrary, Mr. Wordsworth seems always to estimate metre by the powers, which it exerts during (and, as I think, in *consequence of*) its combination with other elements of poetry. Thus the previous difficulty is left unanswered, *what* the elements are, with which it must be combined in order to produce its own effects to any pleasurable purpose. Double and tri-syllable rhythms, indeed, form a lower species of wit, and attended to exclusively for their own sake, may become a source of moderate amusement. . . ." Coleridge is no doubt right about the *"in consequence of,"* as the most sophisticated modern linguistic studies of poetic language are showing. In his own thoughts on metrical matters, Coleridge is most concerned with such questions as getting the German versions of Greek meters into English, and so forth, the kind of thing that occupied Southey and Landor as well. A tantalizing fragment from an earlyish notebook[22] seems to indicate an awareness on Coleridge's part of the problems that result from thinking of a meter as something "super-added": "Metre distinct and artificial—till at length poetry forgot its existence in those forms which

---

21. Southey, for one, ventures deeper into these waters than one might have supposed. He is naturally concerned to defend the English adaptation of the German stressed hexameter which he used so skillfully in the otherwise ill-fated *A Vision of Judgment*. Although as confused in his terminology (in such concepts as "accent" and "emphasis") as any eighteenth-century prosodist, he nevertheless shows some sophistication in grasping the notion of phrase stress. See *Poetical Works* (London, 1838), Vol. X, pp. 198 f. Southey is perceptive in other ways as well; in discussing the complicated stanza-form of *Thalaba*, he correctly observes, *op. cit.* p. 199, that his variations of line length are bound to commit him to monosyllables in English unlike German and Latin (a phenomenon the present author observed in the development of the double dactyl). He observes that "the English greatly exceeds the ancient one in literal length," so that, given typographical conventions, it gets too long for the page. He sees this, perhaps rightly, as causing the break-up of the fourteener couplet into the ballad stanza, claiming that "that fine measure of the Elizabethan age" thereby suffered "diminution of its powers."
22. *Notebook*, ed. K. Coburn (New York, 1957), Vol. I, note 786.

were only hieroglyphics of it." Yes; but whether he really means this to be true of phylogeny or ontogeny, of poetic process in literary history or internalized creation, we cannot be sure.

Romantic metrical theory, as informal a body of thought as it is, finally avows the emblematic, framing, defining role of metrical format as consistently as does that of Whitman, Hopkins, or some of the poets of our own day. Even more clearly, perhaps, the stylistic revolutions of English Romantic poetry which look forward to the intent, if not the methods, of some of the manifestoes of its devouring offspring, Modernism, can be fully understood only in the light of the programs of meter, the wisely schooled heart of poetry, as well as the profuse strains of actual rhythmic instances.

X
"HADDOCKS' EYES":
A NOTE ON THE THEORY OF TITLES

In Book III of the *Aeneid,* Aeneas recounts how he and his men arrived at Leucata and how he took a brazen shield formerly belonging to the Greek Abas and fixed it to the entrance pillars, and marked the event with a poem (*"postibus adversis figo et rem carmine signo"*). The poem, or inscription, is a single line: AENEAS HAEC DE DANAIS VICTORIBUS ARMA ("These arms Aeneas took from conquering Greeks"). Ben Jonson, seizing on one meaning of *"carmen,"* remarks in his *Discoveries*[1] that the verse in question is a one-line poem, arguing that "Aeneas calls it a Poeme, or *Carmen*" which makes it so. Jonson's point is one that he would never, in all probability, have allowed to operate generally, namely, that calling an utterance or inscription a poem makes it one. A totally eclectic world of artistic style and form like our own, self-righteously wary of persuasive or stipulative definitions of "art," of "poetry," or of any genres of these, must nonetheless start from just such a premise. Although it has been frequently observed that titles of Modern poems, for example, while apparently perverse, are frequently of great importance, no general theory of titles and titling has ever been propounded. Borgesian joking about how, by a mad affirmation of synecdoche, a list of titles might constitute the ultimate library, is

---

1. *Timber, or Discoveries,* in *Works,* ed. Herford and Simpson (Oxford, 1947), p. 635. The Virgilian lines are III, 287-88.

about all we have. Nevertheless, the crucial functions of titles of literary works include a basic designative or even ontological power.

I do not mean to imply, of course, that an untitled poem or painting is not a poem or painting at all. In the first place, titles began to seem necessary in either case at a certain point in history, although once that point had been reached, it began to seem necessary that every opus in either mode should have one. Second, a maker's refusal to give a work a title itself has a covert titling function: "Untitled," "*Chant sans paroles*," "Painting No. 6, 1954," "Poem" are all easily recognizable as examples of familiar title conventions. Neither do I mean to suggest that before short poems, for example, began to be designated by what we might call analytic or expressive titles, their intended mode of existence is not to be thought of as that of the short poem per se. What I should like to do here is to consider briefly various species of titles and the different kinds of relations they bear to, and effects they exercise upon, certain literary texts. For reasons beside those of economy, I shall concentrate upon the short lyric poem.

The problem of titles shows up again, at another level, in the definition of genres. Professors Wellek and Warren, after drawing their admirable distinctions between the various classes of genre, can only conclude with the recommendation that genre ought to be "conceived as a grouping of literary works based, theoretically, upon both outer form (specific meter or structure) and also upon inner form (attitude, tone, purpose—more crudely, subject and audience)."[2] The way in which we ascribe to any literary work membership in a particular class or genre is by means of an interpretive act similar, but not identical, to the one by which we decide to call it a poem at all. The question of intention is relevant in both cases. The notion of what sort of poem a text purports to be, of what conventions it seems to engage and associate itself with, is merely a special case of what we might call the text's purporting to be a poem.

It will be readily seen that this act of calling an utterance a poem, or a poem of a specific type—an act of framing the utterance or of present-

2. René Wellek and Austin Warren, *Theory of Literature* (New York, 1949), p. 241.

ing it for a particular kind of consideration—is very much like giving it a designative subtitle. Whether it is the author of the text or some subsequent editor or scholiast who does this does not for the moment matter. What is important, however, is that a title is, or contains implicitly, a kind of statement of literary intention; and one might speculate on the ways in which titles of literary works, and particularly of short poems, seem to exercise the same kind of framing or presentational function as the use of a conventional meter in an age of canonical metrical styles may be said to do.[3]

Some of the rhetorical implications of the uses of titles seem to have been grasped, in another context, by Kenneth Burke. In discussing what he feels to be the relationship between ideas and images, he remarks that "the rhetorician uses 'titles' (either imagined or ideological) to identify a person or a cause with whatever kinds of things will, in his judgment, call forth the desired response."[4] Actually, Burke is thinking of titles in the sense of "epithets" here, and he tries to reserve for epithet a middle ground between metaphor and abstraction.

We generally employ the word "title" in several senses, of course, but it is interesting that the non-literary uses of the word shed some light on this framing aspect of the literary name. A noble or clerical title is not so much the name of the rank itself as it is an entitlement to property, powers, certain forms of address, etc., and it may be observed that a title, in this last respect at least, designates or at least directs certain forms of behavior toward its holder. So, too, the status of any work of art *qua* work of art seems to direct a special sort of attention to it. Aestheticians have at times pondered the way a useful or ordinary object can attain this status simply by direction or presentation: an ancient pot from one civilization becomes an objet d'art in the proper context of another one. The so-called "ready mades" of Dada and surrealist art or the more recent *objets trouvés* become works of art by being *so named* (almost like racehorses, roses, and apples), *not by be-*

---

3. For the titling, labeling, or framing aspects of meter, see the discussion in Chapter VII. Early in the history of titles we get peculiar reversals, in the double-title format (e.g., "*Twelfth Night or What You Will*"), of title and label: "*The Spanish Tragedy or Hieronymo Mad Again*" ought, we feel, to go the other way.
4. Kenneth Burke, *A Rhetoric of Motives* (New York, 1950), p. 86

ing found or conceived of in some other frame. Anyone may "find" a text: the poet is he who names it, "Text."

This brings to mind, particularly with respect to pictures, the problem of labeling. Nelson Goodman has discussed this with great acuity in his *Languages of Art;* but in his example of a picture of a person "as" a young man, "as" President, etc., etc.,[5] he needs of necessity to avoid precisely the problem posed by the labeling of poems, and of poetical pictures (and there may be more of these than he appears to think). I am not thinking just of, say, the title (Reynolds's own) "Mrs. Siddons as the Tragic Muse"—that is a description not only of a particular picture, but a classifier of the picture in a well-established genre. It is simply that many portraits from a particular period are also by way of being emblems, and that since a museum "title" for such a picture is by way of being a heuristic label, we must conclude that many paintings from before the eighteenth century, when painters began to entitle their own works, have the wrong names.

But let us consider for a moment the functions of some particular conventions of titling a poem. We may take as a text to start with a well-known literary joke about titles. In *Through the Looking Glass,* the White Knight's reading of the parody of Wordsworth's "Resolution and Independence" is introduced by an exchange which has been frequently commented upon by logicians as an example of a set of metalanguages, in this case names, names of names, names of names of names, etc. The White Knight announces at first that

> "The name of the song is called '*Haddocks' Eyes.*'"
>
> "Oh, that's the name of the song, is it?" Alice said, trying to feel interested.
>
> "No, you don't understand," the Knight said, looking a little vexed. "That's what the name is *called*. The name really *is* '*The Aged, Aged Man.*'"
>
> "Then I ought to have said 'That's what the *song* is called?'" Alice corrected herself.
>
> "No, you oughtn't: that's quite another thing! The *song* is

---

5. Nelson Goodman, *Languages of Art* (Indianapolis, 1968), pp. 27-30. Also see the whole discussion, pp. 21-43.

called '*Ways and Means*': but that's only what it's *called*, you know!"

"Well, what *is* the song then?" said Alice, who was by this time completely bewildered.

"I was coming to that," the Knight said. "The song really *is* '*A-sitting on a Gate*': and the tune's my own invention."

While logicians might observe that there is a confusion of use and mention in the last case (the song, after all, can be only what it is, and cannot be said to *be* its name or even one of them) I should like to point out that Lewis Carroll selected his four successive titles from four quite different conventions of naming shorter poems. The first of these ("what the name of the song is called") is "*Haddocks' Eyes*," or what we might call an essential title. From the long list of the old man's improbable modes of self-employment one item is taken to stand for the whole, and the Haddocks' Eyes are a symbol of his endeavors:

> He said, "I hunt for haddocks' eyes
> Among the heather bright,
> And work them into waistcoat-buttons
> In the silent night.
> And these I do not sell for gold
> Or coin of silvery shine,
> But for a copper halfpenny
> And that will purchase nine.

This first mode of titling reflects the modern convention of plucking from a fiction—usually a short story or a Broadway drama—either the name of a symbol patently at work in it, or of a passing utterance, lit up in momentary epiphany simply by being so used, in order to entitle the work. It will be noticed that such an act of displacing can both seem to underline the significance of the name or phrase and to create some initial suspense about how and why the work was so entitled—in fact, about what the title convention indeed has been.

Let us proceed to the others. "The *name* of the song" itself, "*The Aged, Aged Man*," identifies its subject and calls more attention than do the others to the poem's narrative frame. It is, of course, a title of the same genre as "The Leech-Gatherer.'" *"Ways and Means"* ("what the song is called") underlines a topic and moralizes upon the whole confrontation in a stolidly pragmatic manner. It is rather like the running heads on the right-hand pages of Victorian novels. Even more, of course, it is like " 'Resolution and Independence.' "

Finally, *"A-Sitting on a Gate"* picks out the repeated short line that ends the poem and treats it as a kind of refrain, entitling the poem with it. It suggests that the poem is a simple, old song, so well known that it has become folklore. As always, there is method in the madness of the looking-glass world. The confusing layers of titling style may very well be aimed at satirizing the puzzling situation faced by the Victorian child when confronted with various titles, and versions of titles, given by editors, or by common reference to the same wellknown poem. (Alice, throughout both books, is constantly being menaced by improving poetry.) But Dodgson's spoof of titles, in their logical capacities as proper names and descriptions, reminds us that there do indeed exist various conventions of titling poems. It also shows that such conventions tend to urge upon us one or another reading of the poem. In this case, we are made to think successively of (1) a symbolic representation of enterprise gone mad; (2) of a Romantic encounter with a worthy "character" (in all literary and modern colloquial senses); (3) of a moral homily à la Isaac Watts; and finally (4) of a pseudo-folk or archaic lyric known only by its refrain—an old song, in fact.

In listing and classifying styles of titling short poems, certain misleadingly extreme situations should be considered at the outset. Where the author, as far as is known, does not give his poem any title at all, some other presentational device is probably being used to do the title's work. In an age of unequivocal, canonical metrical styles, for example, we have a situation where the "inner" and "outer" form differentiated by Professors Wellek and Warren will tend to coincide. Thus, in the eighteenth century in England, the form of the Horatian or the Pindaric ode would render the designation "Ode" in the title redundant, and only the topic really need be specified. As we shall see shortly, it is only in the early seventeenth century in England that the topical or what I have called the "essential" title form appears at all. Before then, it is obvious that a song-text, or a sonnet on an Italian model, for example, is a song or a sonnet; and that subject, occasion, and audience are being specified, in good measure, by the form itself. Neoclassic nostalgia for the perfect association, in ambiguity, of meter, tone, occasion, and range of subject might also be seen as a longing for a great golden age in which poems needed no titles whatsoever. Being entitled, as it were, by birth to their genre and authority, they were like an aristocracy that preceded an arriviste nobility.

At the opposite pole from the case of the poem that is, comprises, or embodies its own title, is that of the poem whose title is usually thought of as being an integral part of the work itself. This seems to be most common in post-symbolist lyrics in English; Wallace Stevens, for example, has frequently been cited as a writer whose titles function with indirection, apparent perversity, or some symbol-making quality that is characteristic of the fundamental methods of his poetry. If they direct a particular kind of attention to the poems that they head, it is much more an analytic or interpretive role that they play than more properly a genre- or type-defining one. Like the titles of many of Paul Klee's paintings, too, they seem often to add another dimension to the contextual frame in which the poem or picture is to be read. (Consider his late, heavily calligraphed oil that looks as if it had been hung on its side, despite the fact that there is no format for orientation—then we read the title which is, indeed, "Lying Down.") In general, surrealist paintings have the titles of poems, and the relation of title to picture is that of post-symbolist poem to *its* title. Although mistakenly assumed by inexperienced viewers of paintings to be intended as merely *épatant*, the relation of name to image was frequently—particularly in a major painter like René Magritte—a profound one, and, despite its obliquity, the Magritte title ultimately does serve to direct the viewer to a proper reading of the picture. Frequently an art-historical debate about the iconography of a particular Renaissance or baroque picture can be as pragmatically directed as a quarrel in the field of connoisseurship: in the second case, the decision to be made is whether to catalogue this painting as actually by Blotto Blotti or not; in the first case, it is whether this picture of a girl with a stag barely visible in the background is in fact a picture of Prudence.[6]

Perhaps the limiting case of the extremely shocking mode of titling is that of the context-providing motto to the raw pictorial core in some experimental images used by Gestalt psychologists, and later popularized in the form of the parlor game known as "Droodles," where the significance of the image itself remains ambiguous until resolved by the "title."

Between these two extremes of the completely redundant title ("Sonnet"; "Symphony in D Major," in the case of a musical work; "Allegory of Vanity," in the case of a cataloguer's name for an untitled painting), on the one hand, and titles like "Le Monocle de Mon Oncle" (or the often apparently cryptic names given to hymn-tunes in the English church) on the other, it might be possible to construct a typology of conventions of titling poems since the seventeenth century. (I am assuming here that there is a kind of "cultural lag" in conventions of titling works of music and paintings, that they have arisen by and large since the early nineteenth century, largely on the model of poem titles.) We might then distinguish among occasional descriptions (those of Marvell's "Horatian Ode," or Jonson's Cary and Morison ode, for example); topical descriptions; indications, particularly in seventeenth-century lyrics, of the subjects of meditation; Romantic pseudo-occasional headings (like that of Wordsworth's "Tintern Abbey"); and many more. Furthermore, we might order this spectrum

---

6. Picture titles are still mostly labels given by curators. Often titles which were simply tags or subject labels become hallowed and almost scriptural, e.g., Dürer's "The Great Piece of Turf," the Rembrandt "Hundred Guilder Print," etc. Again, Aristotle's *Metaphysics* was simply the scroll that came after the *Physica*. When a painter himself decides to change the title, it can be trivial (imagine an abstract expressionist of the middle nineteen-fifties changing with a shrug, "Number 4, 1954," to "Margie"). On the other hand, when Whistler retitled his 1862 picture of Jo Hiffernan, "The White Girl," as "Symphony in White, No. 1: The White Girl," he was making an aesthetic statement. It involved Paterian all-art-approaching-the-condition-of-music, allusion to Gautier's poem "Symphonie en blanc majeur" and the view that British art which rejoiced in subject matter was to be shunned. Eventually, his own repertory of abstract title forms ("Arrangement in Color X or Y," "Nocturne in W") became most influential. See also Richard Bernheimer, *The Nature of Representation* (New York, 1961), pp. 88-109; 154-202.

along the axis from redundancy to maximum informativeness set up by our two polar cases. But such a formalistic criterion for classifying titles (and here again the problem is curiously like the separation of genres) would then lead, I think, to some observations relevant to literary history as well. By and large, the increasing historical and formal and aesthetic self-consciousness of lyric poetry during the past five centuries, its developing allusiveness and its growing claims to independence first of music and then of other forms of literary discourse, are all mirrored in the historical evolution of titles.

To trace this evolution lies outside the scope of these necessarily brief remarks. We might look at the point in the literary history of the past few centuries at which the question of titles begins to have some interest for the literary theorist. While Dante's decision to entitle his poem a "Commedia" is indeed a significant one (as well as one to which he gave some thought, as we can see from his discussion of it in his letter to Can Grande), the case of the long poem, like that of the treatise whose subject is clearly labeled in a more or less formal Latin or Greek title, is a rather special one. But if we examine the titles that short lyric poems are given during the sixteenth century, we find that they are most often, like those in Tottel's Miscellany, little more than editorial glosses which have been placed at the head of the poem rather than as marginal rubrics. I think that it will be hard to find a group of short poems antedating Donne's *Songs and Sonnets* of 1633 that contains a significant number of examples of what we loosely think of as modern titling, or of what I have referred to as expressive or essential descriptions. (In the sixteenth century, tunes seem to have titles, drawn from their texts, before words do.)[7] Donne's lyrics are, of course, unique in their time as speculative-dramatic lyrics, but even Ben Jonson's metaphysical poems, of which he wrote many, are given titles only in the 1640 posthumous folio. Donne's titles seem often to bear an

---

7. This is undoubtedly because there was far more informal need to refer to them orally than there was for designating Classical poems, which were referred to by book and line numbers, opening phrases, etc. A study of the title changes of seventeenth-century song-texts in various printed and ms. sources would be instructive. One might start with Edward Doughtie's splendid notes to *Lyrics from English Airs* (Cambridge, Mass., 1970).

indirect or almost perverse relation to the poem when considered as mere labels of subject or topic. In "The Relic" and "The Canonization," for example, the object or process named in the title only becomes anything like a topic after several narrative, dramatic, and dialectical turns, and after at least one stanza. In "The Flea" or "The Good Morrow," on the other hand, the subject of the title is more immediately confronted as the subject of the poem. In "The Broken Heart," only in the last two stanzas does the emblem of the fractured organ itself become the center of attention.

It may be that the early baroque is a period which for some unexplained reason generates an interest in the purportedly sui-generis short work of art which needs a title to classify it. Relevant musical examples would show the difference between the merely labeling sort of title of short keyboard pieces like many of William Byrd's—"The Carman's Whistle," "Sellenger's Round," etc., which merely indicate the name of the familiar melody upon which the piece bases its variations, and the case of original compositions by Giles Farnaby. His fanciful titles (indeed, for pieces called generically "toys" or "fancies," meaning that they were not standard pavane-galliard dance-form pairs, or the usual sort of keyboard fantasia-variation set) are legendary: "The New Sa-Hoo," "Giles Farnaby's Dreame" (the latter modeled on Elizabethan book titles), etc. More remarkable than these, however, are the titles given to the pieces in his "ordres" for the harpsichord by François Couperin at the end of the seventeenth and the beginning of the eighteenth century.

But it may be in the emblem book of the sixteenth and seventeenth centuries that the origin of titles for short poems may be found. In general, pictures are not given titles by their painters until the nineteenth century; either the pictures are famous, and some label or subject-matter designation follows them about, or they are frequently untitled (and often, as a consequence, misread). Dürer's great *Melancholy* has inscribed in it the simplest kind of emblem label, indicating the allegorical figure depicted. But in the emblem books themselves, the kinds of rubric and heading which eventually came to adorn and complicate the page prefigured various modes of titling. Sometimes, as in Alciati's original 1531 *Emblemata* and its subsequent editions, the page would be surmounted by a title or label indicating what virtue, vice, or condition was being depicted, below which would occur the picture and below that the allegorizing verse. Later on, marginal scholia citing topoi in Horace, other ancient writers, or Scripture would accumulate; often, the title heading would itself be a tag or phrase, what we now would call (and was called then for different reasons) a *motto*. These are all extensions of the names of allegorical figures attached to or part of pictures of them, going back to medieval tradition, but they now become far more generalized, and attached to objects (or, in the later, Dutch proverbial emblems, to genre scenes).

Donne's concrete titles may I think be explained without recourse, however, to rhetorical notions of subjects for discourse, or metaphysical ones like essences. Donne's "Songs and Sonnets" are frequently extremely complicated versions of emblems. Just as the allegorizing mottoes in Renaissance emblem books seized upon a conventional object, mythological character, or event literally depicted above it and proceeded to moralize upon it by means of poetic conceits, so do Donne's poems serve as moralizing emblem verses upon those objects or events represented in their titles. The difficulty is that these poems all too often embody a dramatic situation, and that the tone is extremely complex, rather than merely avuncularly tutorial or hortatory as in most emblem verses, where, at most, the object itself will address a reader or patron. In the famous opening line of "The Flea," for example, the tone is almost mock-emblematic: it is as if the protagonist were starting out by reading some conventional emblem verse to his lady and then, in the middle of the first line, putting the book down and getting extremely personal ("Mark but this flea, and mark in this / How little that which thou deny'st me is"). The poem usually known as "Love's Alchemy" is entitled in most mss. simply "Mummy," the dead preserved flesh supposedly scraped off mummies and sold as medicines throughout the Middle Ages and the Renaissance, although the concept does not enter the poem until the last line, where women are described as being, although "at their best, / Sweetness and wit, they are but Mummy, possess'd." Here the revision substitutes the name of a process for that of a more concrete entity, but was perhaps justified as redeeming the title from an undue perversity occasioned by too great a delay in the reader's discovery of its significance.

In any event, Donne's titles provide a conventional literary context against which the dramatic and dialectical qualities of the poems themselves may work, in this case to produce a new sort of lyric, neither song nor emblem nor occasional verse nor dramatic musical dialogue, but a mixture of all of these. Their influence is observable throughout the first part of the century, and it is only with the growing consciousness of the necessary relation between genre and form that emerges in Neoclassicism that the metaphysical titling convention is replaced by another one, in which a topic label is conjoined with a usually redundant formal description, and in which, for a while, songs are simply called "Song."

Donne's most remarkable follower, from the point of view of the short poem's title, is George Herbert. The titles of the poems in *The Temple* are all clearly his (there are no textual problems with regard to the canonicity of variously titled versions, as with Donne). Moreover, Herbert's titles, like his forms, are amazingly radical, in that their expressive character is in each case part of the poem's fiction.

Often Herbert's titles supply either a text, a topic, or an emblem, "The Bunch of Grapes," "Jordan," "The Holy-Scriptures," "Coloss. 3.3 Our Life Is Hid with Christ in God," each proposes a text for its poem's unique blend of homily and private hymn. And each employs the text with a different degree of explicitness, the contrast Jordan-Helicon (including also, perhaps, Alpheus, Mincius, etc., the other emblematic streams of classical poetry) being implied only, a paraphrase of the Colossians text being "hidden" in its poem in a kind of diagonal acrostic shift pattern, etc. The emblem titles can be explicit, like "The Church-Floor" (beginning, "Mark you the floor? . . ." and thus similar to Ben Jonson's "The Houre-Glasse" and Donne's flea poem). On the other hand, they can be so deeply implicit, as in "The Collar" and "The Pulley," that they can no longer be said to be standing in for the missing pictured object; one is tempted to say that the emblem exists only outside the poem and is itself being adduced in a peculiarly puzzling and thereby helpful way, as a gloss. The images of the poem itself are an alternative expressive model of what the emblem might be read as—the gap between them is rather like the might and complex monosyllable *"or"* which so often connects Milton's metaleptic chains of similes. So many of Herbert's titles are those of partial or absent emblems that to read down the table of contents of any edition of *The Temple* is to move through a vicarage of symbols.

Even Herbert's topic-like titles get turned over and over to exhibit many of their facets of potential figurativeness. "The British Church" and "Self-Condemnation" represent two different modes of topicality. A taxonomic tour through *The Temple* might well provide an excellent start for a study of the typology of poem title. Some of Herbert's titles are enough like those of modern poetry, in their systematic obliqueness, to lead straight, perhaps, to those of Wallace Stevens. To put it another way: both Tennyson's "Mariana in the Moated Grange"—as intelligent critics since John Stuart Mill have understood—and Browning's "Childe Roland to the Dark Tower Came" would be more easily accessible to less sophisticated readers if stripped of peculiarly oblique Shakespearian allusions in their titles. They would also be worse poems; but from the point of view of the way in which titles continue to do complex work of labeling and glossing, they have an off-putting quality. Suppose that they had been given early-Yeatsian, quasi rubric titles, "She who Will Not Be Returned for Waits in Her House" and "After all the Quests Are Over, He Seeks the Dark Tower," for example? The magical grit of the extrapolated Shakespearian phrases, in the case of each poem, that secreted the pearl of a new fiction about them, could as well have been left unacknowledged, as far as most nineteenth-century readers were concerned. The actual titles are rich, and were (as the history of Browning and Tennyson criticism shows) vastly puzzling.

When modern poems are extremely short and in addition seem generically inventive, the role of the title increases in importance. Thus, in a one-line poem like Apollinaire's magnificent evocation of the single-stringed *tromba marina*, the line of the logarithmic spiral around helical sea shells, the string-line-verse that is the heart of water ("*corps d'eau*") and, perhaps, the music from a bandstand near the sea, the title seems to serve as a first line (brief as it is), and I am tempted to punctuate it with a colon:

> Chantre
> Et l'immense cordeau des trompettes marines

Ezra Pound's celebrated "In a Station of the Métro" is really a sort of long-lined *haiku;* we might rewrite it[8]

> In a station of the Métro,
> The apparition of these faces in a crowd—
> Petals on a wet, black bough!

It is these matters with which a useful typology of literary titles must concern itself. The rhetoric of the title—not merely what it directs the audience's attention to, but how, and with what gestures (flourish? jab? insinuation? deadpan pseudo-labeling? etc.) it does the directing.[9] The titles of short poems by Stevens, Robert Frost, and Auden (those he added to earlier, untitled pieces in the *Collected Poems*) are useful texts for a variety of rhetorical modes as well. Along with such questions there should also be considered the literary history of fashions in the titles of larger forms—the vogue for Shakespearian and Biblical quotation in serious popular novels in the early decades of the twentieth century, the subsequent vogue for truncated quotations (perhaps in the face of that earlier vogue, viz. Joyce Cary), deadpan approximations to an anti-rhetorical world of linguistic analysis (Henry Green), and so forth. I suppose, after all, that all of the above remarks have in their way constituted a plea for a systematic study of titles in their various guises and functions. Along with two other unwritten studies—

---

8. See Pound's own comment on this in "Vorticism," *The Fortnightly Review*, 96 N.S. (1 Sept. 1914), 467; also, Hugh Kenner, *The Pound Era* (Berkeley, 1971), p. 184.

9. Again, with respect to paintings, the eye-catching titles of Victorian anecdotal or narrative paintings were intended to startle the observer and lead him into puzzling out the anecdote through the meticulously revealed details.

a *History of Examples* and a *History of Diagrams and Schemata*[10]—it would be of great value for the study of the nature of genre and of representation.

10. For a needed start, see Goodman, pp. 170-77 and 228-31, for some observations on diagrams. The basic question, of course, is how one can tell, at any point in history, whether the intention of the picture is to schematize or not, which can be answered only by the art historian with his grasp of the history of rendering cenventions. Clearly, Villard de Honnecourt's thirteenth-century stick figures were intended to be diagrammatic, while many other minimal renderings of the human figure in earlier mss. were not.

XI
OBSERVATIONS ON THE EXPERIMENTAL

I have discussed experimental forms earlier in these pages, particularly with respect to Milton and the Romantics, but I should like to raise a few questions about metrical experiment generally. It is a concept which has achieved such sanctity in twentieth-century America—as if a final fulfillment of an Emersonian dream—that not only its value but its nature as well has gone unquestioned at any depth. The tradition can be sketched out with a few broad strokes.

1. "*Étonnez-nous!*" the injunction to the young Orpheus-Jean Cocteau, is prefigured by Emerson's Merlin in a most famous passage:

> He shall not his brain encumber
> With the coil of rhythm and number;
> But, leaving rule and pale forethought,
> He shall aye climb
> For his rhyme.
> "Pass in, pass in," the angels say,
> "In to the upper doors,
> Nor count compartments of the floors.
> But mount to paradise
> By the stairway of surprise."[1]

1. Ralph Waldo Emerson, "Merlin," ll. 29-38.

No number, no weight, no measure—we live in no dearth in the American Universe. But there is no specification of exactly what rhyme the bard was seeking at that altitude. Once the shells of structured form are broken, what then? Emerson's own verse guards against excessive self-description (save for an emblematic moment or two, viz. in a largely three-beat accentual context, the flying Blakean fourteener: "The soaring orbit of the muse exceeds that journey's length"). But he does succeed, by the end of "Merlin" in modulating the hard smitings of the short, elastic accentuals through a kind of Herbertian close —a mended rhyme when the poet becomes one with his (and our) fate and, even matching odd now, redresses "The partial wrong, / Fills the just period, / And finishes the song." The song itself finishes with a Marvellian stave of measured evening music at the closure (echoing the end of "Upon Appleton House"):

> Subtle rhymes, with ruin rife,
> Murmur in the house of life,
> Sung by the Sisters as they spin;
> In perfect time and measure they
> Build and unbuild our echoing clay.
> As the two-twilights of the day
> Fold us music-drunken in.[2]

By the end of the poem, the unstated rhyme is of verse with the world (jingling has long since died away). The manifesto in "Merlin" concerns vision and form, but the poem itself is content to embody them both in its own figure of redeemed rhyming, ringing its celebration of the bargain with what must be.

2. In a corresponding passage in "The Poet" (not the one about the plummeting critics), the necessity of rhyming verses with nature is made most explicit about organic expression "the new type which things take when liberated."

> Like the metamorphosis of things into higher organic forms is
> their change into melodies. Over everything stands its daemon or

---

2. "Merlin," ll. 124-30. The "echoing clay" also suggests the "Coy Mistress" poem, ll. 26-28.

soul, and, as the form of the thing is reflected by the eye, so the soul of the thing is reflected by a melody. The sea, the mountain-ridge, Niagara, and every flower-bed, pre-exist, or super-exist, in pre-cantations, which sail like odors in the air, and when any man goes by with an ear sufficiently fine, he overhears them and endeavors to write down the notes without diluting or depraving them. And herein is the legitimation of criticism, in the mind's faith that the poems are a corrupt version of some text in nature with which they ought to be made to tally . . .

The figure for truth to nature is not one of rhyming with it here, but of the tradition of the word itself. Within the terms of that image, the remainder of the passage can make a characteristic Emersonian play on the relation between the natural and the textual in which rhyme becomes the first term of a series of visions of patterning:

> A rhyme in one of our sonnets should be not less pleasing than the iterated nodes of a seashell, or the resembling difference of a group of flowers. The pairing of the birds is an idyl, not tedious as our idyls are; a tempest is a rough ode, without falsehood or rant; a summer, with its harvest sown, reaped and stored, is an epic song, subordinating how many admirably executed parts.

The play is the same as the one in the great passage in "Nature" in which the phases of the day become historicized and textualized at once ("The dawn is my Assyria; the sunset and moon my Paphos, and unimaginable realms of faerie . . .")[3]—in both instances the correspondences of the texts work two ways, and the point is not that one can throw away one's history book and one's *Odyssey* now that one knows what dawn and summer are, but that one needs both members of the pair, each to read the other with. For a theory of poetic form, however, the reading goes only one way, and the larger *architektonike* of *Leaves of Grass* was to loom up with the force of fulfilled prophecy. Organic form is to be the emblem, then, of the authenticity of the text, although the precise nature of the form is not made clear.

3. From the Preface to the 1855 edition of *Leaves of Grass:*

3. Emerson, *Nature,* Part III ("Beauty").

The profit of rhyme is that it drops seeds of a sweeter and more luxuriant rhyme, and of uniformity that it conveys itself into its own roots in the ground out of sight. The rhyme and uniformity of perfect poems show the free growth of metrical laws and bud from them as unerringly and loosely as lilacs or roses on a bush, and take shapes as compact as the shapes of chestnuts and oranges and melons and pears, and shed the perfume impalpable to form.

The relation between the revolutionary form of Whitman's poetry, and the terms in which that form is glossed, explained, defended by the poet himself is almost canonically set forth here. The concepts of form themselves (rhyme—and in the literary sense, rather than the extended one of "verse," the principle of uniformity, of stichic poetry or "verses") are dealt with in an almost allegorical way. The profit of rhyme is that of Emerson's words that rhyme with things, the virtue of lineation and pattern that it enables the expressive effects of poetic language to work within its powerful framework. But for the book whose pages are no barren leaves, the poetry not "distilled from other poems," there can be no reductive reading of the myth of form. There can be no manifesto about the prophetic force of the verse of the English Bible, of the way in which its rhythms of parallelism and antithesis keep echoing with the sound of accentual patterns that rhetorical structures keep sending out. Its bard will not discuss the way in which he so often makes lyric strophes of long lines, so that the movement from line to line is more like the logical and narrative movement from larger units to each other in previous poetry. He will not talk about ode-like and even operatic structures, and how their deep form, their essential inner structures of parts and wholes are preserved even without localized linear measure. He will not, in fact, discuss his method, his prosodic intentions, the source of the melodies to which he was writing—or rather, more properly, the stream of *durchkomponiert* music on which his patterns often floated. In a much later statement about his verse structure, written about himself in the third person, he virtually goes back to Emerson's prescription. Again, he misreads it to the degree of taking the pairing of natural and textual forms as an injunction to substitute one for the other. Here, in rejecting the *architektonike*, he chooses the protean meta-form of the sea, the cadences of Poseidon, warring away ever over the Athenian shore:

> The want for something finished, completed, and technically beautiful will certainly not be supplied by this writer, as it is by existing esthetic works. For the best poems both the old and the later ones now accepted as first class are polished, rhymed regular, with all the elegance of fine conceits, carefully elaborated, showing under all the restraints of art, language and phrase chosen after very much has been rejected, and only the best admitted, and then all joined and cemented together, and finally presenting the beauty of some architectural temple—some palace, proudly rising in proportions of marble, entered from superb porticos and adorned with statuary satisfying the art sense and that of form, fulfilling beauty and inviting criticism. Not so his poetry. Its likeness is not the solid stately palace, nor the sculpture that adorns it, nor the paintings on its walls. Its analogy is *the Ocean*. Its verses are the liquid, billowy waves, ever rising and falling, perhaps wild with storm, always moving, always alike in their nature as rolling waves, but hardly any two exactly alike in size or measure, never having the sense of something finished and fixed, always suggesting something beyond.[4]

What is most significant about the wave analogy is, after all, the crucial sense of boundary, the discreteness of each wave. The image here is not that of the traditional, undifferentiated, flowing stream of eloquence. In oracular poetry like Whitman's, like Rimbaud's (as Northrop Frye has observed), the sense of line terminus is crucial; each line has become a larger unit of utterance. The Pythian priestess may have mouthed hexameters; the later Romantic sibylline leaves, scattered, pieced together, form a text with a more jagged right-hand edge. But the fact of linearity is axiomatic for the reading of Whitman. The particular rhythms are the product of the protean shaping of the language: all of the devices of cataloguing—the anaphora of varying

---

4. Quoted from Horace Traubel, *With Walt Whitman in Camden* (Boston, 1906), Vol. I, p. 414.

length, the Classical ode forms ("Eidolons"), the free elegiacs, the epigrams of greater length. But they all depend upon the integrity of the line as a unit. There can be no enjambment in oracular poetry. It is the prototype of the kinds of free verse which use line terminus as syntactical marker, cutting only at clausal or phrasal breaks. Where there are several equal choices, the *length* of the line becomes a crucial rhythmic matter (i.e. in a catalogue of three-word phrases as names of the entities listed, will each line constitute an item? will there be an ad hoc convention of, say, three per line, to be expressively violated when certain lines then combine six or more?). Patterns like these become rather like schematic markings of musical structures; Whitman's *rhythmic* modalities might be graphed by some latter-day Puttenham to demonstrate the sheer dramaturgy of the introduction of the sudden short line in the parade of longs, of the gradual lengthening or narrowing, of the generation of intermediate wave cycles. The musical periods are no longer those of classical form, but rather Mahlerian. The oceanic force gnawing at the base of the palace of art, in Whitman's image, still manifests its power in waves and not in engulfing, darkening flood.

4. There is, of course, always the tradition that the bard and the magician shall not explain how it was done. There is always, even in the most learned and informed accounts by scholar-poets of what their formal practice, indeed, is, an element of hedging. Thus, Milton in the apology for the verse of *Paradise Lost* tells his slightly perplexed audience how to read the poem (see pp. 92-94 above); but the influence, upon his form for English heroic verse, of the blank verse of Shakespearian and Jacobean tragedy goes utterly unstated. Blake, unlike Whitman, still implies that there are terrific, mild, and prosaic modalities in his verse. But the actual prosodic basis of his radical revision of official English meter is, as we have seen, a series of styles based on the fourteener, with a range of strict and loose versions of it that parallel, in his own oeuvre, the fortunes of the iambic pentameter line in the history of English poetry. He never discusses this at all. It is certainly not through want of knowledge of what he is doing, or of the language in which to express it.

Of all the scholar-poets, Hopkins comes closest to specifying his metrical intentions with great precision.[5] But just as his prosodic terminology seems to come from the poems themselves, each term of tension or extension being violently metaphoric, so the lines of "Harry Ploughman" seem to describe the ploughing of furrows, as J. Hillis Miller has pointed out, of Hopkins's own verse. Aside from telling us that his verse is free-accentual, that many of his poems are extensions of the sonnet form (by which he means, of course, the Miltonic-Wordsworthian sonnet, not the Shakespearian kind), the expressive language and even the detailed scanning marks on his texts often seem to be part of a scattered meta-poem, an ungathered *ars poetica* and written in no expository verses.

2

Aside from what remain, for whatever reason and with whatever conscious volition, mysteries of skill which, being revealed, might destroy the magic of the art, there is a third source of confusion about the nature and purpose of formal revolution or revision. This stems from the inability, rather than the unwillingness, of the poet to explain what he is doing and why he is doing it. I leave aside the case of the poet who keeps silent on the subject. With Whitman, Browning and Emily Dickinson are perhaps the two most original poets of the nineteenth century. In Dickinson's case, there is, of course, no metastatement at all, save what can be extracted from the poems. We can find hundreds of metaphors for her choice of metrical mode, but no bald statement of it. Using a base of the so-called "common meter" of hymnody—the accentual version in 4-beat and 3-beat alternating lines of the tetrameter-trimeter *abcb* rhyming quatrain also loosely called "ballad stanza"—she derived an intense, chromatic, often deliberately soured, solo hymnody of her own. Just as George Herbert's poems are in a sense the hymnody of the rectory itself, the liturgical year of private devotion, so hers are the hymnody of the attic. Browning's use of pointed blank verse upon which to weave a fabric of dialectic also goes

5. As, even more clearly than in the Preface to the poems, in a letter to R. W. Dixon, October 5, 1878. See also Geoffrey Hartman, "Hopkins Revisited," in *Beyond Formalism* (New Haven, 1970), pp. 231-46.

unmentioned by him, although he is perfectly capable of saying that he has mapped the speech-rhythms of Donne and Webster onto the Shelleyan flow of ideas. Both Browning and Dickinson develop characteristic speaking tones from their verse forms; both bring out the accentual content in extreme rhetorical ways. It is as if, in both of their cases, the old *ethos* of poetic modality in English, wherein accentualism is associated with speech sound and the sound of thought, while syllabism reflects singing,[6] were being constantly re-enacted.

But there are those poets who are unable truly to explain what their idiosyncratic modality of meter in fact is, and who nonetheless endeavor to do so. Modernism has somehow sanctified the manifesto as a literary form by itself, drawing on a tradition that goes back to the association of Romantic art and poetry and revolution in nineteenth-century Paris. The art of the manifesto is that of a certain kind of rhetoric; given the necessary ironies of historical repetition of which Marx was so keenly aware, the second go round of the manifesto—in futurism, surrealism, and dada—was always flirting with farce. At the very best, manifestoes go in for widly persuasive definitions: thus, in the Pound-Flint-H.D.-Aldington rules for the aspiring Imagist, the third one is typical of an injunction of great openness: "As regarding rhythm: to compose in the sequence of the musical phrase, not in sequence of a metronome."[7] The point here is that it really means nothing. Some musical phrases are metronomic, some not; the ones which are not are always playing off the expectation of the metronomic (rubato, or the flowing quality of phrasing which extends beyond bar lines). In any sense, this is a kind of high-sounding rubbish for: "To measure lines in syntactic units, not in number of syllables, or number of contrastively heavy stress-accents, nor in a combination of these." The *vers libre* imported from French had to leave behind it the French syllabic evenness, and even the meaning of "libre" (i.e. of undetermined number of syllables—no French verse of that period could evade syllabism

6. I do not, of course, mean pure or unstressed syllabics, which, in English, are purely visual. See Chapter XII.
7. Ezra Pound, "A Retrospect," in *Literary Essays* (New York, 1954), p. 3.

totally) became a different matter in English, when the prominence of stress accent would cause it to be heard even when unplanned.

Thus, to try to scan free verse by counting the number of stresses and concluding that, in any event, the poem under discussion is roughly assembled of four- and five-stressed lines, may be merely to assert a trivial correlation built into the structure of English (Yvor Winters's analysis of Stevens's "The Snow Man" is a case in point). It may have been the poet's intention, for example, to use as a roughly governing principle of composition a line of about 24 typeface ems in width; the probability is that—unless his syntax is most distorted, his density of short, emphatic monosyllabic imperatives and expletives unduly high, his latinate polysyllables likewise—most of his lines will have three or four stresses, if counted in accentual-syllabic terms. But it would surely be wrong to hold the stress-patterning to be the principle.

The foregoing comprises the sort of question that an explanation, or even a reasonably prepared injunction, about Imagist free verse ought to involve. But poets of the period kept harping on innaccurate musical analogies, presumably because of their power to cow, if not to charm. This is clearly a different matter from the meta-poem about style that occurs in Emerson and Whitman, and in tortured, fragmentary form, in among the genuinely helpful scholia, in Hopkins. It is instead a matter of misplaced specificity.

A most influential instance of this is the way in which William Carlos Williams discussed his prosodic practice. As important a poet and visionary he was, his metrical remarks are those of a cranky autodidact who has never had anyone serious to talk to. The magnificent realization of the line-and-stanza patterning in some of the poems in *Spring and All*, for example, lend themselves to the analysis that all poetic verse does. But the impulse that leads modernist American poets to act out a cracker-barrel reading of "Merlin" is very strong, for an obsession with form has been widespread in American poetry. Dr. Williams would denounce "the cultured patter of iambic pentameter" and then in the following sentences go on to refer to "the struggle antedating Shakespeare among the English who were giving up qualitative verse for accentual verse."[8] Since "qualitative" in prosody refers to non-accentual properties of syllables (vocalic and consonantal features, etc.: alliteration or assonance would be qualitative relations between syllables), either this is palpably false; *or* Williams meant "quantitative" (and in which case the statement is even more palpably false—the few quantitative experiments discussed earlier in these pages were largely contemporaneous with Shakespeare, and they were always isolated). Or, indeed, "qualitative" may have had some secret meaning for Williams, in which case it was rather coy of him, under such emphatic circumstances, not to come out with it. But clearly this is not the case, and we are faced with another instance of the strategy of the imagist manifesto.

So, too, in the case of Williams's celebrated "variable foot." I do not mean here the metrical form of Williams's later verse, of poems like those in *The Desert Music;* that is a triadic strophic pattern, the lines of variable length, but graphically marked and, in general, syntactically bounded:

The powerful effect of the graphic schema of the broken line had been demonstrated by Pound much earlier, when he saw an essential symmetry between the scholarly space added between half-lines of early Germanic poetry and the word boundary frequently marked by a stronger syntactic juncture at the caesura of the Classical quantitative line.[9] Schematically, Pound mapped the line like this

---

8. W. C. Williams, in *Poetry,* XCIII (March 1959), 416.
9. The great number of hyphenated compounds in the early cantos is significant, too, I think. They suggest in common both Greek and German compound words, as opposed to the prepositional phrase compound (*the x of y,* rather than *the y-x*) of romance tradition, which he may very well have associated with accentual syllabism and the legacy of Chaucer.

He introduced it in Canto II, after preparing the way with his resonant accentual six-beat "Ear, ear for the sea-surge, murmur of old men's voices." The assimilation of the Germanic accentual and the Classical divided hexameter (actually, the caesura is a linking device in quantitative verse, always occurring *within* a foot) led him to a metrical pattern for a freely accentual line. The graphic schema has since been adopted by many free-verse systems because it has become a conventional form; that is, if framing, underlining, allusive power is to be gained from it, it is for the same reasons that a poem of Sapphic stanzas may so operate.

But for many American poets there must be a mystique to cover what is in fact a line of tradition they have found for themselves. Pound's successors have held matters of form in great sanctity, and have derived poem formats from *The Cantos* but with elaborate explanations which evade the question of the tradition and employ instead a whole hierarchy of fictions. At the lowest level these are trivial but widespread. Every language has a sense of itself and of other languages, a characteristic picture of its structure, and a characteristic disposition to view the structures of other languages in a particular way.

Consider, for example, the relation of French to English. Unless the English-speaker is bilingual from birth, he will tend to hear French words with a stress accent which they do not in fact possess. This can be seen in the two conventions, one British, one American, for the absorption of recent French borrowings: thus, French *"ballet," "garage"* become British "bállet," gárage" and American "ballét," "garáge," etc. When I was studying French in high school, it occurred to me that the French *alexandrin* line had two basic patterns, one anapestic tetrameter, the other trochaic hexameter, the variation of which I found rather inexplicable, or rather, irrelevant, in any poem I learned:

> Plus me plaît le séjour qu'ont bâti mes aïeux
> Que des palais romains le front audacieux;
> Plus que le marbre dur me plaît l'ardoise fine . . .[10]

the patterns being, in the case of these lines,

10. Joachim Du Bellay, *"Regrets."*

(but) ·· / ·· / ·· / ·· /
·· / ·· / ·· / ·· /
/ ·· / · / ‖ · / ·· / · / (.)

Similarly, the line in Racine's *Britannicus*, which I had "heard" as a student *"Approchez-vous, Néron, et prenez vôtre place"* came alive properly in its French metrical frame when I heard Marie Bell of the Comédie Française read it properly with a contrastive stress only on *"vôtre,"* which my fictional anapestic tetrameter would hardly have allowed. The correspondence between Richard Strauss and Romain Rolland on the subject of the French word stress which the German composer cannot believe does not exist is most revealing.[11] In the summer of 1905, while working on the setting of Wilde's French text of *Salomé*, Strauss complained that the French do not sing the way they speak (not true, with respect to stress) and asked if a phrase should be set "de chevéux," "de chevéux," or "de chevéux." Rolland, instead of telling him that the accentuation was purely a matter of the musical rhythm and that any one of these was possible (save for the fact that, at the end of a sentence, clause, or extrapolated phrase, the first of these or even "de chevéux" would be mandatory), blustered and fussed about weights and durations of syllables, never having had the occasion to make the appropriate observations about the structure of his own language.

Little fictions about sound patterns like these haunt many programmatic statements of prosodic theory by poets. It is obviously true that one may know how to do something and yet not know how to describe what he is doing, the skills for doing the thing and doing the describing being not necessarily entailed by each other. Some of these non-useful fictions include those generated by the confusion, in so much modernist poetics, between *speech* and *prose*. Pace *le bourgeois gentilhomme*, they are not the same; prose, or rather the many proses, the many conventions of structure, is not what we speak. So-called "prose rhythms" are as conventionalized as those of verse form, or else they are the

11. Richard Strauss and Romain Rolland, *Correspondence*, ed. Rollo Myers (Berkeley, 1968), pp. 68-75.

rhythms of speech misnamed. Graphic form divorced from phonetic realities can easily, as shall be seen in a subsequent discussion, control imagined or inferred sound patterns.

Thus, for example, anyone with any knowledge of linguistics will find such an account of the way his verse is assembled as that of the late Charles Olson to be, at best, a kind of meta-poem.[12] The physiology of breathing, its relation to articulatory phonetics, of that to acoustic phonetics, of that to phonemics, of that to the graphemics of syllables and word boundaries, of that to the conventionalization of line structure—all of these operate at different levels, but in the structure of verse their effects do not jump levels. Olson may have believed that his rate of respiration was reflected in how long a string of characters would extend itself on a page; or he may have known that whatever he said *about* his practice was oracular and therefore not to be questioned. His most interesting remarks concern his use of the typewriter. The typewriter's graphic "measure" of one em per character (as opposed to the flexibilities of typesetting) certainly provides a kind of substitute for the "numbers" of accentual-syllabic verse. But Olson's account of its *role* in composition, in theory of the relation of graphic pattern to larger poetic intention, etc., does not put the matter properly, or even verifiably. He resorts to fictions about sound when they are not there. And indeed, the one fiction which he might genuinely have employed as a poet should—a fiction which might be classed with Hopkins's metaphoric extensions of the term "stress" to embrace its prosodic, mechanical, and emotional all at once—would have been at least rooted in one acoustical actuality. For the clatter and bang of typewriter keys, creating an audible rhythm of their own as a function of the longer or shorter words being given visual form through their agitation—the clatter of letters and the short breath of the space bar's intercalations:

12. Charles Olson, "Projective Verse," in *The New American Poetry, 1945-1960*, ed. Donald Allen (New York, 1960), pp. 386-97. On the other hand, the elaborate poetic record of another poet who uses the typewriter, A. R. Ammons, and in particular of the way his lines are generated, is thoroughly mythologized. Ammons's "Essay on Poetics" and passages in his long "Hibernaculum"—both in *Collected Poems* (New York, 1972) never partake of the pseudo-technical crankiness of contemporary academic *vers libre* and "open" theorists.

these might well be the muse's voice for a poet who wrote directly on the typewriter.

But poetic formats derive from so many modern written forms: the run-on sentences of *archie and mehitabel*,[13] the "Camera Eye" and biographical portrait sections of John Dos Passos's still underrated *USA*, the visual fields of poster and display composition and the rhetoric of varied typeface, for example.[14] And their source is seldom credited by poets who give putative accounts of their method. Ultimately, there is at work the power of an ideology about experiment which descends, in successive misreadings, from Emerson. In practice, there is also the terrifying foreshortening of modern aesthetic history; the gestures of the avant-garde become academic in a matter of minutes, and revolutionary young poets of the middle nineteen-fifties were piously using spellings like "sh/d" and "w/d" because Pound did in *The Pisan Cantos* and in his letters. At the present time in the United States, there is a widespread, received, free-verse style marked by a narrow (25-30 em) format, strong use of line-ending as a syntactical marker, etc., which plays about the same role in the ascent to paradise as the received Longfellow style did a century ago. Magazine verse then was written in it, as magazine verse today derives from the original voices of W. S. Merwin and James Wright, for example. The very look of the received poem on the page jingles and tinkles today the way neat, accentual-syllabic rhyming once did.

A final word about innovation through historical revision. Ezra Pound's totally anti-Whitmanian move, early in his career, was to throw off the pressures of the parental generation, the still-living and the recently dead, by submitting to the control of venerable ghosts. In its way, this constitutes a reversal of the reduction in the reading of Emerson's great analogy in *Nature* mentioned earlier: "broad noon shall be my England of the sense and the understanding; the night shall be my Germany of mystic philosophy and dreams." Pound's read-

13. The run-on sentences, deliberately under-punctuated, in Allen Ginsberg's "America" are an example.
14. See Chapter XII. The effects of the typographical have been noted since the eighteenth century. G. C. Lichtenberg remarked that a page of German in roman type seemed to him like a translation, for example.

ing was to substitute the historical for the personal, and to map his vision onto the history of culture: his Latin Middle Ages, his Cathay, his Venice, his Rome, his Hellas, indeed, his Georgian London. At the opposite pole from the organic fiction for the generation of *authentic* form was his historical one, and the ways in which translation and pastiche led to invention for him are now well understood. But here, as always, there is the matter of what even the highly conscious, the programmatically learned goliard like Pound will see as being central.

I am thinking now of what so many of Pound's exegetical critics apologize for still: the great weight of archaism in the early poems and then retained, here and there, as echoes in *The Cantos*. I should like before concluding to look at the effect of deliberate archaism, particularly in the Cavalcanti translations; it certainly represents a period in his own poetic style, just as surely as the mode of *Cathay* does. But it is hard to resist quoting, in the context of these observations on poetic versions the following, from Pound's translation of Cavalcanti's canzone "*Donna mi Prega*":

>   In memory's locus taketh he his state
>   Formed there in manner as a mist of light
>   Upon a dusk that is come from Mars and stays.
>   Love is created, hath a sensate name,
>   His modus takes from soul, from heart his will;
>
>   From form seen doth he start, that, understood
>   Taketh in latent intellect
>   As in a subject ready—
>   place and abode,
>   Yet in that place it ever is unstill,
>
>   Spreading its rays, it tendeth never down
>   By quality, but its own effect unendingly
>   Not to delight, but in an ardour of thought
>   That the base likeness of it kindleth not.[15]

---

15. Ezra Pound, "Cavalcanti," in *Literary Essays*, pp. 155-56. The discussion of this translation in Donald Davie, *Ezra Pound: Poet as Sculptor* (New York, 1964), pp. 102-19, is superb.

This manner, which Pound's most energetic interpreters have found to be Pre-Raphaelite, is hesitant in many ways: the hedged commitment to trying for the internal rhymes, which causes him to break up some lines and not others (there are few he even tries for here: the broken line at "ready—/place and abode" covers such a case), rhyme intermittently, etc. The archaisms, though, can hardly be thought of as Pre-Raphaelite, but rather a kind of deliberate, framing (one might also say, in the sense in which it has been used before, *metrical*) device. In any case, it is not the simple, sensuous, and passionate speech of the following lines from a translation of Dante's so-called "Stony Sestina" (after the Lady Pietra to whom it is written, and after the image in the terminal word of the original fifth line—the one which hinges in the middle of the poem). They comprise the last twenty-one lines of the translation:

> A while ago, I saw her dress'd in green,—
> So fair, she might have waken'd in a stone
> This love which I do feel even for her shade;
> And therefore, as one woos a graceful lady,
> I wooed her in a field that was all grass
> Girdled about with very lofty hills.
>
> Yet shall the streams turn back and climb the hills
> Before Love's flame in this damp wood and green
> Burn, as it burns within a youthful lady,
> For my sake, who would sleep away in stone
> My life, or feed like beasts upon the grass,
> Only to see her garments cast a shade.
>
> How dark soe'er the hills throw out their shade,
> Under her summer-green the beautiful lady
> Covers it, like a stone cover'd in grass.

The stoniness of the lady is echoed in the original by her name—*Donna Pietra*; by the way in which the assonances of the terminal words (*ombra, donna; erba, verde*, etc.) are orchestrated in the shifting line juxtapositions, the modulations of the imagery are effected. The translator here has done some of that with his *shade, lady:* the point is that not only is this version astonishingly accurate, but that its direct, high tone never falters. The syntax is masterful, the enjambments in the original being matched by those of the English version; where the syntax is high and indirect ("damp wood and green"), there is a specific reason. In this case, strangely enough, it is not to translate that typically Italianate construction (the original reads *"legno molle e verde"*); nor is it merely the exigencies of line ending. The high tone is accomplished because of the Miltonic character of the construction—it was he who brought it into his own English, and used it so remarkably as a device of imagery. One moves from the dampness of the wood out to its greenness in a kind of narrative progression. The two forms, the "*a, b* X" and "the *a* X, and *b*" differ in the way in which the adjectival order is used: in the first, the precedence is possibly euphonious, conventional, or trivial. In the second, the scanning process and the metrical line terminus both home in on the predicate *b*. Its use here is no whim, nor is it a mechanical, eighteenth-century Miltonism. The translator here is Rossetti, and his version, a half-century before Pound's lines, may be one of the great lyric poems in English. It sounds more "modern" than any of Pound's at the time, save for the poems in *Cathay*.

But the point here is not to indulge in pernicious casuistry; it is to show that the archaizing element in the Pound may be a rather profound matter, part of a deep attitude toward style and a self-consciousness about it. Perhaps it is more like a Chattertonian style of pastiche than we have been able heretofore to think. The matter of Romance was not only an alternative to the mythopoetic world of the American Romantic tradition—the dialectic of landscape and selfhood and their mutual intrusions. An emphatic and intense show of coping with it became for a while as authentic a way to "drink, and be whole again beyond confusion" as, for example, E. A. Robinson's deep draught of English literature, even to the point of his reconsecrating society verse to real poetic purposes.

Here, then, is another instance of true experimentation that may not, within the perspective of rapidly unrolling literary history, be subsequently understood as such for some time. It is additionally significant,

I think, because it outwardly manifests what so much post-Modern experimentation with poetic technique does not avow—the internalization of other prior models, that they may be incorporated into the new poetic being. The dialectic of innovation is always a subtle one, and the very concept of *originality* has shifted its ground since the founding of the formal conventions of poetry in English, from being at the source of a stream of tradition to drilling one's own Helicon, wherever one may be standing in time or place. But to be ignorant of the underground stream that is bursting forth at the time is, after all, not to know the ground upon which one is standing.

XII
THE POEM IN THE EYE

Ut pictura poesis: a poem is like a picture, says Horace in his *Art of Poetry*, raising the question of a problematic correspondence that has become increasingly interesting now that the phrase has ceased being a tag line as it was in the eighteenth century. *A poem is like a picture*, and of course Horace meant, and went on to mean, *in that* one sort may demand a close-up, intimate scrutiny, while another looks best from far away; he goes on to parallel those lines about various modes of scale and scope with another about *haec amat obscurum, volet haec sub luce videri*—this one loves the dark, that one wants to be seen in the light—and fears not, he goes on to say, the critical gaze of judgment. But here the simile abandons its fidelity to painting, and the moralizing thrust outgrows the comparison. The other resemblance between the two arts in Horace is in the opening image of the insane painter putting parts of a picture together the wrong way, where the basis of the comparison is one of a mimetic structure assembled from significant parts. Throughout the rest of his poem, Horace uses conventional musical images in analogies—different instruments for modalities and styles, strings being plucked, etc.—without explanation and far oftener than his allusions to painting. It is significant that subsequent literary history, particularly in the baroque and rococo, applied Horace's phrase as a far more general tag.

As we have seen, criticism has always been interested in the ways in which poetry is more or less *like* and more or less *about* music, and, in particular, with some of the characteristics of poetic language that make any *reading* of a poem, even a silent one, something very like a performance intoned aloud. Reading, in other words, becomes a matter for the inner ear, eliciting songs sung in poetry's private, purely linguistic kind of music. But here I shall be concerned with reading in another sense. That sense is more like one of *scanning*, in the non-prosodic usage (one I have almost borrowed back from art historians and architects, when they talk of "reading" a picture, or an elevation, or some architectural detail). The poem in the eye is a kind of picture, and one of the things we do when we read a poem is to discern visual structures, to make out parts, wholes, relationships, to see patterns in sub- and total contexts, and so forth. Our ability to do this will depend, in the use of pictures, upon the way in which prior associations, previously understood graphic conventions, are engaged by the particular versions of those conventions in the individual style of the picture. All pictures look more like other pictures than what they are pictures *of*.

So, probably, with poems. Our reading of a poem involves not only matters, on a high linguistic level, of primary discernment, in the sense of being able to "read" someone's handwriting, say. There are other levels of this scanning, making out, all the way up to those of, for example, genre recognition; one reads poems in the way in which one reads English, reads sentences, reads rapidly or uncomprehendingly, rather than just in the sense of reading something *in* English. There is a parallel ambiguity with visual representation; consider these exchanges: "What are you drawing?"—"A house" and "What are you drawing?"—"A picture. Of a house." In the first case, the colloquial ellipsis is more than that: the word is being used in the sense of *mimesis*, representation—its proper paraphrase is "What are you depicting?" In the second case, the word means to make, to construct a new sort of thing, on a plane, to make a designed surface. And yet the position I mentioned before essentially maintained that these senses must always be somehow combined, in that one is always depicting not a house, but some depiction of a house—one draws a picture by depicting some picture, by drawing not from life but, in a sense, by tracing a kind of picture that he already sees. So, too, with poems. They are more like each other than they are like reality, and it may even be true that they are more *about* each other in this way as well. A full reading of a poem will depend upon recognition of its genre, and of its version of that genre. It is significant that, as far as all contemporary art—music, poetry, painting—is concerned, when someone says "I don't understand it," he usually means "I don't recognize its genre or type; what *sort* of picture or poem or whatever is it?"[1] But this is patently less true in the case of music, whose tones have, until recently, been available for no other purpose than for musical art (as Paul Valéry remarked longingly to a composer—whereas he, on the other hand, needed to employ the same language with which he communicated with the grocer). Picture genre and poem genre are in this way quite alike.

In moving from the ear's domain to that of the eye, I should like in the following remarks to do several things with the various kinds of likeness between poem and picture. One of these is to investigate the ways in which the poem on the written or printed page is *read* in some of the senses outlined above. Another is to go into the ways in which poems deal with picturing, with the visual world. Finally, I should like to discuss a few parallels between these two matters in the history of English and American poetry, and in modern poetry in particular. Strangely enough, entering the realm of the eye would lead us into history more than did traveling about in the ear's country—I say strangely enough, because we ordinarily think of music as being purely (or at any rate, primarily) temporal, and of pictures as being spatial. And yet as far as language is concerned, an utterance is a thing of the moment, and an inscription can endure, and be consulted, read, reconstructed, misunderstood, or whatever, later on. Even the memory's system of storage and retrieval was thought of, until very recently, as a kind of visual model, from the Lockeian language of slates and impressions and so forth on up. And even the first disc recordings were so obviously

1. This point arose in conversations with Stanley Cavell.

the vocalization of visible inscriptions that the phonographic reproducer was, imaginatively speaking, very much like a person reading aloud a code he alone knew.

So that if one were to diagram the way in which the two senses cut through poetic language, the ear and the eye would be axes at right angles to each other, and would suggest the perpendicular axes along which Yeats, in *A Vision,* suggested that the peculiar identity of poems might be graphed. Not literally, of course: in a far more grandiose way he was purporting to talk about human history and its greater cycles, but when he set up his polarities, he was saying something important about the way in which the personal, immediate, occasional status of a poetic utterance meshes with the conventional and historical. We may view this in the contracted perspective of stylistics (where the problem becomes the famous one of "Tradition and the Individual Talent"), or in a more expanded view like that of the picture analogy (where the axes are representation, *about*-ness, on the one hand, and generic identity, representation of the genre or type, on the other). Yeats puts *past* and *future* as contraries on one axis (not, you will notice, past and present); the other pair couples and contrasts *now* and *eternity*. It is on the second of these axes that I would pose the ear, the individual talent, the voice, the *parole;* on the first are ranged the eye, the tradition, the mask through which that voice sounds, and the *langue*. The ear responds to the dimension of natural experience, the eye to that of convention.

I have drawn a similar distinction elsewhere between the concepts of meter and rhythm in the formal analysis of poetic language.[2] The poem's aural dimension engages the concept of rhythm, but here I shall be concerned with apparent form and meter. Certainly any poem exists in both of these dimensions; but just as poetry's sense of itself, its fiction about its own nature, remains a musical, an auditory one throughout a good deal of its history, a visual concern just as surely begins to emerge after a while. This concern, like the musical one, is a matter of the likeness of poetic language to essential utterance on the one hand, and to inscription on the other.

2. See Chapter VII, above.

My concern, then, shall be with the printed poem. Tortured debates about poetic ontology have taken up the problem as to whether any mere copy, any inscribed instance constitutes the poem; similarly, recent prosodic theory has attempted to replace the views of older metrists by appealing to a kind of linguistic prosody based upon the structural analysis of language as speech. I am more concerned with the way in which poems are aware of each other, of poetry of the past. We may wonder, in the realm of rhythm, whether an actual musical setting could do any more than disrupt the web of a poem's linguistic patterning, smashing the "silken skilled transmemberment of song" as Hart Crane called it. Metrically, we must look not only at the frame on which the web is woven, but at the shape of the rhythms and patterns that inscriptions, rather than utterances, take up in the air.

An early perception of the dual nature of a line of verse, the interpenetrating attributes of utterance and inscription, can be found in a passage of St. Augustine's. It is characteristically concerned with time, the temporal and the timeless serving here in lieu of the more usual contrast between the aural domain, whose room is in time, and the visual, which extends in space. I quote from A. D. Nuttall's unusually sensitive translation:

> So it is that a metrical line is beautiful in its own kind although two syllables of that line cannot be pronounced simultaneously. The second is pronounced only after the first has passed, and such is the order of procedure to the end of the line, so that when the last syllable sounds, alone, unaccompanied by the sound of the previous syllables, it yet, as being part of the whole metrical fabric, perfects the form and metrical beauty of the whole. But the versifier's art itself is not dependent on time in the same way; its beauty is not portioned out in temporally measured units. It is simultaneously possessed of all those virtues which enable it to produce a line—a line which is not simultaneously possessed of all its virtues but which produces them in order. For the beautiful thing shows the last footprints of that beauty which art itself constantly and immutably watches over.[3]

3. St. Augustine, *De Vera Religione*, XXII, 42, tr. A. D. Nuttall, quoted from his *Two Concepts of Allegory* (New York, 1967), pp. 44-45.

The famous passage in the *Confessions* (XI, xxvi-xxvii)—in which the reading, acoustical, and mental scanning of a line of verse, and the remembering of its passing moments and sections, is used as a great example of phenomenological clocking—seems to lie behind this magnificent appreciation of the dual nature of the line of verse. We may take the historical view that oral (and, of course, simultaneously musical) poetry came to be preserved in inscription (or, conversely, died and was entombed in it); or we may, again following Augustine, maintain that the vocal pronouncing of signs, words, "is occasioned by the deep of this world, and the blindness of the flesh, which cannot see thoughts; so that there is need to speak aloud into the ears." In either event, the inscription and the utterance are locked in a dialectical relation of prior-secondary, of primary and antithetical. The field in which that dialectic operates is the domain of language itself, at least the rich, fruitful ground showing forth what the hidden deep structures have caused to blossom.

Whatever position the historian may take, the poet himself feels his metaphorical "singing" of a poem, his actual "writing" of it, and his potential ability, once it is finished, to "speak" or "recite" it all to coexist at once in some strange way. Historically, there is nothing to say save that all poetry is originally oral, and the earliest inscriptions of it were clearly ways of preserving material after the tradition of recitation had changed or been lost. But from earliest times on, these inscriptions were primarily encodings of the spoken poem, and even long after actual sung texts were not the only lyric poems, conventions and genres were maintained through the written conventions of inscribing poems, and the text was by no means to be thought of as a thing in itself. Greek poetic meter, as we have seen, is a patterning both of the sounds of the language in ways perfectly acceptable to that language's sense of itself (i.e. long and short syllables are viable entities, etc.) and of the *ictus*, the upbeat-downbeat contrast, the tonic stress of musical rhythm that the language itself, with its pitch accent, did not supply. It was only when Latin poetry adapted this Greek meter for its own uses, when conflict arose between the penultimate stress of the Latin language and the Greek meter's canonical ictus patterns (having nothing to do with speech stress, but with applied downbeat), that anything like an abstract, like a visual meter, developed. A metrical loan from the poetry of another language always tends to show up, in the borrowing tongue, as an inscriptional coding: consider pure syllabics from the French, of the kind first used by Marianne Moore and W. H. Auden in very different ways—one cannot scan them by ear, but only by counting on one's fingers, for the rules that define syllabification are purely graphical ones. An archetypal instance for English poetry, then, of the rhythmic aural pattern being accommodated to a visual, in this case, graphic one, is that of Latin poetry. Post-Saturnian Latin verse calls for the suppression of certain sound features prominent in Latin, just as does pure syllabic verse in English; but there is always a tendency for the banished sounds to return like ghosts, haunting the visual regions from which they were exiled. The aural stress pattern *bumpety bum-bum*, keeps appearing at the end of Virgilian hexameters. On the other hand, all the lost sounds, the original pronunciation of Greek and Latin, the dying cadences of an earlier language or moment of history become constellations on our pages, even as old and discarded scientific models, for example, become translated, on their deaths, into available poetic mythology.

In one sense, then, all Classical tradition comes through the eye. When the gap is so great, there is no real loss to a subsequent language in a subsequent age; Classical influence on English poetry, insofar as it involves patterning of language, goes on perfectly well in the visual domain, given the syntactical rigidities of English as opposed to Latin. Where the gap is narrower, however, peculiar things can happen, as in the case of the Elizabethan poets' sense of Chaucer's meter. Because they did not understand the use of syllabic "e" in Chaucer's elegantly strict accentual-syllabism, because, indeed, the sixteenth century was inventing Chaucer's iambic pentameter all over again through not being able to read his notation of it correctly, they assumed that Chaucer wrote in "riding rhyme," a rough accentual, nursery-rhyme sort of tetrameter (as witnessed by Spenser's imitation in *The Shepheardes Calender* of what he thought Chaucerian verse was).

2

This aspect of poetry's visual dimension, the graphic conventions of meter and the way in which abstract schemata, metrical and grammatical, are to be located along that dimension, constitutes the eye's gaze out over time. In order to approach this area, I should like to start out with some extreme cases of poetry's picture-like properties, and then move on to some more significant but less obvious ones. In calligraphic traditions of various Eastern languages, the decorative, and occasionally the pictorial element of a written text can be extremely important. There is insufficient room here to go into some of the oriental traditions of decorative inscription: the fantastically complex patterned poems of some Persian grammarians, for example, or the abstract shaping of manuscript texts. In Islamic aniconic tradition, calligraphy, interlace, abstract patterning are all involved. The putting of texts into figures, as George Puttenham was able to remind his English readers in his *Arte of English Poesy* (1589) has an oriental cast to it; not only do Westerners tend to associate ornateness of surface to Eastern impulses, but to consider the role of schematic patterns such as acrostics in Semitic tradition, the integrity of the written texts of the Hebrew bible, and so forth. In view of the fact, for example, that representational images were not permitted to contaminate, in orthodox Jewish tradition, the scriptural text, and that even the scribal variation of the relative scale of a single letter of the text of the Pentateuch was forbidden, there are no illustrated Hebrew bibles as such. But in some medieval European Hebrew bibles probably made for rich and rather less scholarly owners, the masoretic textual notes are shaped in a bewildering and inventive array of animal and bird and plant forms, sometimes with a direct or oblique reference to something in the text the notes deal with or neighbor on, sometimes not.[4]

---

4. There are also quasi-posters—mappings of liturgical texts in the shape of the menorah or seven-branched candelabrum. One cabbalistic tradition so shapes the 67th Psalm, as part of a secret reading of it (in this case, the format is more than decorative.) An excellent collection of oriental patterned texts is in Berjouhi Bowler, *The Word as Image* (London, 1970). An analogous Western tradition of the architectonic patterning of inscriptions has interesting implications for con-

The point about the whole Islamic tradition, and in particular the Turkish and Persian sources which Puttenham claimed for his abstract patterns,[5] is that the scribe would merely calligraph a pre-existent text in the pattern in question—the text had in no way, unless it was a scribal addition or an occasional inscription, been cast in the shape. The central Classical tradition in the West from Alexandrian times on was a different matter.

From the late seventeenth century in England on, shaped, patterned, or "figured" poems have been considered the essence of the trivial or tricky. "The first species of false wit which I have met with is very venerable for its antiquity," writes Addison in the *Spectator* in 1711, "and has produced several pieces which have lived near us as long as the Iliad itself: I mean these short poems, printed among the minor Greek poets, which resemble the figure of an egg, a pair of wings, an axe, a shepherd's pipe and an altar." He was referring to the famous texts (Alexandrian—hardly near as old as the *Iliad* itself!) which were introduced to Renaissance Europe in the printed editions of the Greek bucolic poets, and in the Planudean version of the Greek Anthology.[6] Three of them, by Simmias of Rhodes, (fl. *ca*. 300 B.C.) were extremely well-known in antiquity. They are all written in carefully constructed lines of Greek verse, and the shaping is managed by shortening or

---

temporary verse; it has been studied by John Sparrow in *Line Upon Line* (Cambridge, 1967) and, more fully, in his *Visible Words* (Cambridge, 1969). For reproductions of patterned poems from the Greek *technopaignia* on, see Charles Boltenhouse, "Poems in the Shapes of Things," *Art News Annual*, XXVIII (1959). It might be noted here that throughout this chapter, I shall not be discussing so-called "concrete poetry" which is, properly speaking, a branch of graphic art; see above, p. 100, note 16, and my article on "Concrete Poetry" in *Encyclopedia of Poetry and Poetics*, 2nd ed. (Princeton, 1975).
5. See A. L. Korn, "Puttenham and the Oriental Pattern-Poem," *Comparative Literature*, VI (1954), 289-303. Puttenham's *Observations* was edited by G. D. Willcock and Alice Wallser (Cambridge, 1936); the parts discussed here are available in *Elizabethan Critical Essays*, ed. G. G. Smith (Oxford, 1904), Vol. II, pp. 67-141.
6. I have used the texts, readings, and, in some instances, the translations of J. M. Edmonds, in his Loeb edition of *The Greek Bucolic Poets* (London, 1912), pp. 485-511. W. R. Paton gives different readings in his version of them in the Loeb edition of *The Greek Anthology*, q.v. from which the "Egg" and "Altar" poems are reproduced below.

lengthening lines by the addition or loss of extra feet, and by centering or shifting the lines. Simmias' "Axe" was written to be inscribed on a bladed axe, a votive copy of the one traditionally thought to have been used in making the Trojan horse. It is really a fancy inscription, in the familiar reversed-lozenge shape that Puttenham in his discussion of shapes for poems called the Tricquet (or triangle) Displayed:

```
xxxxxxxxxxxxxxxxxxxxxxxxxxxxxxxxxxxxxxxxxxxxxx
 xxxxxxxxxxxxxxxxxxxxxxxxxxxxxxxxxxxxxxxx
     xxxxxxxxxxxxxxxxxxxxxxxxxxxxxxx
        xxxxxxxxxxxxxxxxxxxxxx
            xxxxxxxxxx
              xxxxxx
              xxxxxx
            xxxxxxxxxx
         xxxxxxxxxxxxxxxxxx
      xxxxxxxxxxxxxxxxxxxxxxxxxx
   xxxxxxxxxxxxxxxxxxxxxxxxxxxxxxxxxxxx
 xxxxxxxxxxxxxxxxxxxxxxxxxxxxxxxxxxxxxxxxxxxx
```

An additional peculiarity was that its lines were arranged: 1, 3, 5, 7, 9, 11, 12, 10, 8, 6, 4, 2—they thus formed couplets of equal lines. Printed Renaissance texts added another, final line, inserted as the handle of the axe between the two blades, as in this edition of Theocritus, Paris, 1561, reproduced on the page opposite.

Simmias' "Wings," however, are another matter. Similar in meter to the previous poem, but centered differently to give the shape of wings hinged at the top, it is also to be read in normal linear order. They are the wings of Eros: the poem opens with familiar inscription-rhetoric: "Behold the lord of the deep-bosomed earth, capsizer of heaven" and so forth. Eros goes on to explain that he was born under the reign of Neccessity, when all beings were kept apart by her grim power, were the creatures either of (and here the gap between the wings occurs) air or Chaos.[7] The effect in English is something like this at the central point:

7. Paton, and some of the Renaissance texts, give a different reading here.

THE POEM IN THE EYE

*all creatures were kept
far apart, moved they
in Air,*

*or Chaos.
The swift-flying son
of Kypris and of Achilles*   etc.

Two presentations of the "Wings" (reproduced on p. 256) show the vertical format in which they were printed in early editions. The more elaborate version, in woodcut borders, is from a Venice Theocritus of 1543, the other, from the Paris, 1561 text.

The "Egg" poem, possibly, like the "axe" to be inscribed, is most complex and allusive. It also has the top-and-bottom-line numbering system. It starts out by describing itself (a speaking egg, like so many

ΘΕΟΚΡΙΤΟΥ ΠΕΛΕΚΥΣ.

VISION AND RESONANCE

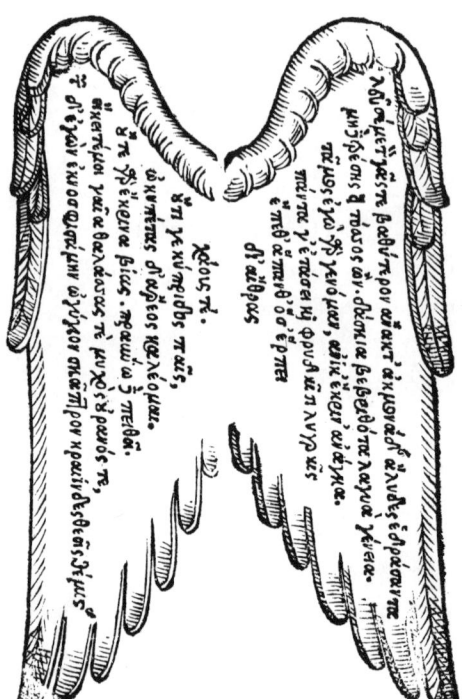

of the objects in emblematic poetry of all kinds that is either addressed in the text, or addresses the reader in it), as the egg of the "Dorian nightingale" (the poet? the poem itself?). It goes on to tell how the loud-voiced herald of the gods "took it up from beneath its dear mother's wings and cast it among the tribes of men, bidding it increase its number onward more and more—keeping always the due order of rhythms—from a one-footed measure up to a full decameter. . . ." The poem is about poetry, about creation and tradition (there is a long parenthetical bucolic simile), and about its own shape (one that "grows" as one reads it—from top and bottom "out" toward center). It is also about what the shape represents, the egg of generation. As an emblematic text it reads the meaning of its own device, but it also alludes to the abstract shape that the reduced convention of represen-

ΣΙΜΙΟΤ ΩΟΝ

Κωτίλας
τῇ τόδ' ἄτριον νέον
πρόφρων δὲ θυμῷ δέξο· δὴ γὰρ ἁγνᾶς
τὸ μὲν θεῶν ἐριβόας Ἑρμᾶς ἔκιξε κάρυξ
ἄνωγε δ' ἐκ μέτρου μονοβάμονος μέγαν πάροιθ' ἀέξειν
θοῶς δ' ὕπερθεν ὦκα λέχριον φέρων νεῦμα ποδῶν σποράδων πίφαυσκεν
θοαῖς ἴσ' αἰόλαις νεβροῖς κῶλ' ἀλλάσσων ὀρσιπόδων ἐλάφων τέκεσσιν
πᾶσαι κραιπνοῖς ὑπὲρ ἄκρων ἰέμεναι ποσὶ λόφων κατ' ἀρθμίας ἴχνος τιθήνας
καί τις ὠμόθυμος ἀμφίπαλτον αἴψ' αὐδὰν θὴρ ἐν κόλπῳ δεξάμενος θαλαμᾶν μυχοιτάτῳ
κἆιτ' ὦκα βοᾶς ἀκοὰν μεθέπων· ὅγ' ἄφαρ λάσιον νιφοβόλων ἂν' ὀρέων ἔσσυται ἄγκος
ταῖσι δὴ δαίμων κλυτᾶς ἴσα θοοῖς δονέων ποσὶ πελύπλοκα μετίει μέτρα μολπᾶς
δίμφα πετρόκοιτον ἐκλιπὼν ὄρουσ' εὐνάν, ματρὸς πλαγκτὸν μαιόμενος Βαλίας ἑλεῖν τέκος
βλαχαὶ δ' οἵων πολυβότων ἂν' ὀρέων νομὸν ἔβαν τανυσφύρων ἐς ἂν' ἄντρα Νυμφῶν
ταὶ δ' ἀμβρότῳ πόθῳ φίλας ματρὸς ῥώοντ' αἶψα μεθ' ἱμερόεντα μαζὸν
ἴχνει θένων . . . ταν παναίολον Πιερίδων μονόδουπον αὐδὰν
ἀριθμὸν εἰς ἄκραν δεκάδ' ἰχνίων κόσμον νέμοντα ῥυθμῶν
φῦλ' ἐς βροτῶν, ὑπὸ φίλας ἐλὼν πτεροῖσι ματρὸς
λίγειά μιν κάμ' Ἶφι ματρὸς ὠδίς
Δωρίας ἀηδόνος
ματέρος.

tation (here, by parallel longer and shorter lines) must needs assume: egg, and expanding shape.

Aside from Simmias' three poems, the so-called *technopaignia* (or tricks—Ausonius' word for them) officially included a "syrinx" by Theocritus. The shape was simply made of shortening couplets; an interesting point is brought up in scholarly debate about whether the array of unequal lines is intended to represent the now-canonical organ-pipe outline of the panpipes, or whether the representation is either an abstract picture of pitch variation, or the length of the stopped pipes—in Theocritus' time, it is argued, the actual shepherd's pipe was boxlike, with reeds of equal length being stopped by wax plugs. Whether the shape is pictorial or abstracted, however, the poem's language is complex and allusive, invoking Pan as the offspring of her who slept with nobody (i.e. Odysseus as "Noman," alluding to a myth of Pan as the son of Hermes and Penelope). Pan's pursuit of such nymphs as Echo, Pitys and, finally, Syrinx herself are all mentioned—the latter, of course, concretized in the actual instrument. The poet himself is referred to in the poem as "Paris, son of Simmias"—Paris, because he was a judge among gods (Theo+kritos, or Theocritus), and Simmias as inventor of the shaped poems. The syrinx poem concludes with an injunction to play sweetly to Echo (in the poem's arch language, to the mute maiden who is the invisible Calliope—mute because she can only reflect another sound, even as the moon might be called "invisible" or "silent"). The poem is a highly complex emblem of poetry itself.

The version reproduced below is from an edition of bucolic poets published in Heidelberg in 1604:

ΣΎΡΙΓΞ.

Σύριγξ ἄνομ' ἔχεις, ἀδί δέ σε μέτρα ζφίης
Οὐδενὸς ἐωάτειρα, μακρηπολέμοιο ὃ μᾶτερ,
Μαίας ἀϋπάτροιο θοὸν τέκες ἰθυντῆρα,
Οὐχὶ Κεράσαν, ὅν ποτε θρέψατο ταυρεπάτωρ.
Ἀλλ' ἀπέλειπες ἇ αἶθε παρ῾Θ' φρένα τέρμα ζάκυς,
Οὗ 'νομ' ὅλον δίζων, ὃς τᾶς μιερπ῾Θ' πόθον
Κούρας γηρυόνας αἶθε τᾶς δυεμώδε῾Θ'.
Ὃς μοίζα λιγὺ πάξεν ἰοςεφάνω
Ἕλκ῾Θ' ἄγαλμα πόθοιο πυρίζφαράγυ,
Ὃς σβέσεν ἀνορέαν ἰσαυδέα
Παππόφονυ, Τυρίας τε ἀφείλε῾ζ,
Ω.ς τόδε τυφλοφόρων ἐρατὸν
Πᾶμα Πάρις θέ῾ζ Σιμιχίδας
Ψυχάν. ὦ βρι῾ζζάμων,
Στή῾ζας οἶσρε δέ῾ζας,
Κλωποπάτωρ, ἀπάτωρ,
Λαρνακόγυε, χάερις,
Ἁδὺ μελίσδοις
Ἕλλοπι κούρᾳ.
Καλλιόπᾳ
Νηλεύσω.

The group known in the Renaissance includes two altar-shaped poems, one by Dosiadas, who appears to have known the "Syrinx," the other by Besantinus (perhaps L. Julius Vestinus, one of Hadrian's secretaries):

ΒΗΣΑΝΤΙΝΟΥ ΒΩΜΟΣ

'Ολὸς οὔ με λιβρὸς ἱρῶν
Λιβάδεσσιν, οἷα κάλχη
Ὑποφοινίῃσι τέγγει·
Μαύλιες δ' ὕπερθε πέτρης Ναξίας θοούμεναι
Παμάτων φείδοντο Πανός· οὐ στροβίλῳ λιγνύϊ
Ἰξὸς εὐώδης μελαίνει τρεχνέων με Νυσίων.
Ἐς γὰρ βωμὸν ὁρῇς με μήτε γλούρου
Πλίνθοις, μήτ' Ἀλύβης παγέντα βώλοις·
Οὐδ' ὃν Κυνθογενὴς ἔτευξε φύτλη
Λαβόντε μηκάδων κέρα,
Λισσαῖσιν ἀμφὶ δειράσιν
"Οσσαι νέμονται Κυνθίαις,
Ἰσόρροπος πέλοιτό μοι.
Σὺν Οὐρανοῦ γὰρ ἐκγόνοις
Εἰνάς μ' ἔτευξε γηγενής·
Τάων ἀείζωον τέχνην
Ἔνευσε πάλμυς ἀφθίτων.
Σὺ δ' ὦ πιὼν κρήνηθεν, ἣν
Ἰνις κόλαψε Γοργόνος,
Θύοις τ' ἐπισπένδοις τέ μοι
Ὑμηττιαδᾶν πολὺ λαροτέρην
Σπονδὴν ἄδην· ἴθι δὴ θαρσέων
Ἐς ἐμὴν τεῦξιν· καθαρὸς γὰρ ἐγὼ
Ἰὸν ἱέντων τεράων, οἷα κέκευθ' ἐκεῖνος
Ἀμφὶ Νέαις Θρηϊκίαις, ὃν σχεδόθεν Μυρίνης
Σοί, Τριπάτωρ, πορφυρέου φὼρ ἀνέθηκε κριοῦ.

the initial letters reading down form an acrostic dedication to that Emperor: "O Olympian, may you sacrifice for many years"). Both altars speak to the reader; the second one reads itself as an emblem: the dark blood of sacrifice does not stain me, it says, going on to point out that it is no material sacrificial altar built of gold or silver, but built by children of heaven aiding the earth-born Nine (Heliconian muses), etc. *Not marble, nor the gilded monuments of princes*, says the altar, *but this powerful rhyme*. . . . It looks forward to the most famous English pattern poems of the seventeenth century.

The first English figured or shaped poems were possibly influenced by French texts, themselves modeled on the *technopaignia* (Rabelais's bottle ode in the fifth book of Pantagruel may be remembered; there are also some wings by Mellin de Saint-Gelais). Stephen Hawes, in

260 VISION AND RESONANCE

The Convercyon of Swerers (1509), has a pair of wings, in black letter; actually there are two pairs of wings, separated by brackets, and the poem can be read in three versions—down the main wing shape (first slowly widening then contracting Skeltonic lines), down the outer wings, or across at the lines on which they meet.[8] There are also many learned exercises in Latin from the period (Richard Willis's *Poematum Liber* of 1573, etc.). But it is really George Puttenham, in the treatise mentioned earlier, who gives a systematic treatment to the patterning of the printed poem as part of the lore of poetic structure.

Puttenham's chapter on the subject is included in the part of his treatise dedicated to "Proportion," which includes prosody and versification. He discusses "Proportion by Situation," by which he means rhyme scheme and stanza pattern, and adduces diagrams, rather than the more modern *abab*, etc., notation, to describe the former. In his treatment of improvisatory, ode-, or madrigal-like strophes, he indicates that there is an almost limitless variety possible: "there are as manie or more proportions of them which I referre to the makers phantasie and choise, contented with two or three ocular examples and no moe"—he then reproduces a few patterns like the following:

etc.

(It will be noticed that these are line-length schemata.)

Puttenham's next section is "Of Proportion in Figure." He himself is aware only of what he calls "Anacreons egge" among the *technopaignia*, but he introduces a whole array of abstract geometrical forms "whereby the maker is restrained to keepe him within his bounds, and sheweth not onely more art, but serveth also much better for briefnesse

8. A good transcription of the text is by R. T. Davies, ed., *Medieval English Lyrics* (London, 1963), p. 259.

and subtiltie of device." Circles, lozenges, triangles, squares, all normal or halved and rejoined, provide him with the shapes to be made up by varying lines of verse. Only the pyramid and the pillar are in any way obvious emblematic shapes (save for the rondel, the circle of perfection, allegorized in two poems as the cosmos and the monarch). A columnar poem to Queen Elizabeth is made to be read up from bottom ("By this noble pourtrayt/Tall stately and strayt/Is plainely exprest/ And seene afarre/The sounde Pillar/Of Albion's rest . . .") to top, ending up with

> Is blisse with immortalitie.
>   Her trymest top of all ye see
>   Garnish the crowne
>   Her just renowne

The extra syllables form the capital, as they do, at the beginning, the base.

It is significant, incidentally, that Puttenham proceeds almost immediately after giving these examples to a discussion of emblems and devices; rather than treating them under his next category, "Ornament" (which is all rhetorical), he associates his own exemplary column and rondel poems with emblem verse, in that they presented a picture and then glossed it, in typical fashion. Puttenham, in fact, allegorizes all his abstract shapes (square:earth; sphere:heavens; spire:fire (through the old Greek falsè-etymology from *pyr*—); triangle:air; lozenge:water. The square for him is also an emblem of constancy (as it is for us, still, in the colloquial pejorative adaptation of "foursquare"). In connection with it, he introduces rather casually a most important notion. He declines to give an example of a square-shaped poem, he says, because "in goode arte all your ditties, Odes and Epigrammes should keep and not exceede the number of twelve verses. . . ." He sees the essential rectangularity on the page of those verse forms whose shapes, even today, we overlook as being a trivial consequence of typographical necessities. Indeed, a freshman textbook today which defined verse forms in the following way would be thought insane:

Sonnet :

Ballad :

Elegiacs:

(Nevertheless, this is a layer of phenomenon of which we as readers, naïve or learned, are always aware. We shall return to this later on.)

During the earlier seventeenth century, wings and pillars and, in particular, altars flourished. Joshua Sylvester wrote whole series of them as dedicatory poems. Browne, Herrick, Wither, and others all employed shaped poems and stanzas occasionally. The altar *format* (if I may here introduce the term to distinguish it from metrical, or generic, *form*) is easily available to accentual-syllabic couplets, with greater or lesser number of syllables and a typographer to center and justify the resultant lines into the shape (whether or not the outlining set of rules, so frequently used, is employed to emphasize the already obvious).

Here is Herrick's "Pillar of Fame" at the conclusion of *Hesperides:*

The pillar of Fame.

FAMES pillar here, at last, we set,
Out-during *Marble, Brasse,* or *Jet,*
Charm'd and enchanted so,
As to withstand the blow
Of overthrow:
Nor shall the seas,
Or OUTRAGES
Of storms orebear
What we up-rear,
Tho Kingdoms fal,
This pillar never shall
Decline or waste at all;
But stand for ever by his owne
Firme and well fixt foundation.

Herrick's poem connects the shaft to the lower part of the abacus, and to the base, by means of interlocking rhyme. The pillar is monumental, not sacramental: the vicar Herrick's verses are not those of the priest Herbert, nor could they do more than commemorate themselves, and the whole vision of poetry they celebrated, other than elegantly.

George Herbert's altar poem, as might be expected, is another matter.[9] The altar is broken because the voice of the supplicant is; it is also, perhaps, the ruin of a classical one (as far as its architectural shape is concerned), broken like a heart, perhaps also, more covertly, broken because it violates some of the traditional shaping of the familiar *technopaignia.* The poem is a farrago of biblical allusion, but the central figure of stony-heartedness, and the theme of the building of

9. Critics of Herbert since Joseph L. Summers—see his *George Herbert: His Religion and Art* (London, 1954), pp. 140-43—have generally seen that "The Altar" and "Easter Wings" were no trivial typographical jokes. The first of these, incidentally, is the opening poem of the section of *The Temple* called "The Church," containing all the short poems. Summers is enlightening on later misreadings of the altar shape, including treating it as a communion table. The altar shape was more ubiquitous in seventeenth-century verse than has been perceived. A glance at the ms. poems of Joseph Beaumont in the Wellesley College Library reveals what the misleadingly set up printed edition (ed. E. Robinson, 1914) does not—a mass of altars, lozenges, and "tricquets displayed."

altars (Exodus 20:25) intertwine inevitably. Unlike Besantinus' original Greek poem, the altar does not speak (the first person in Herbert's lyrics must refer to himself), but it does claim more authenticity for the poem-prayer-altar than for a stone one, and makes ruefully witty play with the possibility that the heart doing stony work risks turning stony.

The Altar.

A broken A L T A R, Lord, thy servant reares,
Made of a heart, and cemented with teares :
Whose parts are as thy hand did frame;
No workmans tool hath touch'd the same.
  A H E A R T alone
  Is such a stone ,
  As nothing but
  Thy pow'r doth cut.
  Wherefore each part
  Of my hard heart
  Meets in this frame,
  To praise thy Name:
That, if I chance to hold my peace,
These stones to praise thee may not cease.
O let thy blessed S A C R I F I C E be mine,
And sanctifie this A L T A R to be thine.

(Herbert's self-conscious format here can be considered as an extreme instance of what pervades *The Temple:* a quest for authenticity of form, as befitting textual, rhetorical, and spiritual occasion. And as always, the quester is ever wary of the traps set by novelty and ingenuity, to which he must nonetheless turn in full knowledge of their dangers.)

But perhaps the most remarkable instance of shaping in the seventeenth century is Herbert's "Easter Wings." This Easter poem celebrates the theme of descent that there may be ascent, of diminution in order that the augmentation may follow. The relation between "down so that up" and "less so that more" is strangely metaleptic, and it is in fact the poem's own figure of "in so that out," realized both in the shape on the page and in the reader's scanning of the text, that forms the connecting and generalizing link. But this is only half the image. The down-up and the poor-rich are celebrated in both stanzas, but the over-all figure is that of wings—angelic, poetic "as larks, harmoniously," and ultimately spiritual: all the wings of ascension. In the 1633 edition of *The Temple*, the wing emblem, a Christian transformation of the wings of Eros by Simmias, is made obvious by the way the text is printed, with the lines running vertically, like the Greek ones.

Easter-wings.

Lord, who createdst man in wealth and store,
   Though foolishly he lost the same,
      Decaying more and more,
         Till he became
            Most poore:
            With   thee
         O let me rise
      As larks, harmoniously,
   And sing this day thy victories:
Then shall the fall further the flight in me.

My tender age in sorrow did beginne:
   And still with sicknesses and shame
      Thou didst so punish sinne,
         That I became
            Most thinne.
            With   thee
         Let me combine
      And feel this day thy victorie:
   For, if I imp my wing on thine,
Affliction shall advance the flight in me.

When the page is turned to allow a lateral reading of the lines, the poem emerges as an instance of one of Puttenham's standard types, the "Tricquet Displayed," in fact, with an off-centering to the left to point up the wing shape:

Each stanza then figures the "in so that out," with the *peripeteia* (in this case, one almost wants to say *pterypeteia*) turning on the juncture of the two short lines "Most poore: with thee . . ." and "Most thinne. With thee." The juncture is a very powerful "but." Ultimately, the poem even prays for the effectiveness of the prayer itself, and fulfills its figural realization of the Alexandrian type of the poem about poetry. Much more than the epigrammatic altar poem, the "Easter Wings" seems to create the pattern of its picture, as we read it, rather than being forced into it. And as such, it is a rather blatant, didactic example of the way in which Herbert is always using form. Here, it is emblem and format as well, together and separately. The grace by which these are all managed is a matter of Herbert's being so at home in the kind of meter that the form demands (paired, reciprocating stanzas with short and long lines locked in by flexible rhyming pattern) that the rhetoric of this poem is not strange to his voice.

The twentieth century saw a renewed interest in his kind of patterned poetry.[10] Perhaps influenced by some of the experiments of the *futuristi,* Guillaume Apollinaire wrote many *calligrammes,* as he called them, calling for all sorts of typographical collage and montage, as well as shaping. Dylan Thomas used the lozenge and reversed lozenge in his "Vision and Prayer," following Herbert in the way he allowed his reversed lozenges (looking very much like centered Easter wings) to contract into the word "I" in the short central line, etc. More recently, we have had Gregory Corso's huge, fold-out "Bomb" in the shape of a thermonuclear mushroom and shaped poems by May Swenson and other poets including myself. These are by no means to be lumped together with "concrete poems"—for this discussion, concrete poetry is a purely graphic art; since a true concrete poem cannot be read aloud, it has no full linguistic dimension, no existence in the ear's kingdom. A

---

10. Aside from specifically emblematic shapes, modern American poetry has been obsessed with vaguely allusive ones, some of which have been discussed earlier. Hart Crane, for example, saw the third page of "Cutty Sark" from *The Bridge* "as a 'cartogram,' if one may so designate a special use of the calligramme. The 'ships' should meet and pass in line and type—as well as in wind and in memory, if you get my rather unique formal intentions in this phantom regatta seen from Brooklyn Bridge." (Letter to Edgell Rickword, January 7, 1927, in Hart Crane, *Letters,* ed. Brom Weber, Berkeley, 1965, p. 283). It would have to be said that, given the prevailing accentual-syllabic movement of even this section, the breaking-up and italicizing and off-centering of lines in "Cutty Sark" displays a formal intention to cope with the text of *The Waste Land,* as does a good bit of *The Bridge*—the question is more of format than of emblem.

concrete poem remains, in the often-quoted terms which Plutarch ascribed to Simonides, "mute poetry," and therefore, picture.[11]

In all of these cases, the shaping of the text into an emblem (or, in the case of Herbert's "Easter Wings," an abstract paradigm as well) has been part of a special genre or type. That genre came under great abuse in the sixteenth and seventeenth centuries from Montaigne on: thus the Elizabethan scholar Gabriel Harvey attacked Simmias of Rhodes as "a foolishe idle, phantasticall poett," and the convention as a whole he calls "mere fooleries, vices taken upp for virtues apish devices, frivolous boyishe grammar schole tricks." But this dispraise was probably a stock device itself, for Harvey's pamphleteering enemy, Nashe, accused Harvey himself of having "writ verses in all kinds as in a form of a pair of gloves, a dozen of points, a paire of spectacles, a two-hand sword, a poynado, a colossus, a pyramid, a painter's easel, a market-cross, an anchor, a pair of pothooks." Not very likely. Ben Jonson, too, sneered at shaped poems, as did Samuel Butler: attacking

11. Obviously, some of e. e. cummings's typographical effects seem, particularly within individual poems, to straddle the border. But such devices as his use of unexpected lineation and unexpected cutting—not of syntax on even morphemes, but graphic members of words (like the diagraphs t/h, s/h, etc.) are all an extension of the extreme left-hand edge of the enjambment spectrum proposed earlier. Two poems of Christian Morgenstern, however, might perhaps be adduced to make the contrast between concrete poem (or graphic art—in most cases, it will be admitted, a cartoon with a punch line, rather than what is loosely called a "graphic") and shaped one. First, the famous *"Fisches Nachtgesang"* ("Night Song of the Fish"), which is a poem schema made up of the "∪− ∪− ∪" marks of Classical scansion, contextualized by the title so that we think of slowly gaping and closing fish mouths, under water, making their silent music. The second, a poem about funnels, is not concrete, albeit funnel-shaped:

      Zwei Trichter wandeln durch die Nacht.
      Durch ihres Rumpfs verengten Schlacht
         fliesst weisses Mondlicht
           still und heiter
            auf ihren
            Waldweg
             U. S.
              w.

"Two funnels wander in the night; through the narrowed shaft of their trunks white moonlight flows quiet and gay on their woodpath, etc."—with the literalization of *"und so weiter"* augmented by the rhyme, the "forth" of "and so forth" introduced in funnel language (where "forth" is the narrowed "down") and in the vanishing-point perspective language of walking, especially in moonlit woods.

the minor seventeenth-century poet Edward Benlowes he said that "as for temples and pyramids in poetry, he has outdone all men that way; for he has made a gridiron and a frying-pan in verse, that, besides the likeness in shape, the very tone and sound of the words did perfectly represent the noise made by those utensils!" And Dryden, finally, advised Shadwell to "choose for they command/Some peaceful province in acrostic land,/There thou mayest wings display and altars raise,/ And torture one poor word ten thousand ways." The burden of all these denunciations is upon the superficiality, the literary version of taking the letter for the spirit. And yet the fact remains that from the early sixteenth century on, all poems are in some sense shaped.

3

Most poems are in the shape of poems, not of pictures. This is to say that by the middle of the sixteenth century, the look of the poem on the page had begun to assume a canonical importance, and patterns of versification and typographical arrangement to play a small but definite role in the history of form. Consider, for example, the convention of line indentation in the Classical elegiac couplet, where the second line, the pentameter, is indented. Now, all Elizabethan writers of metrics knew that the poulter's measure, that couplet consisting of a line of twelve syllables rhyming with one of fourteen and supposedly invented by Surrey, is really a version of the special 3-3-4-3 ballad stanza (just as fourteener couplets are a graphic rewriting of the normal one). When poulter's measures appear in pages of sixteenth-century miscellanies, they are set up with the shorter line indented; even though the order, beginning with the short line, is reversed, the general effect of the poem on the page is one of Classical elegiacs. The acutely classically conscious Renaissance critical eye responded to this, and it may have helped account for the growth of the form. Surely the authenticity of an elegiac look on the page was as significant as the anthologist's possible desire to save space in setting up the poems. The ballads in the tradition of the Courtly Makers, then, become newly dignified typographically. And if this seem too far-fetched, we have the case of Ben Jonson's careful distinction, in the setting up of his 1616 folio *Works,* between two kinds of heroic couplets in English. Ordinarily, where the English couplet is being used for the Classical one, the second line, although the same length, is indented. But there is one instance, in the *Epigrams* section, where he is using couplets, as in Chapman, Marlowe, and subsequent tradition, to stand for hexameters. This is in the mock-heroic *Fabulous Voyage,* a parodic odyssey through the sewers of London. With great care, the verses of the couplets are all aligned flush left, making it clear that they are the English equivalent of hexameters. By the Augustan period, these English couplets have, of course, developed an authority all their own, and the odd fact that they do double duty as versions of hexameters and couplets both, as far as Classical poetry is concerned, is completely unnoticed.

This is merely one small but significant instance. If we look again at some of the emblematic shapings of stanza forms in seventeenth-century poetry, we can see that the impulse to pattern the stanza is often submerged beneath a different one, deriving from the Elizabethan and Jacobean lyrical poem of varying line length, such as Drummond of Hawthornden's "madrigals," which were simply an Italianate lyrical form for epigram. So, for example, the patterned stanzas from Francis Quarles's *Hieroglyphics of the Life of Man.* There is no symbolic picture here, nor no abstract shape of one of the conventional sorts, such as lozenge, reversed lozenge or the like. But the look of such stanzas, which abound in minor seventeenth-century poetry, was clearly a thing in itself, and great care was taken by typographers to preserve the shape in the justification of the lines.

Then, too, Ben Jonson, in the first real attempt to get the Pindaric ode triad into English, labels the strophes in his great Cary and Morison ode "The Turn," "The Counter-Turn," and "The Stand," respectively; he is doing more from a visual point of view than merely dragging marginalia into the middle of the page. The strophic triad was in antiquity a musical strain and a choregraphic pattern as well; it becomes in the adapted so-called Pindaric, as it has long before in the Horatian ode, a block of type on a page, framed in white space. And so too with stanzaic patterning in general: as we move on through literary history, stanza breaks, in poems with a major meditative motion in particular, can become rather complex kinds of linkages rather than merely disruptions of continuity. For what Meyer Abrams has called the Major Romantic ode, in particular, stanzaic form, often extremely ornate, and the far-ranging syntatic and meditative extensions of blank verse, are made to play the same role. When they do, the white space between the stanzas becomes operative and can indeed be *glossed* (with a far more complex glossing than the marginal note one might use to annotate the stanza break between the second and third strophes of Donne's "The Flea"—a simple "Whack!" to indicate that the flea had been so treated by the intransigeant lady).

This consideration of poetry's visual aspect may, indeed, seem as superficial as the shaped poems have been charged with being. But as the metrical traditions of English poetry grow more complex in the seventeenth century, the apparent superficiality of graphic arrangement starts to develop consequences which extend further and further down into the depths of language. I am not thinking now only of the ways in which seventeenth-century theorists themselves were sometimes confused in their ascription of a metrical effect to the ear rather than to the eye. All of the attempts, from those of the Sidney-Spenser circle through that of Campion to develop quantitative verse in English, are really based on games played with written codes alone. The rules about syllable length and so forth were based on an adaptation of rules about the letters of written Latin to those of English. Even granted for a moment that a diphthong in English is a long vowel and the others short, doubling of a consonant after a vowel makes it unequivocally short is a rule that has applied from the thirteenth century *Ormulum* on. Yet the rules of quantitative scansion demand that the doubling of a consonant with another one, even in an adjacent word, lengthen the syllable containing it. All of these attempts at accommodation work out only on the written level, rather like the solution of an acrostic. But given the viability of the English blank-verse line as a thing in itself, a visual matter starts to play an important role.

This is not to say by any means that blank verse is purely visual. But we have already seen (Chapter V) how Dr. Johnson could quote with approval a remark that "blank verse seems to be verse only to the eye."

T. S. Eliot, deciding that Milton was perhaps not so dreadful after all, could in 1947 remark on the similarity between what he called Dr. Johnson's specialized ear and that of the early decades of the twentieth century when it came to free verse.[12] The fact remains that the relation between the eye and the ear is by no means as simple as such remarks suggest. Conventions of inscribing are generally conservative, with a scribal and scholiastic integrity of their own; and Modernist poetry, in particular, tended always to argue for the poetic primacy and the social vitality of the spoken.[13]

In an earlier examination of enjambment, it was seen that line terminus, in some contracted-for regular meter like iambic pentameter, could function like grammatical diagraming, even as stress positioning itself can frequently operate like emphatic underlining for expression, sarcasm, or contrast. Line and strophe and poem structures which do not take shape from the arrangement of audibly prominent phenomena may nevertheless come to play a role in the organizing of sound patterning: there are kinds of quasi-rhetorical notations which format itself can perform. The kinds of linguistic depth which these arrangements of printed surface stir up are beyond my grasp and my subject. Perhaps there is some correlation here, in a notion of poetic language which lies below both sight and sound, with the recent history of linguistic theory, abandoning neo-grammarian philology, the historical paradigms based on the inscription, for the structural linguistics of the school of Bloomfield, Sapir, and their followers, for whom speech was the essential linguistic event, and for whom mere transcriptions of it in a written system remained a kind of ineptly mediating and confusing accident. The current revision of linguistic theory by a philosopher

---

12. T. S. Eliot, On *Poetry and Poets* (New York, 1957), p. 180.
13. And so, apparently, thought Dr. Thomas Sprat, writing in praise of Cowley's "Pindaric" odes, with their improvisatorily varied line lengths: "But that for which I think this inequality of number is chiefly to be preferr'd, is its near affinity with Prose: . . . But now this loose, and unconfin'd measure has all the Grace, and Harmony of the most confin'd." Sprat, a practical man devoted to scientific prose, nevertheless makes the characteristic mistake of Molière's M. Jourdain in confounding *prose* and *speech*, however, claiming that the former "is the style of all business and conversation." T. Sprat, *An Account of the Life of Mr. Abraham Cowley* (1668).

with what is almost an unreconstructed seventeenth-century theory of mind, locates language in mental structures and patterns. But as far as these remarks are concerned, we may locate the syntactical, even the paradigmatic, in the visual domain of poetry. The way in which the printed poem directs attention to grammatical elements, for example, the way in which meter can be used to diagram syntax, is like a set of stage directions, working *through* the eye, rather than on it. Ultimately, it is always with what Wallace Stevens calls "The poem of the act of the mind" that we are concerned.

The question of how poems are shaped like other poems is a vast one. I have dwelt for a while with enjambment because it is a significant part of the larger matter, and because it leads to a consideration of the uneven right-hand margin as a viable criterion for defining verse as opposed to prose, in twentieth-century poetry, at least. Given Dr. Johnson's remarks on Milton's blank verse, it is not surprising that the whole tradition of Miltonic blank verse in the eighteenth century aims only at carrying forward the notion of a long verse paragraph, and not at sharing, let alone going beyond, Milton's "sense variously drawn out from one verse into another." Only Blake, in those violently experimental blank verse poems in *Poetical Sketches*, sought to come to terms with Milton's virtual invention of blank verse as a dialectical and meditative, as well as a dramatic mode.

But the recent use by contemporary poets of purely syllabic verse does indeed appear to present what is "verse only to the eye"—even to the need for practitioners of it to count on their fingers, or otherwise tap out lines when they would never think of so doing in the case of the accentual-syllabic which they always "hear." Pure syllabics are the verse system of French and of Japanese, and the accentual weight of syllables which may be occasioned by phrase or clausal terminus (there being no word stress) is never systematized in the verse. In English, of course, the result is something like

> These two incommensurably sounding
> Lines are both written with ten syllables,
> But so is this, which you can plainly hear.

Sophisticated syllabic verse has an added dimension in modulating its cadences: the contrast between lines like the second and the third in the dummy above is not a matter of an accentual-syllabic line having wandered into the syllabic from iambic pentametersville, but more a matter of a dynamic range which the open criteria about stress provide. Lines 1 and 2 above are not iambic pentameter: in any passage which had declared that convention to be in operation, they would have to be ruled non-metrical. (We might then, indeed as in the case of Hart Crane's more than occasional six-beat lines in a melodious, Shelleyan, five-beat framework, really wonder why they were there, and what went wrong or different.) The allowable displacements in iambic pentameter cannot really be said to constitute too difficult a matter. Whenever we get a line which the iambic pentameter convention cannot dictate to us a proper reading of, then we must assume that the poet is inept, or that he intends to disturb in just that way:

> How many bards gild the lapses of time? (Keats)
> *Read this as "dactyls" and then it will rhyme* (reader)

(The reader here could have been Leigh Hunt, who read it as acephalic anapests.) In fact, this opening line of the splendid sonnet about the voices of precursor poets in one's head being like an evening music, saddened and humanized, in a Wordsworthian way, sounds "That distance of recognizance bereaves"—this opening line, which is indeed quite ambiguous, has a very clear rhetorical function. While we might include it in our stack of pure syllabic lines in the earlier example (as Robert Bridges indeed did), it would stick out as being almost as strongly tightened up in the pitch of patterned accent as line 3 above. No: it is an accentual five-beat and not a four-beat accentual anapestic one *because the sonnet says it is,* and because the sonnet shows us how it is to be read—slowly, with the rhetorical tone of passionate bemusement: *How many bárds! God, how many of them there are and have been! And their voices are all in my head; but they yammer not, neither do they shriek; somehow this is choral. But how many there are, coming rushing in when there is a vacuum of silence to fill!:*

　　　　H󠁯́w many ba󠁲́rds　　gi󠁬́d the la󠁰́ses of ti󠁭́me (!)

The mere displaced positioning of "the" and "of"?

In strict syllabic verses, the control of stress placement is as important as in accentual syllabic verse, but not at the same level of effect. In the latter, misplaced stresses can make lines startling, and overly systematic metrists who are not unduly committed to what poetry is about, perplexed. In syllabic verse, a momentary accentual cadence can function like a momentary rhyme in a strictly controlled blank-verse situation (see the example from Wallace Stevens on p. 132). Often, in uncertain hands, it can do the wrong sort of work. Robert Bridges's experiments with syllabic verse never developed the authority of Marianne Moore's or W. H. Auden's, for example—he was always at his best when there was an accentual richness to nourish his verse. Consider, then, the opening of the programmatically syllabic late poem, "Cheddar Pinks" (written in 1921):

> Mid the squander'd colour
>   idling as I lay . . .

We might be tempted to continue: "*Reading moldy Homer / on the first of May.*" That is, the trochaic rhythm is so strong, the known associations of the longer (four- or three-beat) first line and the indented, shorter (three or two) second one so long, that we are led even to expect the rhyme as well. Here is the movement, in fact:

> Mid the squander'd colour
>   idling as I lay
> Reading the Odyssey
>   in my rock-garden
> I espied the cluster'd
>   tufts of Cheddar pinks
> Burgeoning with promise
>   of their scented bloom
> All the modish motley
>   of their bloom to-be
> Thrust up in narrow buds
>   on the slender stalks . . .

The lower-case initial in the alternate lines may provide a clue to an original impulse to make these longer lines; in fact, if we double them, the tendency to lapse into the trochaic in the longer lines submerges its pounding, and we are left with a strangely Lawrentian cadence. Setting the tone with the original strong trochaic movement, Bridges keeps singing to that tune, as it were; at any rate, the reader keeps humming it. In other words, syllabic meter, "verse only to the eye," can set up all sorts of potentiality for sound effect; it merely frames them and directs attention to them differently.

But there is still the question of *format;* there are more complex and allusive kinds of visual shaping of form in modern poetry than Puttenham could have ever imagined. Consider, for a moment, the following two dummy stanzas:

>   A. Open every door: when the resounding wind
>   Tries to batter it down, you will be wise to lead
>   All that violent weather
>   Into the gentle dark within
>
>   and B. When the wind howls loudly outside your door, never
>   Keep that door shut, but open it instead so that
>   You may make a peaceful guest
>   Of a violent invader

Depending upon whether we are listening or looking, these stanzas are similar or unrecognizable as siblings. The syllabic scheme is a line of twelve, a line of twelve, a line of seven, and a line of eight. This is the meter, so to speak, and both stanzas are written in it. The *shaping,* that is, the particular indentation pattern, suggests that these stanzas are to be considered as versions of, as related to, the German analogues of classical lyric meters as used by Klopstock and Hölderlin, for example, in which stress accent is substituted for length. This worked out rather well, as there were no substitutions allowed in these strophic meters in any case; English poets from Southey, Landor, and Coleridge through Tennyson and Swinburne adopted these Germanized meters, although the Sapphic stanza was the only one that had got much previous use in English verse. (Whenever Romantic or Victorian poets speak of classical experiments, by the way, it is these stress-substitutions to which they refer, not the actual assignment of spurious quantities to written syllables of English that the Elizabethans had tried.)

Now stanza A is a good case of this; aside from the syllabic lines, the stresses are grouped unvaryingly: two lines of [/ · / ·· / / ·· / · /] followed by one of [/ · / ·· / ·] and one of [/ ·· / · / · /] But stanza B has no such distribution, and simply to hear it read aloud would not be to realize that line breaks came where they did. Although it too has the rigorous syllabic scheme for its meter, its rhythm is an irregular one. And yet its shape, also, is that of the alcaic or aesclepedian lyric stanza. I have used dummies to show this more clearly. But consider the meter and the shape of Auden's "In Memory of Sigmund Freud," for example; the purely syllabic meter can yield rhythms as different as A and B, not as separate forms but as rhythmic instances. Moreover the *shape*, the look of the stanza on the page, is part of the meter, although you would never find type B in any traditional adapted classical meter in English or German. Here is a case, then, of a poem-shaped poem: I should say, Hölderlin-shaped, in Auden's case. It is also interesting to note that only from time to time in Auden's poem does he allow the canonical stress rhythm to emerge, as in the last lines, "Sád is Éros, búilder of cíties / And wéeping, ánarchic Áphrodíte"; hereby, the visual music controls even the turning on and off of occasional strains of the audible. Here, unlike the iambic drift possible in the dummy ten-syllable lines, the drift is toward the German accentual versions of the Greek lyric meter. But the stanza format, the patterns of indentation, etc., keep the possibility present that those accentual patterns will actually emerge.

Among the many elements of poetry's visual structure that have emerged since the eighteenth century are those like sight rhymes that have come about as a result of linguistic change; to rhyme "love," "move," and "grove," for example, would not necessarily be to admit the practice of off- or slant-rhyming, so prevalent in contemporary verse. Conventions of indentation are an interesting matter that the formalist historian might study. The crisis in initial capitalization that seems to have come about with imagist poetry is an interesting matter as well; whether or not there was any influence of Classical texts, which do not of course capitalize initial letters of lines, is a matter for historical study. Suffice it to say that lack of capitalization has become the same kind of convention that the avowedly redundant upper-case letter established. But in general, the poem on the page became the essential mode of its existence during the Modern period. We know of course of Mallarmé's obsession, in his later years, with poetic *format;* aside from the typographical experimentation of *Un Coup de Dès,* there was his interest in the structure of the book per se, how pages are scanned, the dynamic of page-turning, and the like, although these matters never involved the deepest sources of his imaginative vision. Mallarmé's kind of attention to format is surely continued, albeit transformed, in Apollinaire's *Calligrammes.*

On the other hand, "free verse" as a category is so open that when we have so designated a poem, we have said nothing, and it becomes necessary to consider this question of *shape*—of format, rather than of metrical form—where nothing is being regularly counted. Even Whitman follows previous traditions of metrical innovation in English verse (Christopher Smart in *Jubilate Agno,* etc.) by working out of the means that the English bible generates for translating Hebrew poetry; whatever his rhetorical accretions of cataloguing, listing, stacking parallel constructions under one another, etc., his lines are always his phrases and clauses. When he uses the visually rhythmic metaphor of sea waves and tides to describe the undulations of his line length, he is making an appeal to a sense of the *natural* that would respond to the correspondence of form with the inner character of his utterance. How various modes of free verse take shape on the page, what occasional sound patternings they may or may not embrace (as in the case of the Auden stanzas, only without, say, either syllabic regularity or stanza shape), are all matters for a theory of graphic prosody.

Just as illuminating, though, is the way in which the increasing importance of format, of shape, manages to engage and control older, aural regularities. The typographic manipulations of e. e. cummings, what we might call his experiments in expressionistic typography, his visual tricks with self-illustrating phrases and words (such as the word "moon" appearing out of parentheses of cloud) are well known. So too in the little poem in which the one word "loneliness" is made to drop down the page, containing between the first "l" and the second, third, and fourth letters, the bracketed, two-letters-to-a-line phrase "a leaf falls." Then the second "l"—punning visually, as throughout the poem, on the identity of the twelfth letter of the lower-case roman alphabet with the first arabic numeral in many typefaces. Then the end. This is all a *haiku*-like evaded simile, so arranged that the vehicle is troped into the tenor. But the vertical drop controls the scanning.

Cummings is capable of another sort of audio-visual subtlety, as in the first two stanzas of the fifty-first poem of *1x1* (1944):

> Sweet spring is your
> time is my time is our
> time for springtime is lovetime
> and viva sweet love
>
> (all the little merry birds are
> flying in the floating in the
> very spirits singing in
> are winging in the blossoming)

Here the graphic arrangement of the lines is slightly skewed, as far as the notation of the rhythm is concerned. There are two stresses per line, in a familiar kind of English jingle; the shifted lineation not only yields up a graphic sub-line "time for springtime is lovetime," lost in the jingle (this is rather like noticing that a poem is acrostic only from the printed text), but even more importantly slows down the scanning of the jingle pattern, and gives a touch of some sort of gravity to the verse, if only because it reveals itself to us a bit more slowly than it would if regularly notated. Here is a strong case of the poem's format by no means notating its meter and rhythm, while yet not being in the least emblematic.

With the importation into Modern English poetry of models and techniques from the poetry of other languages, the role of visual format is again heightened. Much could be said of the interplay between the visual and the aural in Ezra Pound's earlier poetry, let alone the collage-like, palimpsestic, scholia-ridden, diary-entered format of *The Cantos*. I need only mention his attempts to accommodate modes as distant as Alexandrian and Latin epigram, on the one hand, and *haiku* on the other, in his line patterning in the shorter poems in *Personae*. The famous little "Papyrus" is something of a manifesto:

> Spring . . .
> Too long . . .
> Gongula . . .

Here the poem is shaped like a relic of Sappho's, not typographically twisted into something like a jagged edge of torn papyrus, but like the transcription and decipherment of such a scrap in a scholarly edition. "Gongula" is actually a name that appears among the Sapphic fragments,[14] but we might guess that it was a girl's name, even without knowing much Greek. The poem is about fragmentariness, and about the imaginative futility of asking if a broken Hellenistic statue is so beautiful for us just *because* its this and that are broken off. We reconstruct a poem of our own, each one of us as he reads this, more than in the sense in which this is true of all poetry, of all images. Notice, too, the careful metric patterning (one line of one syllable, one of two, one of three), and the assonance and rhyme. But the ellipsis marks are part of this poem's shape, not its heard rhythm.

4

In W. C. Williams's little poem about the red wheelbarrow discussed earlier in this book,[15] so much depends upon a way of seeing, trained and framed by photography's way of cutting out rectangles of scene, and upon poetry's way of cutting and framing bits of language. Indeed, so much has started to depend upon vision, in all of modern poetry.

14. For an inspired guess as to how Pound might have generated the poem from the actual fragment in question, as well as for the best sympathetic treatment of Pound's formal practice I have yet read, see Hugh Kenner, *The Pound Era* (Berkeley, 1971), pp. 5-6, 54, 62.
15. See Chapter V.

And this extends even to poetry's vision of itself. We have come back, in twentieth-century verse, to a new version of *ut pictura poesis*. If eloquence had been musical sound in the imaginative realm of seventeenth- and eighteenth-century poetry, there was also another model for it. Actually, it is hard to tell if this model is visual or aural, so complex is the analogy. An early statement of it is about prose rather than poetry, but in the early seventeenth century, prose style is far more idiosyncratic than verse. Here is Burton writing about his writing in the *Anatomy of Melancholy*, that amazing book of himself:

> I neglect phrases and labour wholly to inform my reader's understanding, not to please his ear; 'tis not my study or intent to compose neatly, which an Orator requires, but to express myself readily and plainly as it happens. So that as a River runs, sometimes precipitate and swift, then dull and slow; now direct, then winding; now deep, then shallow; now muddy, then clear; now broad, then narrow; doth my style flow: now serious, then light; now comical, then satyrical; now more elaborate, then remisse . . . .

Burton glosses his flowing-water language to show how it means flowing language. He need not have done so, for most of those terms were already conventionally applied, in secondary senses, to language as well. "Liquid" for melody, particularly birds' song, can be found as far back as Lucretius.[16] Burton's apology here reminds us of Whitman's talking of his lines as "the liquid, billowy waves, ever rising and falling, perhaps wild with storm, always moving, always alike in their nature as rolling waves, but hardly any two exactly alike in size or measure, never having the sense of something finished and fixed, always suggesting something beyond." Certainly the appeal to the natural, rather than the artificial, is Burton's point as well. But the language about language from the *Anatomy* leads us almost inevitably to some of the most influential lines of poetry written in the seventeenth century, and that helped to make their author, John Denham, acclaimed in the Augustan

---

16. Also see St. Augustine, *Confessions*, XII, xxvii, for what may be a central passage about source and stream, eloquence and tradition. Possibly there is an earlier topos which I am not aware of. (A Hebraic one has the Torah as tree of life.)

age as one of its founding fathers. In *Cooper's Hill,* the poet concludes his description of the Thames with the famous apostrophe to that more-than-river:

> O could I flow like thee, and make thy stream
> My great example, as it is my theme!
> Though deep, yet clear, though gentle, yet not dull,
> Strong without rage, without o'erflowing, full.

Here, poetic language views itself as the totality of the stream, the water which when standing still, has reflecting surfaces and less accessible depths and becomes an inevitable symbol for consciousness, via Narcissus, Milton's Eve, Traherne, and Wordsworth. The running water is part a spatial concept, part an aural one, but the two most promising words here are "deep" and "clear."[17] So much, in the future history of poetry, will depend on them.

The ways in which poetry exercises a pictorial function about what is outside it is also relevant to the ways in which it envisions itself. Descriptions of scene and picture and prospect and landscape in eighteenth-century poetry mirror both literary and pictorial conventions; even as actual landscaping tried to rearrange hundreds of acres of southwestern England into what would look like a painting by Claude, eighteenth-century descriptive poetry was often looking at landscape paintings of what it saw. Keats, then Tennyson, then the Pre-Raphaelite poets modeled description more on the illuminated quality of precise detail, unclouded by painterly interventions and atmospheric perspectives. The amazing thing about so much descriptive vision in romantic poetry is the way in which the imagination invents visionary possibilities for which a technology did not then exist, but for which there is now a trivial technical simulation.

In the opening lines of "Tintern Abbey," for example, there are sev-

---

17. Dr. Johnson, in praising this passage, objects to what he thinks of as a trick of metaphor "for most of the words, thus artfully opposed, are to be understood simply on one side of the comparison, and metaphorically on the other. . . ." He does not see the passage as a schematic means of bringing out the latent metaphorical meanings, almost, indeed, cliché, in the flowing-water language. (*Life of Denham,* in *Lives of The English Poets,* Everyman edition, Vol. I, p. 51.)

eral visual mechanisms working at once. After the five years' interval is announced, and the introductory flourish of sound is heard ("and again I hear / These waters, rolling from their mountain-springs / With a soft inland murmur"), the poet observes that he is once again beholding the

> steep and lofty cliffs,
> That on a wild, secluded scene impress
> Thoughts of more deep seclusion, and connect
> The landscape with the quiet of the sky.

This is a picture of the comparing and remembering mind as well as one of what that mind is seeing and remembering; while the comparing process is on the brink of becoming an overlay of transparencies, there is no conceptual language for it. Wordsworth must adopt the technical vocabulary of associationist psychology, here used metaphorically, to describe the way in which the observed phenomena are consolidated with the remembered ones, and which, finally abandoning all categorical logic, "connect / the landscape" not with the sky, but with its "quiet"—almost, in a slowly developing modern sense of the word, with its silence. Fifty-odd lines later on, this is reaffirmed:

> And now, with gleams of half-extinguished thought
> With many resignations, dim and faint,
> And somewhat of a sad perplexity,
> The picture of the mind revives again . . .

Thought works in gleams of image, just as, before, the scene is like a mind receiving impressions. The grammatical ambiguity of "The picture of the mind" is quite significant, and even if not present by design, it is controlled by some deeper intention: it is both the mind's picture of the scene and the poem's picture of the mind. Wordsworth never reached the point of deriving a picture of the *poem*, although, as Geoffrey Hartman has shown, he was extremely interested in the rhetoric, if not the form, of inscriptions, sepulchral epigrams, and the like.

The principle contribution of modern visual technology is photography, still and moving, as far as the poetic imagination is concerned.

One of the greatest developments in nineteenth-century poetry is the sophisticated kind of transition between stanzas, sections, parts of poems, transitions that need not be glossed or explained. These correspond to the kinds of transition which two generations now, having grown up with moving pictures, can take for granted, and not even find disturbing in dreams. We find traces of this cinematographic vision in modern, as well as in contemporary poetry: the opening pan shot, trucking through the great house and out to the garden and the pool back of it in the beginning of *Burnt Norton,* say, or the cinematic opening sequence of the proem to *The Bridge,* half-consciously brought into a poem which disparages "cinemas, panoramic sleights / With multitudes bent toward some flashing scene / Never disclosed, but hastened to again . . . ." In contemporary verse formats, we frequently find odd sorts of interruption and linkage being developed—extensions of the more archaic white spaces between stanza breaks—in order to handle complex sorts of transition that defy ordinary syntactical punctuation. Even Wallace Stevens, as secure, later in his career in his blank pentameter couplets and tercets, as could be, tried in the first edition of *Parts of a World* to put holes in his lines, adopting a strange sort of double-spacing procedure, independent of punctuation, which he later removed for *Collected Poems.* They were, indeed, quite unnecessary, but it is interesting that he thought once that they might be needed.

I can think of no more startling cinematic tansformation of still picture into motion, even of sound and physical sensation into rushing image, than in a very strange sort of experimental poem, that could only have been written as an informal notebook entry. The format is block, blank-verse paragraph. I quote a whole section of this poem about a journey:

> Antwerp to Ghent
>
> > We are upon the Scheldt. We know we move
> > Because there is a floating at our eyes
> > Whatso they seek; and because all the things
> > Which on our outset were distinct and large
> > Are smaller and much weaker and quite gray,
> > And at last gone from us. No motion else.

> We are upon the road. The thin swift moon
> Runs with the running clouds that are the sky,
> And with the running water runs—at whiles
> Weak 'neath the film and heavy growth of reeds.
> The country swims with motion. Time itself
> Is consciously beside us, and perceived.
> Our speed is such the sparks our engine leaves
> Are burning after the whole train has passed.
> The darkness is a tumult. We tear on,
> The roll behind us and the cry before,
> Constantly, in a lull of intense speed
> And thunder. Any other sound is known
> Merely by sight. The shrubs, the trees your eye
> Scans for their growth, are far along in haze.
> The sky has lost its clouds, and lies away
> Oppressively at calm; the moon has failed;
> Our speed has set the wind against us. Now
> Our engine's heat is fiercer, and flings up
> Great glares alongside. Wind and steam and speed
> And clamor and the night. We are in Ghent.

These lines are, astonishingly enough, by Dante Gabriel Rossetti: they were written on a historic occasion for visionary history, by the way, on a trip which he and Holman Hunt took to Flanders to see the fifteenth-century paintings, in 1849. This was the beginning of their historical moment. And yet the poem is not of their sort; it depicts, if anything, a Whistler, but a Whistler in motion. It is, in fact the title of a famous Turner ("Rain, Steam and Speed: The Great Western Railway"), which he almost quotes. The world whizzing by outside a train window can find no appropriate genre in Victorian poetry, and there is no expansion of format capable of containing this kind of vision. As it stands, this long poem is without results, and remains an amazing experiment. It will not be until such a poem as "An Ordinary Evening in New Haven" that this kind of vision will be overlaid, in the Wordsworthian way, with a similar kind of vision about the world of the poem itself; that the look of poems, square and framelike as they may invariably remain, open and unendingly page-like as their iambic blocks may be, will serve as lenses for the look of things.

A poem's shape, then, may be a frame for itself as it may be a frame for its picture of the world. Traditional meter always had a framing, a labeling or titling faculty: the meter of a poem, as opposed to its rhythm, was some kind of option for a genre status. A modern visual format will be just that, and more. The role of the typewriter in poetic composition is not to be ignored, I think—even though mss. may be composed in longhand, the immediate print-out of a typewriter is available to refer to for a sense of shape,[18] and even though the poem has been patterned in some metrical fashion. And yet the purely conventional role of shape, played throughout history by meter, is still there, and there exist contemporary formats which sooner indicate that the poem is a version of a Poundian canto than reveal the operation of the dubious and muddled principles of so-called "projective verse."

In considering just this sort of confusion between what a poem is doing and what its author claims it is doing, one thinks of the disparity between the effects of W. C. Williams's meter and his interpretation of these. For this and other reasons, I should like to conclude these observations with a look at some lines from one of his, and modern America's, finest poems, one whose shape is still being used, or rather the *outline* of whose shape is still being used, by many poets. It is the first poem of his early sequence called *Spring and All,* and is a version of the *reverdie,* the traditional spring song which one finds in English verse from the thirteenth century on:

> By the road to the contagious hospital
> under the surge of the blue
> mottled clouds driven from the
> northeast—a cold wind. Beyond, the

---

18. Hugh Kenner, *The Pound Era,* pp. 90-91, suggests that hitting the space-bar twice on a typewriter can, indeed, be a kind of marking of time; it is certainly true that, if one were to write a theory of format, the unit spacing of the typewriter, the accentual clatter of the sound of the machine itself (for those who write directly on it) may have some significance. See Chapter XI. We might also observe that just as the verb "sing" became a stock metaphor for "compose poetry," so "write" is becoming one for "type."

>   waste of broad, muddy fields
>   brown with dried weeds, standing and fallen
>
>   patches of standing water
>   the scattering of tall trees
>
>   All along the road the reddish
>   purplish, forked, upstanding, twiggy
>   stuff of bushes and small trees
>   with dead, brown leaves under them
>   leafless vines—
>
>   Lifeless in appearance, sluggish,
>   dazed spring approaches—

This is a poem of discovery, of the gradual emergence of the sense of spring from what looks otherwise like a disease of winter. The "contagious hospital" is both a colloquial usage, by doctors and patients, for the longer name, and a hospital that is itself contagious, that leaks its presence out onto the road. The cold wind will be revealed as a spring wind, but not before the poem's complex act of noticing has been completed. The meter here is a typographic strip about 30 ems wide with a general tendency to break syntax at tight points (lines 3 and 4 are normal, rather than exceptional); but notice the traditional use of discovery-enjambment in lines 2 and 3—"under the surge of the blue" because of its audible dactylic melody aims the syntax at a noun version of "blue," a metonymy for sky. But the next line discovers its mere adjectival use, appositively with "mottled," and the hopefulness of upward motion, the brief bit of visual and perhaps spiritual ascendancy is undercut by the bleakness of the wintry scene, and the totality of the non-greenness, even the exclusion of available blue. For the buds of spring do indeed look, at first, like tumorous nastinesses of the branch. But the poem moves toward the avowal of the discovery: "Now the grass, tomorrow / the stiff curl of wildcarrot leaf." Its real conclusion, however, is revealed in the final moralization: "One by one objects are defined— / It quickens: clarity, outline of leaf." The action of the poem is specifically discovered to be one of *focusing;* as one rotates a knob on the consciousness, the objects are defined, both in the world of the poem and by the poem, by poems in general. In its moralization, the poem is like "The Red Wheelbarrow," a manifesto about poetry. It is full of light, too, which it does not directly confront, the light that, as a younger poet has put it "wipes each thing to what it is,"[19] the light that takes us past what Stevens called "the evasions of metaphor." This is as visual a poem in every sense as one could find, a soundless picture of a soundless world, its form shaped rather than incanted, its surface like that of so much Modern poetry, now reflecting, now revealing its depths and, as the conscious wind of attention blows over it, now displaying the wavy texture of its surface. Put together from fragments of assertion, it has virtually no rhetorical sound. But its shape has become a familiar one—particularly for contemporary poetry of the eye—about its possibilities, betrayals and rewards, about rediscoveries of the visionary in the visual.

19. Alvin Feinman, "November Sunday Morning," in *Preambles* (New York, 1964.

APPENDIX
A POEM FOR MUSIC:
REMARKS ON THE COMPOSITION OF *PHILOMEL* [1]

"Adding music to a good poem," remarks Paul Valéry, "is like using a stained-glass window to light a painted picture." "Music's beauty," he continues, "lies in its transparency; poetry's, in reflection. Light is implicit in one, and implied by the other."[2] By such standards, the differences between literary lyric and song text result in more than a mere difference of genre. While the experience of English literary history would certainly incline one to sympathize with such a view, it would not be necessary to penetrate to the depths of Valéry's aphorism in agreeing with it. Certainly it looks, on the surface, to be less true for French poetry than for verse in English; and while the tradition of the *chanson* in the nineteenth and twentieth centuries is quite distinct from that of German *Lieder* in the nature of the nexus of text and setting, there is no analogue of either, really, in English. Also, we must remember that Stefan George's lyric poems from *Das Buch der hängenden Gärten* do not suffer confusions of color in Arnold Schoenberg's great

---

1. Some of the material in these remarks is adapted from my program notes later published as "Notes on the text of *Philomel*," *Perspectives of New Music*, VI (1967), 134-41. *Philomel* itself, commissioned by the Ford Foundation, was published in a limited edition in London by Turret Books, 1968, © 1967, 1968 by John Hollander.
2. Paul Valéry, *Analects*, tr. Stuart Gilbert (Princeton, 1970), p. 214.

setting, nor, in a minor instance, do Réné Char's texts in Pierre Boulez's *Le Marteau sans maître*.

One attempt to institute an English *Lied* was a very self-conscious one. Tennyson wrote a small *Liederkreis* for the then twenty-four-year-old Arthur Sullivan to set (this was 1866) and for Millais to illustrate (he did, in fact, complete one). Written at the specific suggestion of George Grove, it was entitled *The Window*, or, *The Song of the Wrens*, and Tennyson was never particularly happy with it. Sullivan, he said in 1870, in a letter reluctantly granting permission to publish the cycle, "had been very successful in setting such old songs as 'Orpheus with his lute,' and I drest up for him, partly in the old style, a puppet, whose only merit is, perhaps, that it can dance for Mr. Sullivan's instrument."[3] Actually, one or two of the finished songs are quite good; the one called "No Answer," with its modulating refrain

> And the grass will grow when I am gone,
> And the wet west wind and the world will go on.

is particularly affecting, and if the little song-cycle suffers from secondariness and "puppetry," it is not because of Tennyson's difficulties with Heine, but because Sullivan, like his English contemporaries, had an incurable Mendelssohn problem.

Nevertheless, Tennyson's anxiety about the puppetry of song is a serious matter, given the traditions of lyric poetry in the English language. We may look at the turn of the seventeenth century, in this respect, from two viewpoints. The first of these would see it as the end of the almost stillborn tradition of English art song (the madrigals and ayres), when the strong lines of what would remain for half a century the most intense and profound of shorter English lyric modes (saving always Milton's major alternative) resisted neat musical framing. Conversely, we may view the Jacobean period as the beginning of that great development in English verse, the internalization of music—the deliteralizing of exterior musical structures into a metaphoric and far happier Harmony within, in the rich resources of the rhythms of the

---

3. Quoted in Christopher Ricks's edition of Tennyson (London, 1969), p. 1197; Ricks calls the cycle "an attenuated Maud."

language itself. In either case, given the cooperation of the decline of primary English musical culture after Purcell, Addison's famous contention that "nothing is capable of being well set to Musick, that is not Nonsense" remains, alas, abrasive, rather than merely untrue. John Donne, for all the protestations of his subtly modulated speaking voice, seldom was made a "triple foole" by being set to music. Actually, the roots of the deep rift in English verse between literary lyric and song text can be observed earlier, in the systematic practice of Sir Philip Sidney, who seems to reserve feminine rhymes and trochaic meters for song texts, frequently written as *contrafactum* to pre-existing tunes. The rift widened and grew in the seventeenth and eighteenth centuries, not only under the pressure of the speaking voice and its complex rhythmic consequences in metaphysical verse, but later on as well, when the ode for music, that form of secular cantata text perfected by Dryden, imitated by a host of successors from Congreve through Pope to Christopher Smart, fell away from its musical affiliations and became the model for a type of purely literary lyric poem.

The incompatibility of major lyric poetry in the English language with the traditions of musical setting available to it results from certain linguistic peculiarities of English as manifested in the dominant traditions of English verse; this is probably a matter of stress pattern, and not of the accepted nineteenth-century notion that Italian was a "musical" language because of its vocalic word endings, and English, being so full of consonantal clusters, was not. It is certainly possible in Italian, or even in the consonantal texture of German, to produce strophic verse, written as *contrafactum,* which will nevertheless be nontrivial. It is not so in English, and only the comic poem can maintain rhythmic, as well as schematically metrical, identity of pattern throughout successive strophes. The whole tradition of English *vers de société* is strung along something very like lyric adaptability to strophic musical setting; English and American Protestant hymnody, true ballad opera, and, finally, the Savoy operas of Gilbert and Sullivan, are among other things a demonstration of this.

This has proved true for modern poetry, in particular. While Modernist dogma explicitly rejected exposition, poetry of statement, as belonging to what had been Verlaine's *tout le reste* of "literature," its attitude toward sound, toward internalized music, ruled out the other nether-world of jingle as well, in which strophic hymn and pop song are equally at home. Then, too, any musical setting of a poem is in effect a reductive reading of it, unless the musical apparatus is so complex that it can handle diverse and often contrary rhetorical tonalities, and several layers of reference, at the same moment. Wagner developed just such resources for expanding, rather than reducing, the local textual significance in his heroic poem; he enabled the total musical texture to mirror human consciousness to the degree that emblematic melodic motives could appear either manifestly, in the sung line, or allusively, implicitly, allegorically in a polyphonic sense, by occurring at whatever level of depth in the orchestral score at any given moment. Certainly Hugo Wolf in the *Italienischer Liederbuch* songs was able to handle a rhetoric more complex than usual by virtue of the celebrated independence of his piano parts. In a sense, all Romantic and post-Romantic lyric poetry in English is itself *durchkomponiert*—through-composed—and even if manifestly stanzaic or periodic in structure, totally dependent upon an overriding of the schematic basis by a rush of forward motion and of evolutionary energy.

Tennyson, in the letter quoted before, spoke perhaps half-disparagingly of the composer's ability to set "such old songs as 'Orpheus with his lute' "; it is almost as if the setting of a venerable or well-known text were a quasi-liturgical matter. Famous texts acquire an almost scriptural character in the history of literature. As far as this interpretive or creative dimension of setting of texts to music is concerned, there is less risk of arbitrariness or misreading on the composer's part when he takes such a poem than when he attempts to set to music poems which themselves create or move toward new genres: neoclassically oriented, twentieth-century American composers raided *Chamber Music* and *Pomes Pennyeach* for song texts, but tended to avoid the Crazy Jane poems of Yeats, for example, despite their insistent song format. From this point of view, Samuel Barber's setting of "Dover Beach" for voice and string quartet, or, most particularly, Benjamin Britten's great *Lieder* or his *Serenade* for tenor, horn, and strings—a virtuoso display of his grasp of a wide range of texts—are all instances of handling what Tennyson referred to as "such old songs as. . . ."

But the fact remains that for contemporary poetry, the distinctions in genre between *lyric* and *song* still remain very much like one, not of genre, between *poetry* and *verse*. It is not only post-Modern evolutions of poetic form which account for this: Hardy's "During Wind and Rain," Lawrence's "Bavarian Gentians," and Stevens's "Domination of Black" are all major Modern lyrics, as different in sub-type as they are connected by their ceremonial approaches to death. The first of them is more obviously an instance of that general impulse of Hardy's to write what Yeats called "Words for Music Perhaps." And yet we move into a different region of our sensibility when we turn from admiring any of these to "The Battle Hymn Of The Republic," the songs of Lorenz Hart in *Pal Joey,* or some of Cole Porter, all of which retain for me an electrifying excellence. Songs we sing and delight to hear sung—poems we have read and know and thereby *have:* there is still a great gap here. The true *Lied,* a *chanson* or art song, inhabits a strange nether-world between them as does, of course, the true dramatic song. There is a great moment in the last stanza of Bert Brecht's *"Bills Ballhaus in Bilbao"* when a nostalgic song representing the decline, in successive strophes with a refrain, of one of the Good Old Places itself decays as a correlative of its subject. The refrain consists merely of humming because even its repeated words are forgotten (*"Halt, wie ging das jetzt weiter,"* says the singer *"Ich weiss den Text nicht mehr"*). This is an effect of dramatic poetry, a dialectic of character, scene, and utterance, and remains, with the vexing question of grand opera libretto in English, outside the scope of these remarks.

When, in the summer of 1962 Milton Babbitt asked me to do a text of some sort for a musical commission of his, I was far from writing a seventeenth-century pastiche, and particularly involved in a struggle against wit in my poems, and against talkiness. The former had infected a lot of my contemporaries through the Modernist sanction given to the seventeenth century; the latter was carried to a smaller few by W. H. Auden, and I was trying to emerge from a region of ventriloquism with the ability to articulate something, at least. For this reason, a song cycle seemed impossible for me at the time. In addition, Milton Babbitt is not Benjamin Britten, and his orientation was so deeply Viennese, musically speaking, that I momentarily felt that I should have to try to write in German. His densely textured serial music had been marked by total organization, rather than merely an improvisatory dodecaphonic flavor, and Babbitt's hostile critics condemned him rather for lack of *bêtise* than for frivolity. His setting for soprano and piano of W. C. Williams's "The Widow's Lament in the Springtime" I had long admired; more recently, he had set Dylan Thomas's *Vision and Prayer* for soprano and synthesized accompaniment, a venture growing out of his experiments with a sound synthesizer given Princeton and Columbia by Bell Labs. The present commission was to do a piece for the same soprano, that magnificent interpreter of twentieth-century vocal music Bethany Beardslee, and it was to involve a synthesized score as well. This posed other problems, and I knew from the beginning that a cycle of songs would be ruled out. Moreover, the dramatic possibilities of the contrast between live and canned sound, whether synthesized or not, seemed vast and profound, and even though I was thinking of a lyric text (rather than a dramatic scene per se), I sensed at once the possibilities of a solo ode which might nevertheless be able to echo within itself. I was not thinking, at the outset, of a mono-drama or melo-drama, like Schoenberg's *Erwartung*, although *Philomel* ended up, I suppose, as just that.

Actually, Babbitt and I had discussed the particular myth—the Ovidian story of the raped, silenced girl metamorphosed into the nightingale—earlier, and in a more specifically dramatic context. I had in mind a chamber opera, set in turn-of-the-century *Mittel-Europa;* the royal household would become a minor ducal one, the rape would remain actual, but for the Classical tearing out of the victim's tongue, a conversion hysteria would suffice. A scene I had particularly envisaged was the expressionist transformation of the weaving of the story into the tapestry. But perhaps this is the point to refresh one's memories of certain features of the nightingale myth itself.

The story of the ruined bird whose song pours out of the darkness with a voice restored from incoherence has several sources in classical antiquity. The canonical version for subsequent literature, though, is in Ovid. Earlier Greek mythographers had made Philomela the swallow and her sister Procne the nightingale, but for many reasons the Ovidian story lasted on. The two sisters were, according to the sixth book of the *Metamorphoses*, the children of Pandion, king of Athens. Procne, the older, was married to Tereus, king of Thrace, who took her off to his country where she bore him a son, Itys. After five years, she began to pine for her sister, and Tereus sailed down to Athens and eloquently persuaded Pandion to allow Philomela to accompany him home. But throughout the entire journey back, Tereus lusted for the girl so desperately that upon reaching the shores of Thrace, he took her off into a secluded wood and raped her, and after her threats of exposure, rather than kill her, cut out her tongue. Ovid describes this in a passage of famous grand guignol:

> The mangled root
> Quivered, the severed tongue along the ground
> Lay quivering, making a little murmur,
> Jerking and twitching, the way a serpent does
> Run over by a wheel, and with its dying movement
> Came to its mistress' feet. And even then—
> It seems too much to believe—even then, Tereus
> Took her, and took her again, the injured body
> Still giving satisfaction to his lust.[4]

Outraged and silenced, Philomela remained in captivity for a year, but she contrived to weave her horrible story in pictures and prevailed upon an old woman to take the finished fabric to the queen, her sister. Procne read the tapestry work, and, at the height of the Bacchanal celebrated yearly by Thracian women, went and found her sister, disguised her in the costume of the celebrants, and brought her back to the palace. There, in a fit of hatred and the desire for revenge, inflamed by the Bacchic frenzies, Procne killed her son, Itys, cooked his corpse and served him up to his father, Tereus, for a ritual meal. When he called aloud for his son to be presented to him, Philomela flung the

---

4. This is Rolfe Humphries's splendid translation.

bloody severed head at him and together the two sisters ran from the palace, Tereus following in a murderous rage. He followed Philomela through the woods, but before he could catch up with either of them, he was turned into a hoopoe, the crested, lapwing-like bird who, as the later allegorists pointed out, befouls its own nest. Procne became a swallow and Philomela, a nightingale.

In late antiquity and thereafter, the myth became that of the poet-musician. "*Quando fiam uti chelidon ut tacere desinam?*" cries out the anonymous poet of the late Pervigilium Veneris, speaking as a self-conscious last gasp of pagan culture: "When shall I, like the swallow (he uses the Greek word and the Greek version of the story) quit this silence?" George Sandys, the seventeenth-century mythographer, in his notes on Ovid, ingeniously presents a false etymology of Philomela (actually, *philo-mēlon,* "love of fruit," not *philo-melos*). His comment preserves what is unquestionably the standard Renaissance myth of the nightingale:

> The Nightingall chanting in the solitary woods; deservedly called *Philomela* or a lover of musicke, in that no bird hath so sweet a voice among all silvan musitians: singing fifteene days and nights together, when the leaves begin to afford her a shelter, with little or no intermission. So shrill a voice in so little a body, and a breath so long extended, is worth admiration; shee alone in her songs expressing the exact art of Musicke in infinite variety. Neither have all the same tunes and divisions, which shewes their skill to be more than naturall. They strive among themselves in fervent contention: the vanquished not sildome ending her life with her song, through griefe, or over-straining. . . .[5]

The suffering girl, then, has become the singer who outdoes herself; the bird in Famianus Strada's poem expanded magnificently by Crashaw in "Musick's Duell" herself contends with a virtuoso lutenist and wins by dying of transcendental exertion, and her poetic progeny in English thereafter is vast. Milton's prophetic bird of vision singing

5. George Sandys, *Ovid's Metamorphosis,* ed. Karl K. Hulley and Stanley T. Vandersall (Lincoln, Neb., 1970), p. 300.

out of the darkness; Mark Akenside's "sacred bird" to whose bower we are led by Hesper in "Ode to the Evening Star"; Keats's bird of poetry and passion, half-free of her old mythology; Arnold's horrible mythographic mix-up (his "Philomela" is about Procne, whether as swallow or nightingale, and the secondary mythological power of Philomela's name led him to forget both his Greek and Latin sources); Swinburne's; the Neoromantic nightingales of Robert Bridges ("Alone, aloud in the raptured ear of men / We pour our dark, nocturnal secret") the derivative Philomel in *The Waste Land*, "by the barbarous king / So rudely forced," and even the echo of this in Allen Tate's translation of the *Pervigilium* ("Her act of darkness with the barbarous king").

All these versions of the myth make her the poet or the poem, rather than merely the singer, and in the operatic framework in which it first occurred to me to handle the story, Philomel seemed to be the myth of the soprano, hunted down by the history of music itself, forced to bear the weight of eloquence even when, in operatic tradition, one can't hear a third of the words they sing, and so forth. In the *fin-de-siècle* setting I mentioned earlier, the two sisters would still exhibit the nineteenth-century accomplishment of some skill at watercolor, and instead of weaving the scene of her outrage into fancy work, I wanted the half-mute Philomel to lock herself in her room, painting away at something rather large. The showing of the picture to Procne would have involved the shocking and sudden relevation, both to her and the audience, of a large, violent, de Kooning-like daub manifestly signifying nothing; the following central scene would contain Procne's intuitive "reading" of the abstract picture, with Philomel gesturing or half-singing, according to whether the hypothetical narrative was hot or cold.

But the operatic project had been abandoned some time before, and when the new commission came up, I realized that the transformation scene alone, which I had thought of as an extended scene for the soprano, would make an extended solo vocal work. Babbitt wanted particularly to use, as part of the raw phonetic material upon which his sound synthesizer would work, Bethany Beardslee's own voice, put through many distortions and transpositions. I had thought of the immense problems of realizing the transformation scene in an operatic way—the soprano who had been singing, as the hysterical girl, only choppy nonsense syllables or vocalises, would have, upon her transformation, to break out into both extended melody and coherent language shaping that melody's rhythmic contours. The contrast between internalized, synthetic sound and outwardly directed actual soprano singing seemed almost inevitable. In addition, the relation between live soprano voice and a four-track array of accompanying and enclosing sound called for a dramatic placement of the girl singer in the Thracian woods through which she fled escaping the wrath of Tereus.

Finally, there was the literal presence of a particular soprano; Bethany Beardslee was a very gifted singer whose work I had always liked, and the fact that the commission was to do a work for her heightened my intention to write Philomela's transformation scene, the one in which she lost her inarticulate and ruined humanity and gained a voice she had never before possessed. The basic format of the work, then, called for a central soprano line, augmented, accompanied, perhaps echoed and underlined, by the synethesized score emerging from the four KLH loudspeakers which would share the stage with her. It occurred to me that they could embody voices which might variously represent what she heard in the woods, what she thought she heard, what she fancied she heard inside her own head, and almost anything else. A crucial moment (as it turned out, the very opening) would be that of her own discovery of her new voice, now as a bird. I had also for some time wanted to write a poem about music and pain, and it seemed to be appropriate to a final aria, at the end of the singing.

Aside from a generally tense and somewhat expressionistic flavor provided by the myth, I suppose that I was trying in other ways as well to be attentive to the specific kind of music which would be swallowing up my words (in fact, on hearing one's poem set to music, it is easy to feel raped, rather than consumed). Milton Babbitt's musical lineage stems from Schoenberg, particularly, rather than Webern, and from an almost hermetic mathematical tradition which would want to account for a particular note occurring where it did with as many reasons as one might give for a particular syllable looking the way it does in *Finnegans Wake*. It occurred to me that, since the monodrama would

REMARKS ON THE COMPOSITION OF PHILOMEL

probably either center on, or open with, Philomela's transformation and the recovery of her singing voice, an appropriate mode of handling that transformation might be evolutionary—not, that is, a sudden, baroque shift of perspective, but the result of putting a point of instant under a microscope to reveal a field. The moment would then have the furred edges that even a microdot can easily reveal, and the recovery of speech could be made to occur in a building-up of sung language from its components.

As the text evolved, it fell into three clearly defined sections. The first, which quickly came to start out with the first sub-instant of transformation, I thought of as a kind of prolonged equivalent to a recitative with bits of arioso emerging. Its sounds, which would lead to words, were developed from permutations of the phonemes and clusters of the names *Philomel* and *Tereus*, the pursuer and the chased. Thus the sequences *feel a million, filaments, tears, trees*, the verb *tears*, etc., eventually expanded into more coherent phrase groups and, finally, stanzaic clauses. The restored eloquence could be pulled together out of fragments, as it were, of feeling, of pain. Since it is from fear, outrage, and remembered pain that Philomela's psychic energy in the song is generated, I made her first words *I feel,* worked up not only from her own name, but from its own smaller constituent. Thus the text begins with the taped, synthesized score, which, in this first section would represent the sounds of the Thracian woods initiating, and then commenting in a choral way upon, her singing. It was simply the sound of the vowel phoneme /iy/ (perhaps set with a pure e natural, if the composer so desired):

PHILOMEL	TAPE
	(Eeeeeeeeeeeeeee)
Eeeeeeeeeeeeeeeeeeeee!	
Feeeeeeeeeeeeeeeeeeee!	
Feeeeeeeeeeeeeeeeeeeell!	
I feel—	
Feel a million trees	
And the heat of trees	
	Not true trees—
Feel a million tears	
	Not true tears—

Is it Tereus I feel?

Feel a million filaments;
Fear the tearing, the feeling
Trees, that are full of felony—

Trees tear,
And I bear
Families of tears—

I feel a million Philomels———

I feel trees in my hair
And on the ground, vines,
Honeymelons fouling
My knees and feet
Soundlessly in my
Flight through the forest;
I founder in quiet.

Here I find only
Famine of melody,
Miles of felted silence
Unwinding behind me,
Lost, lost in the wooded night.

My hooded voice, lost.

Lost, as my first
Unhoneyed tongue;
Forced, as my last
Unfeathered defense;
Fast-tangled in lust
Of these woods so dense.
Emptied, unfeeling and unfilled
By trees here where no birds have trilled—

Feeling killed
Philomel stilled
Her honey unfulfilled.

What is that sound?
A voice found;
Broken, the bound
Of silence, beyond

        Not true trees—

        Not Tereus; not a True Tereus—

        Trees filled with mellowing
        Feminine fame—

        Pillowing melody,
        Honey unheard—

        Feeling killed
        Philomel stilled
        Her honey unfulfilled

Violence of human sound,
As if a new self
Could be founded on sound.

Oh, men are sick:
The gods are strong.
Oh, see! Quick! Quick!
The trees are astounded!
What is this humming?
I am becoming
My own song. . . .

                          Oh, men are sick:
                          The gods are strong.
                          Oh, see! Quick! Quick!
                          The trees are astounded!
                          What is this humming?
                          I am becoming
                          My own song. . . .

Throughout all this, I was trying to keep in mind the fact that a good deal of what a soprano sings cannot be heard as language at all—about one third is the usual estimate—but I felt that the short phrases would help, no matter how much might be lost in the sounds of the forest. But for the second section, I wanted there to be several sorts of contrast, not the least being the one effected by a rationalizing of the ambiguous relation, in Part I, between tape sounds and soprano sounds. That is, whatever the composer would do with non-linguistic, quasi-instrumental sounds on the tape, I wanted whatever *voices* emerged from any of its channels to have a clear antiphonal relation to Philomela's quickened singing. It would also have to assume a schematic strophic form, and a rhetoric representing a step beyond her effusion of earlier self-recognition. Part II became a dialogue with various birds of the air; throughout, Philomel questions them, and is always in quest of their help in realizing her new identity as a bird. The tape, as the birds, would echo her. Here, I adopted what has almost always been a satiric and comic device; in the seventeenth and eighteenth centuries, the echo-song was a favorite implement of mockery, the point being to use the echoing last word of a question for a debunking answer. Thus Barnabe Barnes in 1593: "What shall I do to my Nymph when I go to behold her? (*Echo*) Hold her!" or Swift's shepherd: "What most moves women when we them address?" and the echo, of course, coming back with "A dress"; and "Say, what can keep her chaste whom I adore?" "A door"—and so forth. George Herbert uses this technique solemnly in "Heaven" (as he does, in fact, a version of it in the pruning-down of words in the tercets of "Paradise"—*grow* is echoed by *row* and *owe*, both in Eden and in the poem named that). "Heaven" transforms mockery as it begins "O who will show me those delights on high?" and the echo answers "I"; the poem ends with "Light, joy and leisure; but shall they persever?" and the echo concludes, "Ever." This device goes back to classical antiquity, but it seemed wonderfully adaptable to the two voices with which I was working. In particular, the resources of the sound synthesizer would allow me to build echoes not merely from discrete final syllables, but to cut across word and syllable boundaries to accumulate new initial consonantal clusters. This could be effectively intense or horrific, but not necessarily witty and certainly not bitchily humorous. Throughout the second section, then, the tape becomes in turn each of the birds to whom a question is directed:

II
ECHO SONG

PHILOMEL	TAPE
O Thrush in the woods I fly among, Do you, too, talk with the forest's tongue?	
	Stung, stung, stung; With the sting of becoming I sing
O Hawk in the high and widening sky, What need I finally do to fly And see with your unclouded eye?	
	Die, die, die; Let the day of despairing Be done
O Owl, the wild mirror of the night, What is the force of the forests light?	
	Slight, slight, slight; With the slipping-away of The sun
O sable Raven, help me back! What color does my torn robe lack?	
	Black, black, black; As your blameless and long- Dried blood

O bright Gull, aid me in my dream!
Above the foaming breaker's cream!

      Scream, scream, scream,
      For the scraps of your being;
      Be shrill

The world's despair should not be heard!
Too much terror has occurred:
The Gods who made this hubbub erred!

      Bird, bird, bird!
      You are bare of desire:
      Be born!

Oh green leaves! through your rustling lace
Ahead, I hear my own myth race.

      Thrace, Thrace, Thrace!
      Pain is unchained,
      There is change!
      There is change!
      In the woods of Thrace!

  Finally, there was to be the last aria. I had always thought of it as being strophic, and with a somewhat extended refrain—this last notion more than a bit *méchant*, considering the dogmatic commitment of dodecaphonic music to avoid repeated notes, let alone larger sequences. Moreover, I wanted the tape's "voice" and soprano to come together in these refrains, but nowhere else in the aria except as instrumental accompaniment. The relation between tape and singer here was of a fundamentally different nature from that of the first two sections. In the first, the singer was struggling to free herself from the background of forest noises from which her tongueless mewing could hardly be differentiated. In the second section, she was seeking to join a new realm of created being. Here, at the end, she was to reign over a whole kingdom of sound—it was as if, in an antithetical reversal of that great primary text,[6] *Never again would our song be the same./ And to do that to us, the sad bird came.* . . .

  The form that emerged had, I felt, to be both dense and flexible enough to allow all the impulses of through-composition to work for the setting. The strophe consisted of four loose, six stressed lines, the first two linked, in all the strophes, by an assonance of the vowel nucleus /ey/ (as in *pain, change, Thrace,* etc.), and the last two strictly,

---

6. Of Robert Frost; see "Never Again Would Birds' Song Be the Same," discussed above, p. 42.

and varyingly, rhymed. The refrain developed into a kind of shorter tail, slightly varied, its two-stressed lines tightly rhymed, and with the last three lines unchanging, and given to soprano and tape in unison. (This scheme was varied somewhat in the musical setting, but the textual form was retained. The point about this was, I suppose, that although a careful attention to what the setting *might be like* helped me develop certain of the formal structures, they were sure to succumb to the overpowering restructurings of the setting, their own rhythms overridden by the generations of the music. But this is always the case in true art song.) The long, six-beat lines, I realized only years later, probably came about because I had been brooding about such a meter at the time: I was in the next few years to use it excessively in the poems in *Visions from the Ramble*. While the stanzas of the last song were almost expository in their affirmations and even in their syntax, what haunted me while working on the refrain was the immense self-knowledge, even the world-weariness of the *Waldtaube*, the wood-dove, in Schoenberg's *Gurre-Lieder*

> *Weit flog ich,*
> *Klage sucht' ich*
> *Fand gar viel*

emerging for me out of a nest of romantic enforestations, as it were: the woods of *Pelléas*, of the last scene of *Falstaff*, of *Die Frau ohne Schatten* gave some of their shape to what I was making of the Thracian wood. In any event, the mode of the last section is that of song expounding itself:

III
PHILOMEL
Living, growing, changing, being in the hum always
Of pain! The pain of slow change blows in our faces
Like unfelt winds that the spinning world makes in its turning:
Life and feeling whirl on, below the threshold of burning.

(with tape)
I burn in change.
Far, far I flew
To this wailing place.
And now I range
Thrashing, through
The woods of Thrace.

If pain brush against the rushing wings of frightened change,
Then feeling distills to a burning drop, and transformation
Becomes intolerable. I have been raped and had my tongue
Torn out: but more pain reigns in these woods I range among.

                I ache in change,
                Though once I grew
                At a slower pace.
                And now I range
(with tape)   Thrashing, through
                The woods of Thrace.

Crammed into one fell moment, my ghastly transformation
Died like a fading scream: the ravisher and the chased
Turned into one at last: the voice Tereus shattered
Becomes the tiny voices of night that the God has scattered.

                I die in change.
                Pain tore in two
                Love's secret face.
                And now I range
(with tape)   Thrashing, through
                The woods of Thrace.

Love's most hidden tongue throbbed in the barbarous daylight;
Then all became pain in one great scream of silence, fading,
Finally, as all the voices of feeling died in the west
And pain alone remained with remembering in my breast.

                I screamed in change.
                Now all I can do
                Is bewail that chase.
                For now I range
(with tape)   Thrashing, through
                The woods of Thrace.

Pain in the breast and the mind, fused into music! Change
Bruising hurt silence even further! Now, in this glade,
Suffering is redeemed in song. Feeling takes wing:
High, high above, beyond the forests of horror I sing!

                I sing in change
                And am changed anew!
                (O strange, slow race
                That I ran with grace!)
                I sing in change.
                Now my song will range
                Till the morning dew
                Dampens its face;
                Now my song will range
                As once it flew
                Thrashing, through
                The woods of Thrace.

As finally set, a few changes were made in the text, mostly to smooth over movements which would have proved too much even for the most heroic diction. And of course, I discovered my own rhythms to have undergone a more than Ovidian metamorphosis. Not only did the three sections run together (as I had thought they might), but the decomposition of both rhythms and meters in the text had been necessary to allow the floral music to grow. Most important, the musical work was a very successful one.[7] I experienced a personal satisfaction in having elicited from so celebratedly "cerebral" a composer a lusher, more corny composition than had come about from his setting even of some of his beloved poems by obscure German expressionists like August Stramm. And as W. H. Auden remarked a long time ago, the success of a text written for musical setting consists in how well it gets the composer to compose, not in how it looks on the page. As a kind of musical ode, the text of *Philomel* remains for me somewhere in between libretto and literary or abstract lyric. No musical conventions dictated its metrical forms, for Babbit could just as well have set something randomly scattered across the page à la some of the late Charles Olson's disciples; moreover, nothing I have since written looks or sounds in any way like this. Nevertheless, a direct confrontation of what the music might sound like led to its taking shape on the page in a way so independent of the structures of the setting that they dissolve in the music they themselves anticipated.

7. An excellent brief discussion of Babbitt's *Philomel* (which, incidentally, is published by Associated Music Publishers, Inc.) appears in Eric Salzman, *Twentieth Century Music, an Introduction* (Englewood Cliffs, N.J., 1967). "Philomel, for Soprano, Recorded Soprano, and Synthesized Sound," has been recorded (Deutsche Grammaphon 0654,083).

INDEX

Abernathy, Robert, 130n.
Abrams, Meyer H., 270
Accentual-syllabism, 6, 36, 43, 60, 66-70, 81-82, 83, 87, 114, 116, 128-29, 197-98, 202-3, 239-40; in Donne, 44-58; rhythmic effects generated within, 147-60; stress-analogues of Classical meters, 64-70, 107-8, 210
Addison, Joseph, 253, 291
Akenside, Mark, 297; *Ode to the Evening Star*, 297
Alcaics, 69
Alciati, Andrea, 222
Aldington, Richard, 234
Alighieri, Dante, 110n., 121, 220, 242-43
Allen, W. Sidney, 62n.
Ammons, A. R., 239n.
Anacreontea, 24, 75, 169, 180
Apollinaire, Guillaume, 224-45, 266, 277
Archie and Mehitabel (Don Marquis), 240
Aria, 29, 299, 303-5
Aristotle, 219n.
Arnold, Matthew, 148, 297; *Dover Beach*, 292; *Philomela*, 297
Auden, W. H., 92n., 169, 185, 225, 251, 274, 276, 294, 306; *In Memory of Sigmund Freud*, 276; *Sea and the Mirror, The*, 185n.
Augustine, St., 14, 249-50, 280n.; *Confessions*, 250; *De Vera Religione*, 249

Ausonius, 257
Ayres, 17, 29-31, 32-34, 36-37, 71-82, 89-90

Babbitt, Milton, 293, 294, 298, 306; *Philomel*, 297-306
Bach, J. S., 39
Baïf, Jean-Antoine de, 64
Barber, Samuel, 292
Barfield, Owen, 97
Barnes, Barnabe, 301
Barnfield, Richard, 17
Battle Hymn of the Republic (Julia Ward Howe), 293
Beardslee, Bethany, 294, 297-98
Beardsley, Monroe C., 56n., 101
Beare, William, 62n.
Beaujour, Michel, 127n.
Beaumont, Francis, 25, 26n., 193
Beaumont, Joseph, 263
Beaver, Joseph C., 54n., 56n.
Beethoven, Ludwig van, 43
Benlowes, Edward, 268
Bernheimer, Richard, 219n.
Besantinus, 258-59
Bible, 203, 252, 264; *Psalms*, 80, 184, 252n.
Bishop, Elizabeth, 112
Blackmur, R. P., 59
Blake, William, 24-25, 28, 93, 101, 114-15, 117, 189, 196, 200, 204-9; *Jerusalem*, 205, 208-9; *Poetical Sketches*, 114-15, 205, 208, 272; *Songs of In-*

Blake, William (*Cont.*)
nocence and of Experience, 24-25, 200, 205-6
Blank verse, 91-99, 112-16, 193, 198, 200, 204-5, 270-72, 283
Bloom, Harold, 28
Bloomfield, Leonard, 271
Boethius, 13, 14
Boltenhouse, Charles, 253n.
Borges, Jorge Luis, 212
Boulez, Pierre, 290
Bowler, Berjouhi, 252n.
Bowles, William Lisle, 199
Brecht, Bertolt, 185, 293
Bridges, Robert, 68, 273-75, 297; *Cheddar Pinks*, 274-75; *Nightingales*, 297
Britten, Benjamin, 292, 294; *Serenade for Tenor, Horn and Strings*, 292
Browne, William, 262
Browning, Robert, 4, 44, 46, 106, 130, 202, 224, 233-34; *How They Carried the Good News from Ghent to Aix*, 202
Burke, Kenneth, 214
Burns, Robert, 201; *Afton Water*, 201
Burton, Robert, 280
Butler, Samuel, 267-68
Buttel, Robert, 159n.
Byrd, William, 28, 56, 72, 81, 87, 89, 221
Byron, George Gordon, 6th Baron, 202; *Destruction of Sennacherib, The*, 202

Campion, Thomas, 14-15, 32-33, 56-58, 61, 69, 71-82, 89-90, 107-8, 143, 144, 181, 270; *Observations, etc.*, 14-15, 143
Caravaggio, Michelangelo Merisi da, 12
Carew, Thomas, 44, 74, 175
Carroll, Lewis, 110n., 215-17; *Through the Looking-Glass*, 215-17
Cary, Joyce, 275
Cassiodorus, 13
Catullus, 46, 49, 59, 68, 69, 75-77, 86, 107, 144, 158, 172-73, 193
Cavalcanti, Guido, 242-43
Cavell, Stanley, 247n.
Chapman, George, 206, 269
Char, René, 290
Chatman, Seymour, 46n., 98n., 101n., 139n.
Chatterton, Thomas, 21, 189, 243
Chaucer, Geoffrey, 13, 66, 67, 83, 99, 118, 189, 197, 251; *Canterbury Tales*, 197
Chomsky, Noam, 101-5
Clare, John, 105, 201; *Hen's Nest*, 105
Classical prosody, 10-12, 59-70, 80-89, 92n., 107-8, 116, 143-44, 154, 172-73, 250-51; quantity, 59-70, 81-87, 107-8, 236; *arsis* and *thesis*, 11, 62-63, 138
Claudian, 193
Cocteau, Jean, 227
Coleridge, Samuel Taylor, 27, 41, 67, 68, 156, 185, 187, 194-95, 201, 210; *Animae Poetae*, 188n.; *Biographia Literaria*, 194, 210; *Kubla Khan*, 156; *Notebooks*, 210-11
Collins, William, 41
Concrete poetry, 100n., 266-67
Congreve, William, 291
Contrafactum, 17, 27, 291; in strophic settings, 30-31, 51-53
Contrastive stress, 35, 49-56, 101-5
Cooper, Charles Gordon, 92n.
Coperario, Giovanni, 49
Corso, Gregory, 266
"Counterpoint," 5, 21-22, 33, 140
Cowley, Abraham, 193, 271n.
Cowper, William, 113, 200, 201; *Polar Field, The*, 200
Crane, Hart, 95, 249, 266n., 273; *Bridge, The*, 266n., 283
Crashaw, Richard, 12, 297; *Musick's Duell*, 297
Cummings, e. e., 277-78
Curtius, Ernst Robert, 11-12

Daniel, John, 56, 73-74
Daniel, Samuel, 17, 74, 84
Darley, George, 25-27, 201
Darwin, Erasmus, 149
Davenant, Sir William, 192
Davie, Donald, 97, 116, 241n.
De Kooning, Willem, 297
Della Casa, Giovanni, 116
Demosthenes, 171
Denham, Sir John, 151-52, 280-81; *Cooper's Hill*, 151-52, 281
Descartes, René, 16
Dickinson, Emily, 233-34
Digby, Sir Kenelm, 167, 175
Digby, Lady Venetia, 167-68
Donne, John, 44-58, 71, 73, 74n., 75, 129, 138, 166-69, 178, 181-82, 184, 193, 199-200, 205, 220-23, 234, 270, 291; *Anniversarie, The*, 54; *Canoni-*

INDEX

zation, The, 182; Expiration, The, 47-52; Flea, The, 270; Hymn to God the Father, A, 55-56; Love's Progresse, 58; Nocturnal Upon S. Lucie's Day, A, 52-53; Primrose, The, 54; Satyres, 205; titles of poems, 220-23; Valediction: Of Weeping, A, 52
Dosiadas, 258
Dos Passos, John, 240
Doughtie, Edward, 220n.
Dowland, John, 31, 46-47, 72, 74
Drant, Thomas, 84, 87, 107
Drayton, Michael, 172, 178; Poly-Olbion, 172
Drummond of Hawthornden, William, 44, 166, 172-73, 269
Dryden, John, 92, 149, 150, 193, 291
Du Bartas, Guillaume de Salluste, Sieur, 193
Du Bellay, Joachim, 237
Duchamp, Marcel, 127
Dunstable, John, 72
Dürer, Albrecht, 219n., 221

Echoic effects, 131-33, 157-60
Echo-song, 301-3
Edmonds, J. M., 253n.
Elegiacs, 67, 72, 172-73, 200-202, 268-69
Eliot, T. S., 6-7, 106n., 110, 137, 141, 142, 168, 172, 271; *Burnt Norton*, 283; *Tradition and the Individual Talent*, 248; *Waste Land, The*, 266n., 297
Emblem, 56, 57, 181-82, 220-24, 228, 263-66, 269, 278; meter as, 163-64
Emerson, Ralph Waldo, 27, 118-19, 186, 227-30, 235, 240; *Journals*, 118-19; *Merlin*, 227-28; *Nature*, 229; *Poet, The*, 228-29
Empson, William, 149, 155
Enjambment, 37, 74, 91-116, 140-46, 177-78, 204-5, 208, 231-32
Ennius, 61, 84
Epigram, 56, 72-73, 75, 152, 169-70, 206-7, 269, 282
Experiment, 184-86, 202-11, 227-44

Fabry, Frank J., 58n.
Falstaff (Verdi), 304
Fanshawe, Sir Richard, 158
Farnaby, Giles, 221
Feinman, Alvin, 287
Ferrabosco, Alfonso, 33n., 47-51, 73, 75, 179

Fletcher, John, 25, 26n., 193
Flint, F. S., 234
Format, 91, 237, 249, 260-63, 275-77
Foster, John, 17
Fourteeners, 205-9, 228
Fowler, Alastair, 18n., 94
Fowler, Roger, 46n., 100n.
Framing, 135, 160-64, 186, 188-90, 242, 279; titling as, 212-26
Fraunce, Abraham, 85; *Countess of Pembroke's Emmanuel, The*, 85
Free verse, 110-21, 195, 225, 231-32, 234-44, 277-79
Frost, Robert, 42-43, 59, 103, 105-6, 109, 133, 138, 185, 195, 225, 303n.; *Never Again Would Birds' Song Be the Same*, 41-43, 133, 303n.; "sentence sound," 43
Frye, Northrop, 3-4, 189, 192, 231
Fussell, Paul, Jr., 18n.

Gardner, Dame Helen, 47n.
Gascoigne, George, 17
Gautier, Théophile, 219n.
George, Stefan, 289
Gesualdo, Carlo, 12
Gibbons, Orlando, 28, 72
Gilbert, Stuart, 22n.
Gilbert, W. S., 126, 291
Gildon, Charles, 17
Ginsberg, Allen, 240n.
Goethe, Johann Wolfgang von, 31, 33; *Heidenröslein*, 31
Golding, Arthur, 206
Goldsmith, Oliver, 110n.
Goodman, Nelson, 215, 226n.
Graphic meter, 65-66, 83-87, 91, 107, 144, 235-37, 239-40, 252-79
Gray, Thomas, 200
Great vowel shift, 64-65, 83, 128
Greek music, 10-12, 135
Green, Henry, 225
Grierson, Sir Herbert, 44
Grigson, Geoffrey, 201
Grove, Sir George, 290
Guarini, Giovanni Battista, 158; *Pastor Fido, Il*, 158
Guercino (Gian-Francesco Barbieri), 140

Haiku, 225, 278
Hall, Donald, 19n.
Halle, Morris, 46n., 51n., 92n., 101n.
Handel, George Frederick, 29; *Semele*, 29

310 INDEX

Hanslick, Eduard, 21
Hardy, Thomas, 137, 185, 293; *Dynasts, The,* 185n.; *During Wind and Rain,* 293
Hart, Lorenz, 106n., 126, 293
Hartman, Geoffrey, 233n., 282
Harvey, Gabriel, 17, 84, 85-86, 267
Hawes, Stephen, 259-60
Haydn, Josef, 21
Heine, Heinrich, 58, 290
Hendecasyllabics, 59-60, 68, 69
Hendrickson, G. L., 66n., 92n.
Herbert, George, 130, 131, 182, 184-85, 223-24, 228, 233, 263-66, 302; *Altar, The,* 263-64; *Church Monuments,* 182; *Denial,* 131; *Easter Wings,* 265-67; *Paradise,* 302; *Temple, The,* 185, 223; titles of poems, 223-34
Herrick, Robert, 77, 108, 175, 262-63; *Pillar of Fame,* 262-63
Hexameters, 61-65, 67, 85, 87, 91-92, 171-73, 231, 251, 268-69
Hilton, John, 55-56
Hobbes, Thomas, 10, 148, 192
Hoffmann, E. T. A., 21
Hölderlin, J. C. F., 275, 276
Home, Henry, Lord Kames, 17
Homer, 61-63, 65, 172; *Iliad,* 61-63
Hopkins, Gerard Manley, 5-7, 33, 34, 106n., 116, 122-23, 139, 154, 185, 197, 203, 204, 211, 232-33, 235, 239
Horace, 67, 144, 158, 178n., 217, 222, 245; *Ars Poetica,* 178n., 245
Housman, A. E., 125; *Chestnut Casts Its Flambeaux, The,* 125
Howell, James, 175
Hume, Tobias, 73
Humphries, Rolfe, 295n.; translation of Ovid, 295
Hunt, Leigh, 187-88, 202, 273
Hunt, William Holman, 284

Imitative rhythms, 4, 108-9, 116, 144-60
Information theory, 138-39
Ing, Catherine, 52n.

Jacquot, Jean, 47
Jakobson, Roman, 6, 20, 34
Jenkins, John, 39
Jespersen, Otto, 130n.
Johnson, Samuel, 91-92, 152, 164, 271-72, 281n.
Jones, Inigo, 179

Jones, Robert, 32-33
Jonson, Ben, 44, 49-51, 67, 71, 75-77, 93, 108, 117, 129, 134, 137, 141-46, 158, 165-84, 185, 212, 219, 223, 267-69; *Come, My Celia,* 49-50, 75-76, 158, 176; *Cynthia's Revels,* 169; *Elegie on Lady Jane Pawlet,* 175; *Eupheme,* 168; *Execration Upon Vulcan,* 179-80; *Fabulous Voyage, The,* 269; *Fit of Rime Against Rime, A,* 93, 117, 181-82; *Forrest, The,* 169, 176; *Musical Strife, The,* 175; *My Picture Left in Scotland,* 182, *Ode* (Cary and Morison), 53n., 129, 141-143, 219, 269-70; *To Penshurst,* 176; *Pleasures Reconciled To Virtue,* 179-80, *Sonnet,* 181-82; *Timber,* 170-212; *Underwood, The,* 166, 170; *Volpone,* 176
Joyce, James, 22n., 125, 183, 184; *Chamber Music,* 292; *Finnegans Wake,* 298; *Pomes Pennyeach,* 292

Kames, Lord (*see* Home, Henry)
Kastendieck, Miles W., 58n.
Keats, John, 24, 68, 116, 144-45, 153, 156, 158, 160, 187, 273-74, 281, 297; *To Autumn,* 24, 144-45; *Eve of St. Agnes, The,* 156n., *Ode on a Grecian Urn,* 159-60; *Ode to a Nightingale,* 158; *Sonnet: "How Many Bards . . . ,"* 273-74
Kenner, Hugh, 225n., 279n., 285n.
Keyser, Samuel J., 46n., 51n., 92n., 101n.
Klee, Paul, 218
Klopstock, F. G., 275
Knight, W. F. Jackson, 64
Knights, L. C., 205n.
Korn, A. L., 253n.
Krohn, William A., 54n.

Lamb, Charles, 45
Landor, Walter Savage, 202, 210, 275
Lanier, Sidney, 10, 19-21
Lawes, Henry, 36-39, 74, 82; songs for *Comus,* 36-39, 55n.
Lawrence, D. H., 275; *Bavarian Gentians,* 293
Leavis, F. R., 144, 184
Leibnitz, Gottfried Wilhelm von, 10
Levellers, 206
Levin, Samuel R., 100n., 139n.
Lewis, C. S., 39-40, 197

INDEX   311

Lichtenberg, Georg Christoph, 120n., 240n.
Lieder, 58, 31-32, 289-90, 292
Lindsay, Jack, 205n.
Locke, John, 247
Longfellow, Henry W., 65, 240
Longinus (Pseudo-Longinus), 7-8, 171, 190
Lowell, James Russell, 202
Lucretius, 193, 280

Machaut, Guillaume de, 9, 73
Madison, Carol, 141n.
Madrigals, 17, 29-31, 34-36, 72-73, 143, 180; as epigrams, 269
Magritte, René, 218
Mahler, Gustav, 232
Mallarmé, Stéphane, 277
Mandelbaum, Allen, 110n.
Manwaring, Edward, 17
Marlowe, Christopher, 269
Martial, 169
Marvell, Andrew, 4, 77, 108-9, 176, 209, 219, 228; *Horatian Ode, A*, 219; *To His Coy Mistress*, 4, 77, 108, 228n., *Upon Appleton House*, 178
Marx, Karl, 234
Masque, 178-80
Mendelssohn, Felix, 290
Mersenne, Marin, 17
Merwin, W. S., 240
Meter and rhythm, 17-18, 30-31, 32-35, 45, 88-89, 135-64, 187-211, 218, 242, 248, 270-71, 278, 279; in Classical theory, 12-14, 135; in experimental theories, 227-44
Metrical contract, 137, 162-64, 193-211
Mill, John Stuart, 224
Millais, Sir John Everett, 290
Miller, J. Hillis, 233
Milton, John, 36-39, 53, 67, 69, 82, 91-101, 109-16, 117, 119, 125, 134, 145, 153, 156n., 159, 172, 173, 190, 192, 193, 196, 199, 200, 204, 232, 243, 271-72, 290, 296; *Comus*, 38; *Il Penseroso*, 159; *Lycidas*, 192; *On the Morning of Christ's Nativity*, 158; *Paradise Lost*, 34, 91-101, 109-16, 125, 190, 232; *To Mr. Henry Lawes, On His Airs*, 36-38
Minturno, Antonio Sebastiano, 141n.
Modality, 56-58, 160-62, 166-86, 190-92, 218, 232, 234, 245
Modal rhythm, 16
Modes, Greek musical, 170-71, 190-92

Molière, J. B. P., 271n.
Molinêt, Jean, 127n.
Monboddo, James Burnet, Lord, 18
Morgenstern, Christian, 267n.
Morley, Thomas, 72
Moore, Marianne, 92n., 128, 251, 274
Moore, Thomas, 201; *Lalla Rookh*, 201; *Irish Melodies*, 201; *Fudge Family in Paris, The*, 202
Mozart, Wolfgang Amadeus, 39
Music as poetic subject, 79-80
"Music of poetry," 6-22, 28, 40, 43, 44, 46, 55, 63-64, 90n., 96, 118-19, 134, 145, 157, 188, 194, 245, 248, 250, 290-91
Musical prosody, 10, 17-20
Musical setting of texts, 28-38, 45-58, 71-82, 89-90, 143, 218, 289-306

Nash, Ogden, 125
Nashe, Thomas, 267
Necker cube, 104
Newcastle, William Cavendish, Earl of (afterwards Duke), 175
Nuttall, A. D., 249

Oldham, John, 149
"Old Oaken Bucket, The" (Samuel Woodworth), 201
Olson, Charles, 239-40, 306; "projective verse," 285
One-line poem, 212, 225
Orgel, Stephen, 180
Ormulum, The, 272
Ossian, 189
Ostriker, Alicia M., 114n., 115n., 205n.
Ovid, 56, 69, 81, 158, 173, 294-97, 306; *Amores*, 172; *Heroides*, 56; *Metamorphoses*, 294-97
Owen, Wilfred, 130

Palestrina, Giovanni Pierluigi da, 39
Pater, Walter, 22
Paton, W. R., 253n., 254n.
Pavlov, Ivan, 150
Pelleas et Mélisande (Debussy), 304
Pepusch, Edward, 17
Pervigilium Veneris, 296, 297
Peterson, Douglas L., 45n.
Petrarch, 83, 89, 173; Petrarchanism, 23, 57-58, 78, 173, 199
Petronius, 173
Phaer, Thomas, 206
Philips, John, 112-13; *Splendid Shilling, The*, 112-13

Pindar, 144; Pindaric ode, 119, 141, 167, 176, 217, 269, 271n.
Planudean Anthology, 253
Plato, 121, 171; *Cratylus*, 121; *Republic*, 170-71
Plautus, 198
Plotinus, 13
Plutarch, 267
Pope, Alexander, 24, 29, 68, 100-101, 122, 125, 148-54, 156, 291; *Essay on Criticism, An*, 100-101, 122, 148-53; *Summer*, 29
Porter, Cole, 126, 293
Poulter's measure, 268
Pound, Ezra, 39-40, 137, 172, 203, 225, 234, 236-37, 240-43, 279, 285; *ABC of Reading, The*, 39-40; *Canto, The*, 164, 203, 237, 241; *Cavalcanti*, 241-42; *In a Station of the Métro*, 225
Poussin, Nicolas, 140
Praed, Winthrop Mackworth, 126
Prince, F. T., 116n., 117n., 118, 121
Prosodic theory, 3-7, 12, 14-22, 71, 73-74, 135-40, 187-89, 227-44
Proust, Marcel, 147
Purcell, Henry, 291
Puttenham, George, 15, 232, 252-54, 259-61, 265
Pythagoreanism, 12

Quarles, Francis, 269
Quine, W. V., 12n.

Rabelais, François, 259
Racine, Jean, 147, 238; *Britannicus*, 238; *Phèdre*, 147
Recitative, 18, 49, 73-74, 299
Rembrandt, 219n.
Reverdie, 285
Reynolds, Sir Joshua, 215
Rhyme, 17, 81, 83, 92-94, 96, 106, 108-10, 112, 113, 117-34, 180-81, 183, 228-30, 240, 242, 263, 266, 277, 301, 304; "eye rhyme," 122-23; *rime riche*, 118; in enjambed contexts, 108-10
Richards, I. A., 135-36, 156
Ricks, Christopher, 96, 132n., 290n.
Riding-rhyme, 83
Rilke, Rainer Maria, 185
Rimbaud, Arthur, 20, 231
Ringler, W. A., 87n.
Robinson, Edwin Arlington, 243
Rolland, Romain, 238
Ronsard, Pierre de, 46
Rossetti, Dante Gabriel, 105, 242-43, 284; *Antwerp to Ghent*, 105, 283-85; "Stony" *Sestina*, 242-43
Russell, Thomas, 199

Sachs, Curt, 14
Saint-Gelais, Mellin de, 259
Saintsbury, George, 188
Salzman, Eric, 306n.
Sandys, George, 296
Sapir, Edward, 271
Sappho, 107, 144, 279; Sapphic stanzas, 65-66, 107-8, 275
Saturnian, 63, 251
Sayce, R. A., 130n.
Scazon, 68
Schoenberg, Arnold, 289, 294, 298, 304; *Erwartung*, 294; *Gurre-Lieder*, 304
Scholia Enchiriadis, 14
Schubert, Franz, 31-32
Schumann, Robert, 58
Selden, John, 178
Seneca, 198
Shadwell, Thomas, 268
Shakespeare, William, 6, 122, 138, 154, 157, 232, 236; *Merchant of Venice, The*, 156; *Orpheus with His Lute*, 290-92; *Sonnets*, 154, 155
Shawcross, J., 188n.
Shelley, Percy Bysshe, 24, 187, 201, 273; *Esdaile Notebook*, 201; *To a Skylark*, 24
Sidney, Sir Philip, 61, 65, 66, 67, 71, 75, 82-83, 86, 173, 184-85, 270, 291; *Apology for Poetry*, 82-83; *Arcadia*, 86, 184; Sidney family, 176
Simmias Rhodius, 253-58, 265, 267
Simonides, 267
Sitwell, Dame Edith, 157
Skeltonics, 260
Smart, Christopher, 164, 189, 203, 204, 277, 291; *Jubilate Agna*, 164, 203, 277
Smith, A. J., 52n.
Smith, Barbara Herrnstein, 134n.
Socrates, 170
Sonnet, 42, 73, 116, 154-55, 173, 180-81, 198-200, 218, 229, 233
Sound, as poetic subject, 22-27, 40-43
Souris, André, 47
Southey, Robert, 210, 275; *Vision of Judgment, A*, 210n.; *Thalaba*, 210n.
Sparrow, John, 253n.
Spenser, Edmund, 41, 69, 71, 84, 85-87, 88, 132, 133, 154-55, 158, 159, 172, 251, 270; *F.Q.*, 155, 159, 172;

INDEX

metrical experiments, 85-87; *Shepheardes Calendar*, 41, 251; spelling, 124
Sprachgefühl, 4, 129-30
Sprat, Thomas, 271n.
Stanyhurst, Richard, 87n., 107
Star-Spangled Banner, The (Francis Scott Key), 202
Statius, 193
Steele, Joshua, 18-20, 31
Stein, Arnold, 45-46, 48n.
Stevens, Wallace, 8, 132-33, 159, 185, 218, 224, 225, 235, 272, 274, 283, 287, 293; *Ordinary Evening in New Haven, An*, 284; *Domination of Black*, 293; *Monocle de Mon Oncle, Le*, 219; *Notes Toward a Supreme Fiction*, 132-33, 159; *Parts of a World*, 283
Strada, Famianus, 296
Stramm, August, 306
Strauss, Richard, 238; *Die Frau ohne Schatten*, 304
Sullivan, Sir Arthur, 290, 291
Summers, Joseph L., 263n.
Surrey, Henry Howard, Earl of, 83, 268
Swenson, May, 266
Swift, Jonathan, 301-2
Swinburne, Algernon Charles, 21, 25, 65-66, 178, 275; *Sapphics*, 65-66
Syllabic verse, 64, 91, 114-16, 128-29, 251, 272-75
Sylvester, Joshua, 193, 262

Tasso, Torquato, 158
Tate, Allen, 297
Technopaignia, 253-66
Tennyson, Alfred, Lord, 4, 44, 59-60, 69-70, 131-32, 156-57, 189, 224, 275, 281, 290-92; *Window, The*, 290
Terence, 193
Theocritus, 61, 172, 254-55, 257-58
Thomas, Dylan, 266, 294; *Vision and Prayer*, 294
Thomas, Edward, 185
Thompson, John L., 46n., 87n.
Thomson, James, 113
Titles, 212-26; of musical works, 221; of pictures, 213-15, 218-19, 221, 225n.
Tooke, John Horne, 18
Tottel, Thomas, 46n., 220
Traherne, Thomas, 281
Traubel, Horace, 204n.

Turner, Joseph M. W., 284
Tuve, Rosemund, 79n.

Ut pictura poesis, 245-48, 279-87

Valéry, Paul, 92, 116-17, 195, 289; *Au Sujet d'Adonis*, 195
Vathek (William Beckford), 202
Vaughan, Henry, 184
Verlaine, Paul, 21, 292
Vers de société, 106n., 125-26, 291
Villard de Honnecourt, 226n.
Villon, François, 46
Virgil, 40, 63-64, 69, 87n., 91, 116, 173, 212, 251; *Eclogues*, 40; *Aeneid*, 63-64, 212

Wagner, Richard, 39, 292
Wakefield plays, 197
Waller, Edmund, 151
Walton, Izaak, 55n.
Warner, William, 206; *Albion's England*, 206
Warnke, Frank J., 45
Warren, Austin, 192n., 213, 217
Warton, Joseph, 113
Warton, Thomas, 113, 199
Watts, Isaac, 217
Webern, Anton von, 298
Webster, John, 234
Weelkes, Thomas, 28, 34-36, 72; *Hark, All Ye Lovely Saints*, 34-36
Wellek, René, 139n., 192, 213, 217
Whistler, James A. M., 219n., 284
Whitman, Walt, 26, 197, 203, 204-5, 211, 230-32, 235, 240, 277, 280; *Leaves of Grass*, 229-32
Whitney, Geoffrey, 56
Wilbye, John, 28, 143
Wilde, Oscar, 238
Williams, William Carlos, 5, 60, 110-11, 235-36, 279, 285-87, 294; *Desert Music, The*, 235; *Spring and All*, 110-11, 235, 285-87; "variable foot," 236-37; *Widow's Lament in the Springtime, The*, 294
Willis, Richard, 260
Wilson, Edmund, 183
Wimsatt, W. K., 46n., 98n., 101, 119-20, 124
Winters, Yvor, 235
Wither, George, 262
Wittgenstein, Ludwig, 104, 144
Wolf, Hugo, 292; *Italienischer Liederbuch*, 292

Wordsworth, Christopher, 199
Wordsworth, William, 22-24, 39, 118, 137, 153, 164, 188n., 193-96, 215, 273, 281-82; *Lyrical Ballads*, 28, 193-96; *Prelude, The*, 199; *Resolution 96; Prelude, The*, 199; *Resolution and Independence*, 215; *Tintern Abbey*, 281-82; various poems in anapestic tetrameter, 200; *White Doe of Rylstone*, 201
Wright, James, 240

Wuorinen, Charles, 52n.
Wyatt, Sir Thomas, 46, 138

Yeats, W. B., 24, 137, 147, 158, 247, 292, 293; *Long-Legged Fly, A*, 147; *Sailing to Byzantium*, 158; *Vision, A*, 247; *Words for Music Perhaps*, 293
Young, Edward, 113

Zirmunskij, Viktor, 100n.